Collector's Edition
3 Cookbooks in 1

Essential

3-INGREDIENT COOKBOOK

4-INGREDIENT COOKBOOK

5-INGREDIENT COOKBOOK

1,000 Quick & Easy Recipes

Collector's Edition

Essential
3-Ingredient Cookbook
4-Ingredient Cookbook
5-Ingredient Cookbook

1,000 Quick and Easy Recipes

1st Printing March 2005
2nd Printing May 2006

ISBN 1-931294-99-2
Library of Congress Number: 2005922714

Edited, Designed and Published in the
United States of America and
Manufactured in China by
Cookbook Resources, LLC
541 Doubletree Drive
Highland Village, Texas 75077
Toll free 866-229-2665
www.cookbookresources.com

Introduction

This Collector's Edition: **3-Ingredient Cookbook, 4-Ingredient Cookbook** and **5-Ingredient Cookbook** combines much of the three bestselling cookbooks: **The Best of Cooking With 3 Ingredients, The Ultimate Cooking With 4 Ingredients and Easy Cooking With 5 Ingredients**.

You can now find some of the very best recipes from all three cookbooks in one book for the ultimate in convenience and speed in finding quick, easy and delicious recipes.

Families in the United States, Canada, Australia, New Zealand and the United Kingdom are using these fast, easy recipes to prepare dinners at home. No matter how fast our lives move and how much we try to cram in to each day, we need to make time for sharing meals at the dinner table. And this Collector's Edition is the best tool to help you make it happen.

Cookbook Resources, LLC in a cookbook series called "Cooking By The Numbers", first published these three cookbooks in 2000. The cookbooks listed below are included in this series and have sold more than 1,000,000 copies.

The bestselling cookbook series, "Cooking By The Numbers", is packed with fast, easy recipes for everyday use.

The Best of Cooking With 3 Ingredients
The Ultimate Cooking With 4 Ingredients
Easy Cooking With 5 Ingredients
Easy Healthy Cooking With 4 Ingredients
Easy Diabetic Cooking With 4 Ingredients
Easy Dessert Cooking With 5 Ingredients
Easy Gourmet-Style Cooking With 5 Ingredients

We hope you enjoy reading these cookbooks as well as cooking from them. We also hope the recipes make meals at home with family and friends easier and more appealing to everyone who graces your table.

Thank you.
Editors
Cookbook Resources, LLC

Contents

The Best of Cooking with 3 Ingredients

Contents

The Ultimate Cooking with 4 Ingredients

Contents

Easy Cooking with 5 Ingredients

The Best of Cooking with 3 Ingredients

By Ruthie Wornall

cookbook resources® LLC

Best of 3 Ingredient Cooking

Ist Printing – August 2002
2nd Printing – December 2002
3rd Printing – June 2003
4th Printing – September 2003
5th Printing – March 2004
6th Printing – February 2005

ISBN 1-931294-11-9 (hard bound)
ISBN 1-931294-13-5 (paper cover)
Library of Congress Number: 2001099917

Front Cover and Illustrations by Nancy Murphy Griffith

Edited, Designed and Published and Manufactured
in the United States of America by
Cookbook Resources, LLC
541 Doubletree Drive
Highland Village, Texas 75077
Toll free 866-229-2665
www.cookbookresources.com

In The Author's Words

I couldn't cook when I married and needed help. So I began collecting 3 ingredient recipes that were so easy I couldn't ruin them. I tested them by cooking Christmas dinner for my husband's family and nobody knew I couldn't cook. I even fooled my mother-in-law. She proclaimed me a gourmet cook.

Since then I've parleyed not being able to cook into a series of 12, **3-Ingredient Cookbooks** and have proved that quick, easy and elegant recipes don't have to be complicated.

When I first decided to write and sell the books my husband said, "You might sell 100." Now that my sales are pushing 150,000 I take pleasure in reminding him that behind every successful woman there's a very surprised man.

In trying to help myself, I'm delighted to discover that I've helped other people, too. The books have been transcribed into Braille and used to teach cooking in schools for the blind, in hospice programs and in homes for the educable mentally disabled. They have been lifesavers for new brides, busy moms, college students, widowers, children learning to cook, retired people who want to cook the easy way, people with chronic fatigue syndrome, wheel chair chefs and for people with other disabilities.

I've made a career of helping busy people cook "Fast Food at Home." These books have shown them how to use convenience foods in unique ways to create memorable dishes for family and friends. Busy people do have time to cook when they can prepare dinner in minutes with these 3 ingredient recipes.

This book contains recipes in all categories ranging from appetizers and beverages for parties to soups, salads, vegetables, main dishes, breads and desserts which enable you to prepare entire dinners in minutes. It incorporates short-cuts which save time, but don't compromise taste.

When you use these quick and easy recipes you'll find cooking is fun so you won't mind preparing dinners and entertaining, because now it is **EASY TO COOK**.

Happy Cooking!
Ruthie Wornall

Contents

The Best of Cooking with 3 Ingredients

Hamburger-Cheese Dip

1 (32 ounce) package cubed, processed cheese
1 (10 ounce) can tomatoes and green chilies
1 pound ground beef, browned, drained

- Combine cheese with tomatoes and green chilies and heat until cheese melts.
- Stir in meat.
- Serve hot with large corn chips.

Taco Dip

1 (8 ounce) package cream cheese, softened
1 (8 ounce) carton sour cream
1 (1 ounce) package taco seasoning mix

- Beat cream cheese until creamy and combine with remaining ingredients. Mix well.
- Cover and chill. Serve with corn chips.

Mexico City Dip

2 cups sour cream
1½ cups thick and chunky salsa
4 green onions, chopped

- Combine all ingredients and mix well.
- Chill until ready to serve. Serve with corn chips.

Hot Chili Dip

1 (15 ounce) can chili without beans
1 (4 ounce) can chopped green chilies
1 (8 ounce) package shredded cheddar cheese

- Combine all ingredients and mix well.
- Microwave on HIGH until bubbly or bake at 350° for 30 minutes.
- Serve with tortilla chips.

Hot Tamale Dip

1 (15 ounce) can tamales
2 (15 ounce) cans chili
1 (8 ounce) package shredded cheddar cheese

- Mash tamales with fork, mix with chili and place in 9-inch glass pie plate.
- Sprinkle cheddar cheese over tamale-chili mixture.
- Heat in 350° oven for about 25 minutes or until bubbly.
- Serve with corn chips.

Slow-Cook, Simmerin' Mexican Dip

1 pound pork sausage
2 (16 ounce) package cubed, processed cheese
1 (10 ounce) can tomatoes and green chilies with liquid

- Brown sausage in skillet, crumble and drain well.
- Place all ingredients in slow cooker and heat thoroughly.
- Serve hot with tortilla chips.

Creamy Broccoli-Mushroom Dip

1 (5 ounce) tube garlic cheese
1 (10 ounce) can golden mushroom soup
1 (10 ounce) box frozen chopped broccoli, thawed

- Melt cheese with soup. Stir in broccoli and heat thoroughly.
- Serve with raw vegetables or corn chips.

Snappy Broccoli-Cheese Dip

½ cup (1 stick) butter
1 (16 ounce) package cubed, processed jalapeno cheese
1 (10 ounce) package frozen chopped broccoli, partially thawed

- Combine butter and cheese in saucepan on low heat until cheese melts.
- Cook broccoli according to package directions, drain and stir into cheese mixture.
- Continue to heat until broccoli is hot.
- Serve with tortilla chips.

Scoopin' Crab Dip

1 (8 ounce) package cream cheese, softened
1 (6 ounce) can crabmeat, drained, flaked
1 (1 ounce) package dry onion soup mix

- Beat cream cheese until creamy and combine with remaining ingredients. Mix well.
- Serve with shredded wheat crackers.

Beginner Guacamole

3 avocados, peeled, seeded, mashed
1 cup thick and chunky salsa
½ cup cottage cheese, drained

- Combine all ingredients and ¼ teaspoon salt and mix well. Chill.
- Serve as salad with Mexican food or as dip with tortilla chips.

Favorite Vegetable Dip

1 cup cottage cheese, drained
1 cup mayonnaise
1 (1 ounce) package ranch-style salad dressing mix

- Combine all ingredients and mix well.
- Chill until ready to serve.

Cheesy Artichoke Dip

1 (14 ounce) can artichoke hearts, drained, chopped
1 cup grated parmesan cheese
1 cup mayonnaise

- Combine all ingredients and mix well.
- Pour into sprayed baking dish and bake at 350° for 20 to 30 minutes.
- Serve with fresh vegetables, chips or crackers.

Easy Shrimp Dip

1 (1 ounce) package dry onion soup mix
2 cups sour cream
1 cup chopped, cooked shrimp

- Combine soup mix with 2 cups sour cream. Blend well.
- Stir in 1 cup chopped shrimp.
- Cover and chill for 2 hours before serving.
- Serve with crackers, chips, bread or veggies.

Simple Simon's Chili Con Queso

1 (1 pound) package cubed, processed cheese
1 (10 ounce) can tomatoes with green chilies, drained
2 green onions, chopped

- Combine cheese and drained tomatoes in double broiler and heat until cheese melts.
- Pour into serving dish and sprinkle onions or chives over top.
- Serve with corn chips.

Easy Cheese Ball

2 (5 ounce) jars Old English cheese spread, softened
2 (3 ounce) packages cream cheese, softened
1 cup chopped nuts

- In mixing bowl, combine cheese and cream cheese and beat well.
- Shape into ball and chill 4 to 6 hours.
- Roll cheese ball in chopped nuts and wrap in plastic wrap until ready to serve. Serve with crackers, chips or breads.

Sausage-Chestnut Balls

1 pound hot pork sausage
1 (8 ounce) can sliced water chestnuts, drained
1 cup barbecue sauce

- Shape sausage into small balls. Cut water chestnuts in half and put 1 chestnut half in middle of each sausage ball.
- Place on sprayed cookie sheet and bake at 400° for 20 minutes.
- Drain, place in serving dish and pour heated barbecue sauce over sausage balls.
- Insert wooden picks in sausage balls for easy pick-up.

Kids' Steak Kabobs

1 package wieners, cut in 1-inch pieces
1 (8 ounce) jar maraschino cherries, drained
1 (16 ounce) can pineapple chunks, drained

- Alternate wieners, cherries and pineapple on $10\frac{1}{2}$-inch skewers.
- Place on cold broiler pan, broil for 2 minutes and turn.

Pop-In-Your-Mouth Sausage Balls

These freeze well.

2 cups biscuit mix
1 (1 pound) package hot pork sausage
1 cup shredded cheddar cheese

- Combine all ingredients with wooden spoon or use your hands.
- Shape into balls, place on jellyroll pan and bake at 350° for 20 minutes.

Raspberry-Cheese Ball

2 (8 ounce) packages cream cheese, softened
4 tablespoons raspberry preserves
1 cup finely chopped pecans

- Beat cream cheese until creamy. Combine with remaining ingredients and blend well. Shape into ball and roll in chopped pecans. Serve with crackers.

Spinach-Stuffed Mushrooms

24 large mushrooms, stems removed
1 (12 ounce) package frozen spinach souffle, thawed
½ cup grated cheddar cheese

- Preheat oven to 375°.
- Arrange mushroom caps on lightly sprayed baking sheet. Spoon 1 teaspoon spinach souffle into each mushroom cap and top with ½ teaspoon cheese.
- Bake mushrooms for 20 minutes.

On Top Of Old Smokey

2 pounds little smokies sausages
1 pound bacon
1 (1 pound) box brown sugar

- Cut smokies into 1-inch lengths and bacon slices into halves.
- Wrap smokies in bacon halves and secure with wooden picks.
- Place smokies in baking dish and spread brown sugar over top.
- Bake at 350° until sugar melts and broil until bacon browns.

Little Smokey Crescents

1 (8 ounce) can refrigerated crescent rolls
24 little smokies
1 cup barbecue sauce

- Unroll crescent roll dough and spread out flat. Cut 8 triangles lengthwise into 3 triangles each, so you have 24.
- Starting at wide end of each dough triangle, place 1 smokey on dough, roll up and repeat.
- Place rolls on baking sheet and bake at 400° for 10 to 15 minutes or until golden brown.

Tip: Serve with barbecue sauce.

Saucy Barbecued Sausages

This could be served in slow cooker.

1 (18 ounce) bottle barbecue sauce
1 (12 ounce) jar grape jelly
2 (16 ounce) packages cocktail sausages

- Pour barbecue sauce and grape jelly into large saucepan and cook until jelly melts and mixture is smooth. Stir well.
- Add cooked sausage and simmer on low heat for 20 minutes, stirring often.
- Serve hot.

Tip: Cocktail wieners could be substituted for sausage.

Apricot Smokies

½ cup apricot preserves
1 tablespoon prepared mustard
1 package little smokies sausages

- In saucepan, combine apricot preserves and mustard over low heat.
- Add smokies and heat until bubbly.
- Pour into serving dish. Insert wooden picks in sausages.

Sweet 'N Sour Vienna Sausages

1 (6 ounce) jar prepared mustard
1 (10 ounce) jar currant jelly
4 (5 ounce) cans Vienna sausages, drained, halved

- Mix mustard and jelly in saucepan and heat until they blend well.
- Add sausages and heat through.
- Serve in chafing dish. Insert wooden picks in sausages.

Tip: Hot dogs, cut in bite-size pieces, can be substituted for Vienna sausages.

Baked Brie

1 round baby brie
Apricot preserves
Almonds, slivered, toasted

- Coat brie with preserves and bake at 350° for 20 minutes.
- Sprinkle with toasted almonds. Serve with sliced apples or pears and pumpernickel bread.

Cheese Fondue

1 (1 pound) package cubed, processed cheese
1 (10 ounce) can cheese soup
1 (6 to 8 inch) round loaf bread

- In saucepan, melt cheese with cheese soup. Stir constantly to prevent scorching.
- Cut center from bread in cubes. Form bread bowl and place on platter.
- Pour cheese fondue into bread bowl and surround with cut bread cubes.
- Use bread cubes to dip into fondue. You can also eat bread bowl.

Ham and Cheese Pick-Ups

1 (8 ounce) package cream cheese, softened
1 (1 ounce) package dry onion soup mix
2 (3 ounce) packages thin sliced ham

- Beat cream cheese until creamy and stir in soup mix. (If needed, add a little mayonnaise or milk to make cream cheese easier to spread.)
- Lay slices of ham and carefully spread thin layer of cream cheese mixture over each slice.
- Roll ham slices into log and refrigerate 1 to 2 hours.
- To serve, cut into ¾-inch slices and insert wooden pick in each slice for easy pick-up.

Cocktail Ham

1 cup hickory-flavored barbecue sauce
4 tablespoons light brown sugar
1 pound deli ham, cut in squares

- Pour barbecue sauce and sugar into saucepan and mix well. Heat until sugar dissolves in barbecue sauce.
- Add ham and heat thoroughly. Cool then reheat. (This improves flavor.)
- Place in chafing dish and serve with cocktail-size hamburger buns.

Chili Snacks

1 (15 ounce) can chili without beans
1 cup shredded cheddar cheese
Party rye bread slices

- Combine chili and cheese in saucepan and heat until cheese melts.
- Spread on party rye bread.
- If desired, place bread on cookie sheet and bake at 350° for 15 to 20 minutes.

Shrimp Surprise

1 (8 ounce) package cream cheese, softened
½ cup shrimp cocktail sauce
2 (4 ounce) cans tiny shrimp, cooked, drained, chilled

- Place cream cheese in center of serving plate and pour cocktail sauce over cheese.
- Sprinkle chilled shrimp over sauce and surround with crackers.

Sticky Chicky

30 chicken wings
½ cup honey
½ cup soy sauce

- Wash wings, cut into sections and discard tips.
- Pour honey and soy sauce into 9 x 13-inch pan and mix in pan.
- Arrange wings over mixture and chill for 2 hours.
- Turn after 1 hour, so both sides will be "sticky".
- Bake in same pan at 375° for 45 minutes, turning occasionally.

Chinese Chicken Wings

3 pounds chicken wings
1 (10 ounce) bottle soy sauce
½ cup sugar

- Clean wings, snip tips and discard.
- Mix soy sauce and sugar in 9 x 13 x 2-inch glass dish or pan.
- Add chicken wings and turn to coat. Marinate wings for 24 hours in refrigerator and turn often.
- Remove from refrigerator after 24 hours and let set on counter for 15 minutes. Pour off most of sauce.
- Cover dish tightly with foil and bake at 250° for 2 hours.
- Remove foil during last 15 minutes of baking time to brown wings.

Taco Meatballs

1 (2 pound) package ground beef or ground round
2 eggs, beaten
1 (1 ounce) package taco seasoning mix

- Combine all ingredients, mix and shape into small meatballs. Place in foil-lined pan.
- Bake at 375° for about 15 minutes or until brown and drain.
- Serve on platter and insert wooden pick in each meatball for easy pick-up.

Tip: You may use a small ice cream scoop to shape uniform meatballs.

Shrimp Spread

1 (6 ounce) can shrimp, drained, mashed
1 (3 ounce) package cream cheese, softened
Shrimp cocktail sauce

- Combine mashed shrimp and softened cream cheese. Mix until they blend well.
- Stir in enough shrimp cocktail sauce for spreading consistency.
- Spread on crackers.

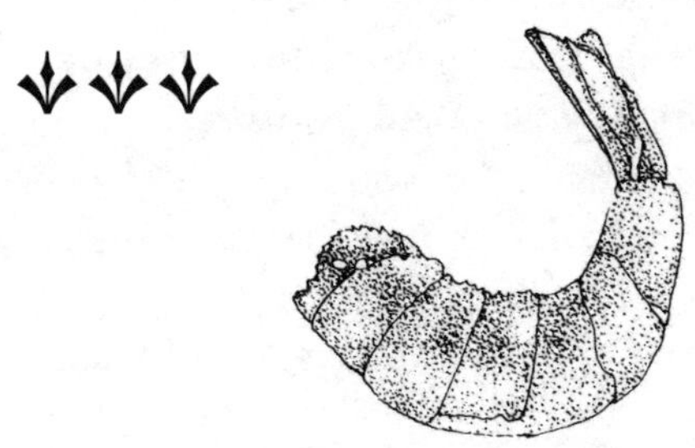

Crabmeat Spread

1 (8 ounce) package cream cheese, softened
1 (6 ounce) can crabmeat, well drained
½ (8 ounce) bottle seafood cocktail sauce

- Spread softened cream cheese on 10-inch serving plate.
- Spread drained crabmeat over cheese and layer with cocktail sauce.
- Cover with plastic wrap and chill for 4 hours.
- Serve with crackers.

Caviar Spread

1 (8 ounce) package cream cheese
½ red onion, finely chopped
1 (2 ounce) jar black caviar

- Place cream cheese in center of plate.
- Sprinkle chopped red onion over cheese and add caviar on top.
- Serve with melba toast rounds.

Spicy Peanuts

2 teaspoons vegetable oil
1½ teaspoons ground red pepper
2 cups dry roasted peanuts

- Heat oil in 10-inch skillet over medium heat. Stir in red pepper and peanuts.
- Mix and cook 2 minutes, stirring constantly, until evenly coated and hot.

Orange-Fruit Dip

1 (8 ounce) package cream cheese, softened
½ cup chopped pecans
1½ tablespoons dry orange drink mix

- With mixer, beat cream cheese until creamy.
- Combine remaining ingredients and mix well.
- Chill. Serve in small bowl in middle of platter surrounded by sliced apples.

Tip: Cut top slice off 1 orange and scoop pulp from fruit. Fill fruit cup with dip.

Strawberries and Dip

1 (8 ounce) carton sour cream
2 tablespoons brown sugar
Fresh strawberries, chilled

- Combine sour cream and brown sugar and mix well.
- Serve in bowl and put in middle of platter surrounded by fresh strawberries.

Strawberry-Spritzer Punch

3 (10 ounce) packages frozen strawberries, thawed, divided
2 (24 ounce) bottles white grape juice, chilled
1 (28 ounce) bottle club soda or carbonated water, chilled

- Place 2 packages thawed strawberries with juice in blender. Cover and blend until smooth.
- In punch bowl, combine strawberries, grape juice and remaining package strawberries. Mix well.
- Stir in carbonated water when ready to serve.

Strawberry Punch

2 (10 ounce) boxes frozen strawberries
1 (12 ounce) can frozen pink lemonade concentrate, diluted, chilled
1 (2 liter) bottle 7-Up or ginger ale, chilled

- Thaw strawberries until slushy and mix in blender.
- Pour lemonade into punch bowl and stir in strawberries.
- Add 7-Up or ginger ale and stir well. (Add a little sugar if punch is too tart.)

Cranberry Punch

2 quarts cranberry juice, chilled
2 quarts ginger ale or 7-Up, chilled
1 (12 ounce) can frozen lemonade concentrate

- Combine all ingredients punch bowl and add 2 cans ice water.
- Mix well.

Party Fruit Punch

2 quarts cranberry juice, chilled, divided
1 (46 ounce) can fruit punch, chilled
1 (46 ounce) can pineapple juice, chilled

- Pour 1-quart cranberry juice into ice trays and freeze as ice cubes.
- In punch bowl, combine fruit punch, pineapple juice and 1-quart cranberry juice. Mix well.
- Add cranberry ice cubes to punch when ready to serve.

Orange-Strawberry Drink

2 cups orange juice, chilled
1½ cups apricot nectar, chilled
1 cup frozen sweetened strawberries, thawed

- Combine all ingredients in blender and mix well.

Strawberry Cooler

1 (6 ounce) can frozen limeade concentrate, diluted
1 (10 ounce) package frozen strawberries, thawed
1 (2 liter) bottle strawberry-carbonated beverage, chilled

- Prepare limeade according to directions on can. Chill.
- Blend strawberries in blender until smooth.
- Combine limeade and berries in punch bowl.
- Stir in strawberry-carbonated beverage when ready to serve.

Mary's D.A.R. Punch

2 quarts orange juice, chilled
2 quarts lemonade, chilled
1 (2 liter) bottle 7-Up, chilled

- Combine all ingredients in punch bowl and mix well.

Christmas Punch

1 (46 ounce) can pineapple juice, chilled
1 (1 liter) bottle ginger ale, chilled
1 (2 liter) bottle strawberry-carbonated beverage, chilled

- Combine all ingredients in punch bowl and mix well.
- Use extra ginger ale or 7-Up, if desired.
- Makes about 20 servings.

Emerald Punch

2 packages lime fruit-flavored drink mix
1 (46 ounce) can pineapple juice, chilled
1 (2 liter) bottle ginger ale, chilled

- Prepare drink mix according to package directions. Chill several hours.
- Pour into punch bowl and stir in pineapple juice.
- Add ginger ale when ready to serve.

Tip: Make an ice ring with additional ginger ale and add to punch bowl. If you don't have a round jello mold, pour ginger ale into any nicely shaped container and freeze.

Holiday Punch

1 package cherry fruit-flavored drink mix
2 quarts ginger ale, chilled
1 (46 ounce) can pineapple juice, chilled

- Combine all ingredients in punch bowl and mix well.
- Add more ginger ale if needed.

Five-Alive Punch

2 (12 ounce) cans frozen Five-Alive juice concentrate
1 (12 ounce) can frozen pink lemonade concentrate
1 (2 liter) bottle ginger ale, chilled

- Dilute juices according to directions on cans and pour into punch bowl. Mix well.
- Add ginger ale when ready to serve.

Pina Colada Punch

1 (2 quart) can pineapple-coconut juice, chilled
2 quarts 7-Up, chilled
1 (20 ounce) can pineapple rings with juice

- In punch bowl, combine pineapple-coconut juice, 7-Up and juice from pineapple rings.
- Float pineapple rings in punch bowl.

Betty's Hawaiian Punch

1 (46 ounce) can Hawaiian Punch, chilled
1 (2 liter) bottle ginger ale or 7-Up, chilled
1 (12 ounce) can frozen lemonade concentrate

- Combine all ingredients in punch bowl and add 2 cups cold water.
- Mix well and serve immediately.
- Makes about 22 cups punch.

Mocha Punch

1 quart coffee, chilled
1 quart chocolate milk
1 quart vanilla or chocolate ice cream

- Mix coffee and milk until they blend well.
- Stir in ice cream and mix until creamy.
- Serve immediately.

Lime Punch

2 (2 liter) bottles 7-Up, chilled
1 (2 liter) bottle ginger ale, chilled
½ gallon lime sherbet

- Combine 7-Up and ginger ale in punch bowl.
- When ready to serve, add lime sherbet and stir well.

Dorothy Townsend's Strawberry Punch

½ gallon strawberry ice cream, softened
2 (2 liter) bottles ginger ale or 7-Up, chilled
1 (10 ounce) package frozen strawberries, thawed

- Combine all ingredients in punch bowl and stir well.
- Serve immediately.
- Makes about 26 punch cups.

Apricot-Orange Punch

1 (46 ounce) can apricot juice, chilled
1 (2 liter) bottle ginger ale, chilled
½ gallon orange sherbet

- Combine apricot juice and ginger ale in punch bowl.
- Stir in scoops of sherbet.
- Serve immediately in 4-ounce punch cups.
- Makes about 35 cups.

Cranberry-Grape Frost

1 (48 ounce) bottle cranberry juice, chilled
1 (46 ounce) can grape juice, chilled
½ gallon raspberry sherbet

- Combine juices in punch bowl and stir in scoops of sherbet.
- Serve immediately.

Tip: Add 1 (2 liter) bottle chilled ginger ale or 7-Up for something bubbly.

Hot Apple Cider

2 quarts apple cider
½ cup cinnamon red hot candies
1 apple, sliced

- Pour apple cider into large pan, stir in red hot candies and simmer until candy dissolves.
- Serve hot in mugs and garnish with ½ apple slice.

Frosty Grape Punch

1 (2 quart) bottle grape juice, chilled
½ gallon raspberry sherbet
2 (2 liter) bottles ginger ale, chilled

- Pour grape juice in punch bowl and stir in sherbet.
- Add ginger ale and serve immediately.

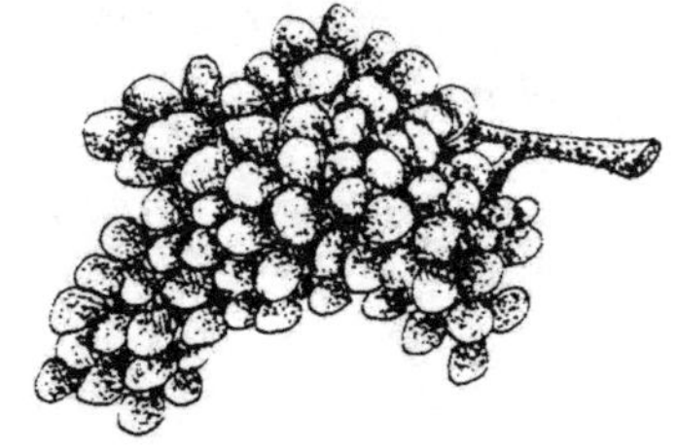

Frosty Orange-Pineapple Punch

2 (46 ounce) cans pineapple juice, chilled
½ gallon orange sherbet
1 (2 liter) bottle ginger ale, chilled

- Pour pineapple juice in punch bowl and stir in sherbet.
- Add ginger ale.
- Serve immediately.

Shirley Temple

4 tablespoons grenadine syrup
4 cups ginger ale, chilled
4 maraschino cherries

- Put 1 tablespoon grenadine syrup in each glass.
- Add ginger ale and stir.
- Garnish with maraschino cherry.

Mock Pink Champagne

2 quarts cranberry juice, chilled
1 quart ginger ale, chilled
1 quart 7-Up, chilled

- When ready to serve, combine all ingredients in punch bowl. (Do not prepare punch ahead of time.)
- Makes 30 (4 ounce) punch cups.

Chocolate Milk Shake

1 cup milk
⅓ cup chocolate-flavored syrup
2 to 3 scoops vanilla ice cream

- Place milk and syrup in blender, cover and blend on HIGH speed for 5 seconds.
- Add ice cream, cover and blend on LOW speed for 5 to 10 seconds.
- Pour into 2 glasses.

Chili-Cheese Bread

1 (16 ounce) loaf French bread
1 cup shredded cheddar cheese
1 (7 ounce) can chopped green chilies, drained

- Cut bread in half lengthwise and spread cheddar cheese over each half.
- Sprinkle chopped, green chilies over top and place on cookie sheet.
- Bake at 325° for 10 minutes.

Sour Cream Rolls

1 cup self-rising flour
½ cup (1 stick) butter, melted
1 cup sour cream

- Combine all ingredients and mix well.
- Pour into sprayed miniature muffin tins and bake at 350° for 15 minutes.

Cloverleaf Rolls

2¼ cups biscuit mix, divided
1 (8 ounce) carton sour cream
½ cup (1 stick) butter, melted

- Combine 2 cups biscuit mix with sour cream and melted butter and mix well.
- Sprinkle remaining ¼ cup biscuit mix on wax paper.
- Drop dough by level tablespoonfuls onto biscuit mix and roll into balls.
- Place 3 balls into each of 12 sprayed muffin cups and bake at 350° for 15 to 20 minutes or until golden brown.

Mexican Corn Bread

1 (8 ounce) package corn bread mix
½ cup shredded cheddar cheese, divided
1 (8 ounce) can cream-style corn

- Prepare corn bread according to package directions and stir in corn and ¼ cup shredded cheese.
- Pour into sprayed skillet or muffin tins and top with remaining ¼ cup cheese.
- Bake at 400° for 15 to 20 minutes.

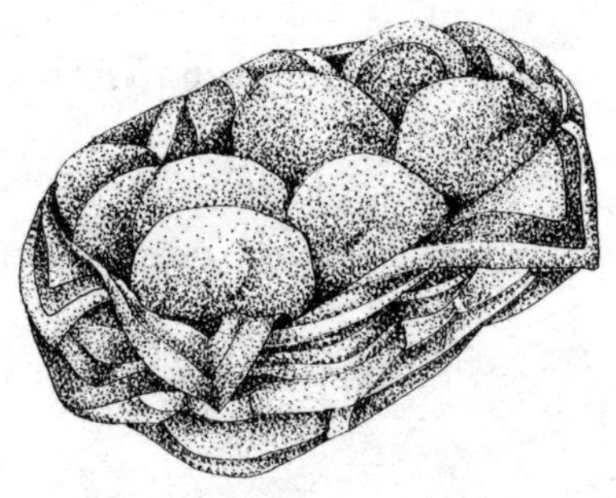

Rosebillie Horn's Zucchini Bread

1 (18 ounce) box spice cake mix
2 cups shredded zucchini
½ cup chopped black walnuts or pecans

- Prepare cake mix according to package directions.
- Squeeze liquid from zucchini, stir zucchini and nuts into spice cake mix and mix well.
- Pour into 2 greased, floured loaf pans and bake at 350° for 50 to 60 minutes.

No-Peek Popovers

2 eggs
1 cup milk
1 cup flour

- Combine all ingredients and mix well. Pour ¾ full into 8 sprayed muffin cups.
- Place in cold oven, bake at 450° for 30 minutes and don't peek.

Mayonnaise Rolls

2 cups self-rising flour
1 cup milk
4 tablespoons mayonnaise

- Combine all ingredients and mix well.
- Pour into sprayed muffin tins and bake at 400° for 22 minutes.

Cheese Biscuits

2¼ cups baking mix
⅔ cup milk
½ cup shredded cheddar cheese

- Mix all ingredients until soft dough forms and beat for 30 seconds. If dough is too sticky, add more baking mix.
- Drop by rounded spoonfuls onto sprayed cookie sheet and bake at 350° for 15 minutes or until light brown.

Buttermilk Biscuits

½ cup (1 stick) butter
2 cups flour
¾ cup buttermilk

- Using pastry blender, cut ½ cup butter into flour until mixture resembles coarse meal.
- Stir in buttermilk and mix until dry ingredients are moist. Turn dough out onto floured surface and knead 3 or 4 times.
- Roll dough to ¾-inch thickness and cut with biscuit cutter. Place on lightly sprayed cookie sheet and bake at 425° for 12 to 15 minutes.

Tip: To make buttermilk, mix 1 cup milk with 1 tablespoon lemon juice or vinegar and let milk rest for about 10 minutes.

Party Biscuits

1 cup flour
1 cup whipping cream
2 tablespoons sugar

- Mix all ingredients and pour into sprayed mini-muffin cups.
- Bake 400° for 10 minutes.

Onion Biscuits

2 cups biscuit mix
¼ cup milk
1 (8 ounce) carton French-onion dip

- Combine all ingredients and mix until soft dough forms. Drop dough into mounds onto sprayed cookie sheet.
- Bake at 375° for 10 to 12 minutes or until golden brown.

Tip: If you like round cut-out biscuits, sprinkle extra biscuit mix on wax paper and spoon dough over biscuit mix. Sprinkle 1 tablespoon biscuit mix over dough and knead 3 or 4 times. Use a little more biscuit mix if dough is too sticky. Pat out to ½-inch thickness and use biscuit cutter.

Ice Cream Muffins

2 cups self rising flour
1 pint vanilla ice cream
2½ tablespoons butter

- Blend flour and ice cream until flour is very moist. Batter will be lumpy. Fill 10 buttered muffin cups until ¾ full.
- Spoon 1 teaspoon melted butter over top of muffins and bake at 350° for 20 minutes.

Yield: 5 to 10 servings.

Orange Butter

1 cup (2 sticks) butter, softened
2 tablespoons grated orange rind
¼ cup orange juice

- Beat butter and rind until fluffy. Gradually add orange juice and beat until it blends well.
- Store in refrigerator and serve with hot biscuits.

Heidelberg Soup

2 (10 ounce) cans potato soup
6 slices salami, cubed
10 green onions, chopped

- Dilute soup according to directions on can.
- In well greased skillet, saute cubed salami and onions and add to soup.
- Heat thoroughly and serve hot.

Guacamole Soup

1 (18 ounce) can spicy tomato cocktail juice
½ cup chopped onion
2 avocados, peeled, seeded, divided

- In saucepan, heat tomato juice and onion for 5 minutes or until very hot.
- Stir in ¾ of diced avocado and heat. Reserve ¼ avocado for garnish.
- Sprinkle avocado on top of soup and serve immediately.

Pat's Chilled Strawberry Soup

2 (10 ounce) packages strawberries in syrup
½ cup cranberries
2 (8 ounce) cartons strawberry yogurt

- In blender, combine all ingredients and blend until smooth.
- Chill 1 to 2 hours before serving.

Tomato-Bacon Soup

1 (10 ounce) can tomato soup
1 (14 ounce) can stewed tomatoes with celery and peppers
½ pound bacon, fried, drained, crumbled

- In saucepan, combine soup and stewed tomatoes and heat thoroughly.
- Sprinkle bacon over soup and serve hot.

El Paso Tomato Soup

1 (10 ounce) can tomato soup
1 (14 ounce) can chopped stewed tomatoes with onion
1 (10 ounce) can chopped tomatoes and green chilies

- In saucepan, mix all ingredients plus 1 soup can water.
- Heat to boiling, stirring often.
- Reduce heat and simmer for 5 minutes.

Senate Bean Soup

2 cups dried navy beans
6 cups water
½ pound ham hocks

- Cover beans in water and soak overnight.
- Drain and pour beans in 6 cups water and cook with ham hocks for 2 to 3 hours or until tender.
- Season with salt and pepper.

Microwave Mushroom Soup

1 (10 ounce) can cream of mushroom soup
1 (10 ounce) can beef consomme
1 (4 ounce) can sliced mushrooms

- Combine mushroom soup and consomme in 2-quart bowl and mix well. Microwave on HIGH for 1 minute and stir.
- Add sliced mushrooms and mix well.
- Reduce heat to medium and microwave 1 minute longer or until hot.
- Stir before serving.

Olive-Egg Salad Spread for Sandwiches

6 eggs, hard-boiled
12 stuffed green olives, finely chopped
Mayonnaise

- Rinse hard-boiled eggs in cool water, peel shells and chop eggs.
- Combine eggs, olives and enough mayonnaise to moisten.
- Refrigerate mixture until ready to use.
- Spread on wheat bread and cut in half for sandwiches.

Tip: You can also add ½ cup chopped pecans to this recipe.

Dorothy Townsend's Ribbon Sandwiches

8 slices sandwich bread (4 whole wheat and 4 white)
1 (5 ounce) jar Old English cheese spread
½ cup (1 stick) butter, softened

- Remove crusts from bread slices.
- With mixer, beat cheese spread and butter until smooth.
- Spread mixture on 4 slices of white bread and top with whole wheat bread slices.
- Slice each sandwich in 3 or 4 strips, wrap tightly with plastic wrap and refrigerate.

Cucumber-Tea Sandwich Spread

1 (8 ounce) package cream cheese, softened
2 cucumbers, peeled, seeded, grated
¾ teaspoon seasoned salt

- In bowl, beat cream cheese until smooth.
- Drain grated cucumber well with several paper towels and combine with cream cheese mixture and seasoned salt. Mix well.
- Spread on crust-trimmed white bread slices and cut in triangles or bars.

Black Olive Spread

1 (3 ounce) package cream cheese, softened
1 (2 ounce) can chopped black olives, drained
1 (8 ounce) package shredded cheddar cheese

- In bowl, beat cream cheese until smooth.
- Combine olives and both cheeses.
- Spread mixture on slices of party rye or pumpernickel bread.
- Serve cold or, if you prefer, broil and serve hot.

Did you know that you can extend the shelf life of olives by transferring them and their brine to a glass jar before refrigerating. Make sure the jar is airtight.

Cherry-Cheese Sandwich Spread

1 (8 ounce) jar maraschino cherries
1 (8 ounce) package cream cheese, softened
½ cup pecans, finely chopped

- Drain cherries and finely dice.
- In bowl, beat cream cheese until creamy and combine with diced cherries and chopped pecans. Mix until they blend well.
- Trim crusts from several slices of white bread and spread mixture.
- Use as open-face sandwiches or make into 3-layered ribbon sandwiches.

Salami-On-Rye Sandwiches

24 salami slices
48 slices party rye bread
1 (8 ounce) jar dijon-style mustard

- Place 1 salami slice folded in half or quartered so that it fits on rye bread.
- Spread mustard and top with second slice of party rye for quick party sandwiches.

Yield: 24 sandwiches.

Anytime sandwiches are made in advance, they can be wrapped and refrigerated in an airtight container. They'll keep for at least a day.

Spinach-Bacon Salad

2 quarts fresh spinach, torn into pieces
8 bacon slices, cooked, crumbled
3 eggs, hard-boiled, chopped

- In salad bowl, combine all ingredients.
- Toss well before serving.

Summer Spinach Salad

4 cups fresh spinach, torn into pieces
½ fresh strawberries, sliced
1 cup halved, seedless grapes

- In salad bowl, combine all ingredients.
- Toss well before serving.

Tip: You may substitute romaine lettuce for spinach. Toss and serve with poppy-seed dressing.

Store spinach leaves that are wrapped loosely in paper towels and tightly sealed in a plastic bag in the refrigerator for up to 3 days.

Spinach-Orange Salad

2 cups spinach, torn into pieces
⅓ cup almonds, slivered, toasted
1 (11 ounce) can mandarin oranges

- In salad bowl, combine all ingredients.
- Toss well before serving.

Spinach-Apple-Walnut Salad

6 cups fresh spinach leaves, torn into pieces
2 red delicious apples, cored, chopped
½ cup coarsely chopped walnuts

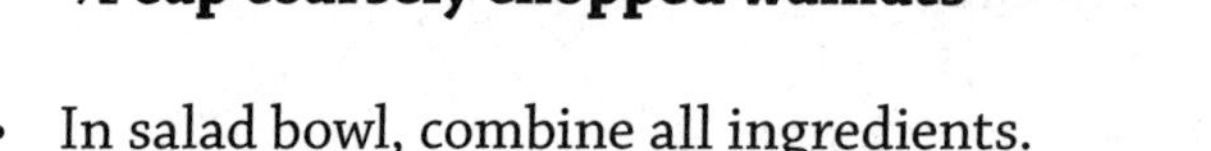

- In salad bowl, combine all ingredients.
- Toss well before serving.

When selecting spinach, avoid limp, damaged or discolored leaves. Look for spinach with crisp, dark green leaves (curled or smooth). Wash leaves in cold water, swishing the leaves gently to clean well. Use salad spinner to dry leaves or lay them on paper towels and blot-dry.

Greek Summer Salad

4 cups fresh spinach, torn into pieces
1½ cups sliced strawberries
⅓ cup crumbled feta cheese

- In salad bowl, combine all ingredients.
- Cover and chill until serving time.

Shrimp and Spinach Salad

1 cup shrimp, cooked, drained
3 cups fresh spinach, torn into pieces
½ cup chopped celery

- In salad bowl, combine all ingredients
- Toss before serving.

Tip: Thousand Island dressing is great with this dish.

Romaine-Artichoke Salad

1 head romaine lettuce, torn into pieces
1 (14 ounce) can artichoke hearts, drained, chopped
1 large tomato, cut in wedges

- In salad bowl, combine all ingredients.
- Toss before serving.

Boston Bibb Lettuce Salad

1 head bibb lettuce, torn into pieces
1 (11 ounce) can mandarin oranges, drained
⅓ cup walnuts

- In salad bowl, combine all ingredients. Toss before serving.

Instant Salad

1 (24 ounce) carton cottage cheese, drained
1 (6 ounce) package strawberry gelatin
1 (8 ounce) carton frozen, whipped topping, thawed

- In bowl, combine drained cottage cheese with dry gelatin. Mix well.
- Fold in whipped topping and spoon into glass serving dish
- Chill for 2 to 3 hours before serving.

Layered Raspberry-Cranberry Salad

2 (3 ounce) packages raspberry gelatin
1 (16 ounce) can whole berry cranberries
1 cup sour cream

- Prepare gelatin with 1½ cups boiling water. Chill until partially set.
- Stir in cranberries and pour half mixture into dish.
- Chill in freezer until firm and spread sour cream over mixture.
- Top with remaining berry-gelatin mixture at room temperature. Chill until firm.

Strawberry-Banana Whip

1 (3 ounce) package strawberry gelatin
1 (8 ounce) container frozen, whipped topping, thawed
2 bananas, sliced

- Prepare gelatin with ¾ cup boiling water and stir until it dissolves.
- Chill until partially set.
- Whip gelatin, fold in whipped topping and blend well. Stir in bananas.
- Pour into glass bowl, cover and chill until firm.

Raspberry-Sherbet Salad

1 (6 ounce) raspberry gelatin
1 pint raspberry sherbet
1 pint fresh or frozen raspberries

- Dissolve gelatin in 1½ cups boiling water, mix well and cool. Add sherbet and mix well.
- Chill until partially set.
- Stir in berries and pour into 9 x 13-inch glass dish.
- Chill until set and cut into squares.

Tip: Don't wash berries until just before using them. Refrigerated berries will not bruise as easily while washing as room-temperature berries.

❖❖❖

Anita McKee's Raspberry Salad

1 (6 ounce) package raspberry gelatin
1 (8 ounce) carton frozen, whipped topping, thawed
1 (10 ounce) package frozen, unsweetened raspberries, thawed

- Prepare gelatin with 1½ cups boiling water and mix well. Do not add any cold water.
- Cover and chill until partially jelled.
- Beat with electric mixer until fluffy, fold in whipped topping and beat until it blends.
- Stir in raspberries and spoon into serving bowl.
- Cover and chill until firm.

Margaret Sinclair's Carrot-Pineapple Gelatin Salad

1 (3 ounce) box orange or lime gelatin
½ cup grated carrots
1 (8 ounce) can crushed pineapple, drained

- Prepare gelatin with ¾ cup boiling water and chill until partially jelled.
- Stir in carrots and pineapple and pour into serving bowl.
- Chill several hours before serving.

Wilma Davis' Cinnamon-Apple Salad

⅔ cup cinnamon red hot candies
1 (3 ounce) package cherry gelatin
1½ cups applesauce

- Heat cinnamon red hots in ⅔ cup boiling water until candy melts.
- Pour over dry gelatin and stir until it dissolves well.
- Chill until partially set. Stir in applesauce and pour into glass serving dish. Chill until firm.

Shamrock Salad

1 (6 ounce) package lime gelatin
1 pint vanilla ice cream
2 bananas, sliced or 2 apples, chopped

- Mix gelatin with 1½ cups boiling water, cool and stir in ice cream.
- Chill until partially set and stir in sliced bananas or apples.
- Spoon into glass serving dish and chill until firm.

Wilma Davis' Cran-Apple Salad

1 (6 ounce) package orange gelatin
2 peeled apples, peeled, chopped
1 (16 ounce) can whole berry cranberry sauce

- Prepare gelatin with 1 cup boiling water and stir until it dissolves.
- Cool. Add apples and whole berry cranberry sauce, mix well and pour into 7 x 11-inch glass dish. Cover and chill until firm.

Lime-Gelatin Salad

1 (6 ounce) package lime gelatin
1 (15 ounce) can crushed pineapple with juice
1 cup cottage cheese

- Dissolve gelatin in 1 cup boiling water and chill until partially set.
- Stir in pineapple and cottage cheese and pour into 7 x 11-inch glass dish.
- Chill until firm and cut in squares to serve.

Lime-Yogurt Salad

1 (8 ounce) can pear halves, drained
2 (3 ounce) packages lime gelatin
1 (8 ounce) carton vanilla yogurt

- Slice pears and stir gelatin into 1½ cups boiling water until it dissolves.
- Divide gelatin into 2 bowls. Blend yogurt into 1 bowl of gelatin and stir pears into remaining gelatin in other bowl.
- Pour gelatin-yogurt mixture into square 9-inch dish and chill until partially thick.
- Let pear mixture set and on top of gelatin-yogurt mixture.
- Chill until firm and cut into squares to serve.

Pam's Creamy Cranberry Mold

2 (3 ounce) packages cherry gelatin
1 (16 ounce) can jellied cranberry sauce
1 cup sour cream

- Dissolve gelatin in 1¼ cups boiling water, stir in cranberry sauce and mix until they blend well.
- Add sour cream and beat with electric mixer until creamy.
- Pour into mold and chill until firm.

Cherry-Cranberry Mold

1 (6 ounce) package cherry gelatin
1 (16 ounce) can whole cranberry sauce
1 (20 ounce) can cherry pie filling

- Dissolve gelatin in 1 cup boiling water and mix cranberries and cherry filling into gelatin.
- Pour into mold or 9 x 13-inch glass dish and chill until firm.

Blueberry Salad

2 (3 ounce) boxes grape gelatin
1 (20 ounce) can blueberry pie filling
1 (20 ounce) can crushed pineapple with juice

- Dissolve gelatin in 1 cup boiling water.
- Chill until partially set and stir in blueberries, pineapple and juice.
- Pour into 9 x 13-inch glass dish and chill until firm.

Pineapple Boats

1 fresh pineapple
1 (15 ounce) can tropical fruit salad, drained
2 tablespoons shredded coconut

- Cut fresh, whole pineapple in half (leaves and all). Remove core and fruit but leave ½-inch thick shell.
- Cube core and fruit from pineapple shell and set aside.
- Fill with drained, tropical fruit mixed with reserved pineapple and sprinkle coconut over top.

Quick Ambrosia

1 (11 ounce) can mandarin oranges, drained
1 (15 ounce) can pineapple chunks, drained
2 tablespoons shredded coconut

- Drain oranges and pineapple, combine fruit and divide among 4 dessert dishes. Sprinkle each with coconut.

Cranberry-Orange Relish

1 (16 ounce) can whole berry cranberries
⅔ cup orange marmalade
⅓ cup chopped walnuts

- In bowl, combine all ingredients and mix well.
- Cover and chill 2 to 3 hours before serving. Serve with pork or ham.

Tip: You may substitute ½ cup sliced maraschino cherries for walnuts.

Jim Wornall's Peach and Cottage Cheese Salad

1 cup cottage cheese
1 (15 ounce) can peaches halves or slices, drained
Maraschino cherries

- Place scoop of cottage cheese in center of salad plate and arrange peaches around it.
- Add maraschino cherry on top of cottage cheese as garnish.

Judy Mueller's Honey-Lime Dressing

¼ cup fresh lime juice
¼ cup honey
¼ teaspoon dijon-style mustard

- In bowl, combine all ingredients, cover and chill.
- Serve chilled over lettuce or fruit salad.

Tip: Judy serves this dressing over a romaine and honeydew melon salad.

Walnut-Cranberry Relish

1 (16 ounce) can whole berry cranberries
1 (8 ounce) can crushed pineapple, drained
½ cup chopped black walnuts

- In bowl, combine all ingredients and mix well. Chill before serving.

Bean and Corn Salsa

½ cup canned black beans, drained
½ cup canned whole kernel corn, drained
1 cup thick and chunky salsa

- In small bowl, combine all ingredients and mix well. Keep chilled.

Tip: Serve with enchiladas or other Mexican food.

Deluxe Asparagus

1 (15 ounce) can cut asparagus with liquid
2 eggs, beaten
¾ cup shredded, Mexican-style 4-cheese blend

- Drain asparagus and reserve 4 tablespoons liquid.
- In bowl, combine eggs and reserved asparagus liquid and mix well.
- Arrange asparagus in sprayed baking dish and pour egg mixture over asparagus.
- Sprinkle cheese over top and bake at 350° for 30 minutes.

Broccoli Casserole

1 (10 ounce) package frozen broccoli florets, thawed
1 (10 ounce) can cream of celery soup
½ cup shredded cheddar cheese

- Cook broccoli according to package directions and drain.
- Spread in sprayed baking dish and cover with celery soup. Sprinkle cheese over top.
- Bake at 350° for 20 to 25 minutes or until hot.

Cabbage Casserole

1 head cabbage, cut, cooked, drained
1 (10 ounce) can cream of chicken soup
1 cup shredded cheddar cheese

- In buttered baking dish, alternate layers of cabbage, soup and cheese.
- Repeat layers and bake at 350° for 30 minutes.

Creamed Corn

2 (10 ounce) boxes frozen whole kernel corn
1 (8 ounce) package cream cheese, softened
Lemon pepper to taste

- Cook corn according to package directions and drain.
- Stir cream cheese into hot corn and stir until heated thoroughly.
- Season to taste with lemon pepper.

Mexican Corn

1 (16 ounce) package frozen corn, thawed
½ cup thick and chunky salsa
¼ cup sliced ripe olives

- Cook corn according to package directions and stir in salsa and olives.
- Cook until hot and drain.

Company Cauliflower

1 head cauliflower, divided
1 cup sour cream, divided
1 cup shredded cheddar cheese, divided

- Rinse cauliflower and separate into florets. Cook in 2-quart covered saucepan in 1-inch boiling, salted water for 8 to 10 minutes or until tender. Drain well.
- Place half cauliflower in greased casserole dish and spread ½ cup sour cream over cauliflower. Sprinkle with ½ cup of cheese and repeat layers. Bake at 325° for 20 minutes or until cheese melts.

Lila Obercrom's Green Beans and Bacon

6 slices bacon
1 cup onion, chopped
2 pounds fresh green beans or 2 (14.5 ounce) cans green beans

- Fry bacon until crisp and drain on paper towels.
- Cook onion in bacon drippings until transparent. Stir onion into beans and cook 1 minute.
- If you cook fresh green beans, add 1 tablespoon water, cover and cook 3 minutes. Uncover and cook 10 minutes longer.
- If you cook canned green beans, 4 minutes of cooking time is enough.
- Crumble bacon and add to beans just before serving.

Green Bean Casserole

2 (15 ounce) cans green beans, drained
1 (10 ounce) can cream of celery soup
1 cup crushed potato chips

- In bowl, combine green beans and soup and pour into sprayed 2-quart casserole dish.
- Top with crushed potato chips and bake at 350° for 25 to 30 minutes.

Basil Green Beans

1 (10 ounce) package frozen, French-style green beans
2 tablespoons (¼ stick) butter
½ teaspoon dried basil

- In saucepan, combine all ingredients, cover and bring to boil.
- Reduce heat, simmer until all liquid is gone and stir as needed.

Green Bean Amandine

2 (10 ounce) packages frozen green beans, thawed
⅓ cup almonds, slivered
3 tablespoons butter

- Cook beans according to package directions and drain well.
- In small saucepan, saute almonds in melted butter.
- Stir almonds and butter into green beans.

Myrtle Hull's Green Bean Casserole

2 (15 ounce) can green beans, drained
1 (10 ounce) can cream of mushroom soup
1 (3 ounce) can french-fried onion rings, divided

- In bowl, combine beans, soup and ½ of onion rings and mix well.
- Pour into sprayed baking dish and bake at 350° for 25 minutes.
- Top with remaining onion rings and bake 10 minutes longer.

New Year's Black-Eyed Peas

Eating black-eyed peas on New Year's Day brings good luck in the new year!

1 (15 ounce) can black-eyed peas, drained
8 slices pepperoni, chopped
2 tablespoons chopped onion

- In saucepan, combine all ingredients and heat thoroughly.
- Serve hot.

Green Pea Casserole

2 (10 ounce) packages frozen green peas
1 cup shredded cheddar cheese
1 (10 ounce) can golden mushroom soup

- Cook peas according to package directions and drain.
- Combine all ingredients in greased casserole dish at 350° for 30 to 35 minutes.

Green Peas Deluxe

2 (10 ounce) packages frozen green peas, thawed
1 (8 ounce) can chopped water chestnuts, drained
1 (10 ounce) can golden cream of mushroom soup

- Prepare green peas according to package directions and drain.
- Stir in water chestnuts and soup.
- Heat well in saucepan or pour into sprayed baking dish and bake at 350° for 25 minutes.

Snow Peas

1½ pounds fresh snow peas
1 tablespoon lemon juice
3 tablespoons butter

- Cook peas in steamer for 3 to 4 minutes.
- Season with lemon juice, butter and salt to taste.

Onion-Rice Casserole

1 (10 ounce) can French-onion soup
1 cup regular rice (not instant)
½ cup chopped celery

- In saucepan, combine all ingredients with 1 cup water. Mix well.
- Cook over medium heat for 25 to 30 minutes or until rice is tender. Fluff with fork.

Julie's Scalloped Onions

6 onions, peeled, sliced
½ (16 ounce) package processed cheese, sliced
3 cups potato chips, crushed

- In saucepan, boil onions until limp and transparent.
- Butter casserole dish and layer onions alternately with cheese and potato chips.
- Repeat layers and bake at 350° for 20 minutes.

Creamed Spinach

1 (10 ounce) package frozen, chopped spinach, thawed
1 (10 ounce) can cream of mushroom soup
½ teaspoon nutmeg

- Cook spinach according to package directions and drain well.
- In bowl, combine spinach and soup and mix well. Simmer for 10 to 15 minutes, stirring occasionally.
- Sprinkle with nutmeg.

Zucchini Casserole

4 zucchini, chopped
1 tube round, buttery crackers, crushed
1 (8 ounce) jar processed cheese spread, melted

- Cook zucchini in small amount of water until tender and drain.
- Alternate layers of zucchini and crushed crackers in sprayed casserole dish.
- Pour melted cheese over zucchini and crackers and bake at 350° for 30 minutes.

Vegetable Casserole

1 onion, chopped
2 (15 ounce) cans peas and carrots, drained
1 (8 ounce) package cubed, processed cheese

- In saucepan, saute onion in butter. Add remaining ingredients.
- Pour mixture into 2-quart baking dish and bake at 350° for 25 to 30 minutes.

Vegetable Christmas Tree

1 head broccoli
1 head cauliflower
24 cherry tomatoes

- Build tree on large tray or platter. Make tree trunk out of broccoli stem.
- Build first row of tree with cauliflower florets, next row with tomatoes and alternating rows. Decrease size of each row.
- Outline tree with broccoli florets.
- Serve with dip of choice.

Charlotte's Onion-Roasted Potatoes

2 pounds potatoes
1 (1 ounce) package dry onion soup mix
⅓ cup olive oil

- Wash, peel potatoes and cut into chunks.
- Pour all ingredients into large plastic bag, close bag and shake until potatoes coat well.
- Empty potatoes into sprayed 9 x 13-inch pan and bake at 450° for 40 minutes or until tender and golden brown, stirring occasionally.

Microwave Potato Skins

4 baked potatoes
1 cup shredded cheddar cheese
4 to 6 slices bacon, fried crisp, drained, crumbled

- Slice potatoes lengthwise and microwave for 3 minutes.
- Scoop out potato, leaving ¼-inch skins, and fill each potato skin with cheese and bacon.
- Place on plate, cover with paper towel and microwave for 30 seconds or until cheese melts.

Yield: 4 servings of 2 potato skins per person.

Skinny Mashed Potatoes

5 large potatoes, cut in 1-inch pieces
3½ cups chicken broth, divided
½ teaspoon white pepper or to taste

- Place potatoes and 2¼ cups broth in large saucepan. Boil on high and reduce to medium.
- Cover, cook 10 minutes or until potatoes are tender and drain, but reserve broth.
- Mash potatoes with 1¼ cups broth and pepper until desired consistency is reached. Add more broth if needed.

Pizza Potatoes

1 (5.5 ounce) box scalloped potatoes
1 cup shredded mozzarella cheese
1 cup pepperoni slices

- Prepare potatoes according to package directions but do not bake.
- Pour into sprayed casserole dish and spread cheese over potatoes.
- Arrange pepperoni slices over cheese.
- Cover and bake at 400° for 30 to 35 minutes.

Gay Herndon's Potato Casserole

5 potatoes, peeled, sliced
1 (10 ounce) can golden cream of mushroom soup
1 cup grated cheddar cheese

- Place sliced potatoes in sprayed 2-quart casserole dish.
- Dilute soup with ½ cup milk or water and mix well.
- Pour over potatoes and bake covered at 400° for 45 minutes.
- Uncover, top with cheese and bake 15 minutes longer.

Boiled New Potatoes

3 pounds small, new potatoes
¾ cup (1½ sticks) butter, melted
6 tablespoons minced parsley

- Cook small, new potatoes in 5 cups boiling water until tender.
- Drain. Sprinkle with melted butter and minced parsley.
- Serve hot.

Did you know that new potatoes should be used within 3 to 4 days of purchase so plan accordingly. Choose potatoes that are firm, are well-shaped, and are not sprouted.

Baked-Onion French Fries

1 (1 ounce) package dry onion soup mix
3 teaspoons canola oil
1 (24 ounce) package french-fried potatoes

- In large bowl, combine soup mix and oil.
- Add potatoes and stir until coated with soup mixture.
- Bake according to package directions and stir as needed.

Glazed Sweet Potatoes

4 sweet potatoes
½ cup packed brown sugar
¼ cup (½ stick) butter, melted

- Pierce potatoes several times with fork. Microwave on HIGH for 10 minutes or until fork-tender and cool.
- Peel and slice potatoes and place in greased baking dish. Sprinkle brown sugar over potatoes and top with butter.
- Cover and microwave on HIGH for 4 minutes then stir. Microwave for 1 or 2 minutes longer and let stand covered for 3 minutes before serving.

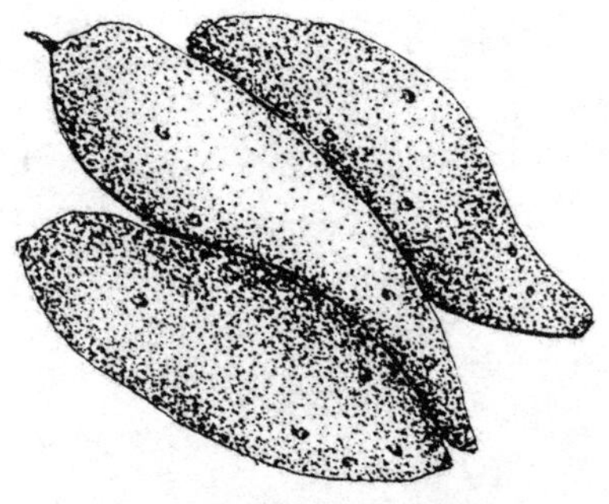

Seasoned Pasta

2 (14 ounce) cans seasoned chicken broth with Italian herbs
3 cups uncooked corkscrew pasta
½ to 1 cup grated parmesan cheese

- In saucepan, heat broth until it boils and stir in uncooked pasta.
- Reduce heat, simmer on medium until pasta is fork-tender. Stir often.
- Pour into serving bowl and sprinkle with grated parmesan cheese.

Carole's Easy Dressing

1 (6 ounce) box cornbread stuffing mix
1 onion, chopped
1 (14 ounce) can chicken broth

- In bowl, combine all ingredients and mix well.
- Pour dressing mixture into sprayed, non-stick 9 x 13-inch baking dish.
- Bake at 325° for 30 minutes.

Rice Pilaf

This rice is great with chicken!

2 cups cooked rice
⅓ cup raisins or chopped dates
¼ cup almonds, slivered, toasted

- In bowl, combine all ingredients and mix well.

Pecan-Rice Pilaf

½ cup pecan halves
3 tablespoons butter, melted
1 (7 ounce) package wild rice

- Saute pecan halves in melted butter.
- Prepare wild rice according to package directions and stir pecans into rice.
- Serve hot with chicken or pork.

Deviled Eggs

6 eggs, hard-boiled, halved
Thousand Island salad dressing
Paprika

- Slice eggs lengthwise, remove yolks and chop.
- Mix with enough dressing to moisten and stuff into egg white shells.
- Sprinkle with paprika and chill.

Glazed-Pineapple Slices

1 (20 ounce) can pineapple slices, drained
2 tablespoons (1/4 stick) butter
3 tablespoons brown sugar

- Arrange pineapple slices in large microwave dish.
- Brush with melted butter and sprinkle with brown sugar.
- Microwave on HIGH for 1 to 2 minutes or until butter and sugar bubble.
- Serve hot with ham or pork.

Artichoke Chicken

8 boneless, skinless chicken breast halves
1 (6 ounce) jar marinated artichoke hearts
8 slices Swiss cheese

- Between 2 pieces wax paper, flatten chicken to uniform thickness.
- Brown chicken breasts on both sides in sprayed or well-greased skillet and arrange chicken in single layer in greased 9 x 13-inch pan.
- Drain artichoke hearts, chop coarsely and spread on top of chicken.
- Lay Swiss cheese over all and bake at 350° for 20 to 30 minutes or until chicken is tender and cheese melts.

Honey Orange-Glazed Chicken

4 boneless, skinless chicken breast halves
¼ cup honey
⅓ cup orange marmalade

- Place chicken in 7 x 11-inch baking dish and set aside. Combine honey and marmalade in small bowl.
- Microwave uncovered for 1 minute or until glaze melts and is hot.
- Stir and spread ½ mixture over chicken. Cover and bake at 350° for 30 minutes.
- Uncover and cook another 10 minutes or until chicken is light brown.

Velma Stewart's Russian Chicken

6 boneless, skinless chicken breast halves
Velma Stewart's Russian Chicken Sauce (below)
Salt

- Pour Velma Stewart's Russian Chicken Sauce over chicken in buttered 9 x 13-inch dish. Bake at 300° for 2 hours.

Velma Stewart's Russian Chicken Sauce:

1 (8 ounce) bottle Russian salad dressing
1 (8 ounce) jar apricot preserves
1 (1 ounce) package dry onion soup mix

- Combine dressing, soup mix and apricot preserves and mix well.
- Pour over 6 chicken breasts in buttered 9 x 13-inch dish and bake at 300° for 2 hours.

Ernie Massey's Italian Chicken

6 boneless, skinless chicken breast halves
½ cup flour
1 (8 ounce) bottle Italian salad dressing

- Remove fat from chicken.
- Roll chicken breasts in flour and place in sprayed 9 x 13-inch pan.
- Pour dressing over chicken, cover and bake at 350° for 1 hour or until tender.
- Remove, cover and bake until golden brown.

Tip: This could be prepared in slow cooker on low.

Chicken Dijon

6 boneless, skinless chicken breast halves
4 tablespoons dijon-style mustard
2 cups finely crumbled seasoned breadcrumbs

- Place chicken breasts in greased baking dish and bake at 350° for 20 minutes.
- Remove from heat and generously spread mustard on both sides of chicken
- Coat with breadcrumbs and return to baking dish and bake at 350° for 1 hour.

Tip: The mustard gives chicken a tangy flavor and makes it moist. Don't overcook.

Chicken Mozzarella

6 boneless, skinless chicken breast halves
½ (28 ounce) jar spaghetti sauce
6 slices mozzarella cheese

- Place chicken breasts in greased baking dish, cover with sauce and bake covered at 325° for 1 hour.
- Remove from oven and top each breast with 1 slice cheese.
- Return to oven and bake uncovered for 10 minutes longer.
- Serve with spaghetti or noodles, if desired.

Tip: Keep in mind that low-calorie cheeses do not have very much fat so they will not melt the same as with regular cheese.

Baked Mexican Chicken

4 to 6 boneless, skinless chicken breast halves
1 teaspoon taco seasoning mix
1 (10 ounce) can enchilada sauce

- Place chicken in pan sprayed with non-stick cooking spray.
- Sprinkle desired amount of taco seasoning mix over chicken.
- Pour enchilada sauce over chicken and bake at 350° for 1 hour or until tender.
- Serve with warmed corn tortillas.

Honey-Mustard Chicken Tenders

1 pound boneless, skinless chicken tenders
3½ tablespoons honey mustard
1 ⅓ cups french-fried onions, crushed

- Coat chicken with mustard. Roll in crushed onions.
- Place on greased baking pan. Bake at 400° for 15 minutes or until chicken is done.

Chicken Parmesan

4 to 6 boneless, skinless chicken breast halves
⅓ cup (⅔ stick) butter, melted
1 cup grated parmesan cheese

- Roll chicken in melted butter first, then in parmesan cheese until they coat well.
- Place chicken in greased baking pan and drizzle a little extra butter over each piece.
- Bake at 325° for 45 to 50 minutes or until tender.

Pepperoni Chicken

6 boneless, skinless chicken breast halves
24 pepperoni slices
6 mozzarella cheese slices

- Brown chicken on both sides in well-greased skillet.
- Place chicken in sprayed 9 x 13-inch pan and arrange 4 pepperoni slices over each piece of chicken.
- Bake at 350° for 20 minutes, remove from oven and top each with cheese.
- Bake additional 5 minutes or until chicken is tender.

Party Chicken

1 (2 ounce) package dried beef, sliced
4 boneless, skinless chicken breast halves
2 (10 ounce) cans cream of mushroom soup

- Spread dried beef slices in bottom of greased baking dish and lay chicken over beef.
- Pour mushroom soup over chicken and refrigerate 3 hours.
- Bake at 275° for 2 hours 30 minutes or until chicken is tender.

Tip: Sometimes I chop the dried beef, mix with soup and pour over chicken before baking. Sometimes I do not refrigerate before baking. It's great either way. I serve with wild rice, cranberry-cherry gelatin salad and green beans.

Irma Mouttet's Sunday Chicken

4 boneless, skinless chicken breast halves
1 (10 ounce) can cream of mushroom soup
1½ cups shredded cheddar cheese

- Place chicken in greased 9 x 13-inch pan bake at 350° for 30 minutes.
- Remove from oven, spread soup over chicken and top with cheese.
- Bake 30 minutes longer.

Apricot Chicken

6 boneless, skinless chicken breast halves
1 cup apricot nectar
1 (1 ounce) package dry onion soup mix

- Arrange chicken breasts in 9 x 13-inch pan and pour apricot nectar over top.
- Sprinkle with soup mix, cover with foil and bake at 325° for 1 hour.
- Remove cover and bake 15 minutes longer.

Be careful when handling raw chicken because of the possibility of surface contamination. You can set raw chicken in a metal colander to wash pieces. Pat chicken dry while still in colander and then transfer to baking dish. Wash hands thoroughly and place colander in dishwasher or use hot, soapy water to wash it.

Judy's Orange-Onion Chicken

4 boneless, skinless chicken breasts
1 cup orange juice
1 (1 ounce) package dry onion soup mix

- Trim any visible fat on chicken. Spray 9 x 13-inch pan with non-stick cooking spray and arrange chicken pieces in pan.
- Pour orange juice over chicken and sprinkle with soup mix.
- Bake at 350° for 30 minutes. Turn chicken and bake 30 minutes longer or until tender.

Baked-Breaded Chicken

4 boneless, skinless chicken breast halves
½ cup mayonnaise
1¼ cups Italian-seasoned breadcrumbs

- Brush both sides of chicken with mayonnaise and roll in crumbs until well coated.
- Place in baking pan and bake at 375° for 4 minutes or until there is no pink in chicken and juice runs clear when pierced with fork.

Baked-Buttermilk Chicken

1 chicken, cut in serving pieces
½ cup buttermilk
1 cup Italian-style breadcrumbs

- Dip chicken in buttermilk and roll in breadcrumbs.
- Place on sprayed non-stick baking pan and bake at 350° for 1 hour or until tender.

Barbequed Chicken

4 boneless, skinless chicken breast halves
1 (12 ounce) can 7-Up
1 (8 ounce) bottle barbeque sauce

- Place chicken in greased skillet.
- Combine 7-Up and barbecue sauce and pour over chicken.
- Bring to boil and simmer for 1 hour or until tender.

Broiled Chicken Cordon Bleu

4 boneless, skinless chicken breast halves
4 slices cheddar or Swiss cheese, divided
4 slices ham or Canadian bacon, fully cooked

- Preheat broiler. Broil chicken breasts 4 inches from heat for 4 minutes.
- Turn chicken over and broil for 4 or 5 minutes or until tender.
- Cut cheese in half, place ½ cheese on top chicken breasts and top with ham or Canadian bacon slice.
- Broil for about 30 seconds and top with remaining ½ cheese slices. Broil until cheese melts.

Chipper Chicken

1 (3 pound) chicken, cut in serving pieces
½ cup (1 stick) butter, melted
3 cup potato chips, crushed

- Dip chicken in melted butter and roll in crushed potato chips.
- Bake in greased 9 x 13-inch pan at 350° for 1 hour or until tender.

Tip: If you don't want to cut up chicken, buy the pieces you want. It's much easier.

Coca-Cola Barbequed Chicken

4 to 6 boneless, skinless chicken breast halves
½ cup ketchup
1 (12 ounce) can cola soda

- Place chicken in large greased skillet.
- Combine ketchup and cola, pour over chicken and cover.
- Cook at 350° for about 1 hour or until tender.

Tip: To get ketchup out of the bottle, insert a straw or knife with a long, thin blade and rotate a few times. Remove and invert bottle.

Irish Chicken

1 (2½ pound) chicken, cut into serving pieces
1 egg, beaten
1½ cups dry potato flakes

- Dip each chicken piece in egg and roll in potato flakes. Repeat with all chicken pieces.
- Melt butter in shallow baking pan, place chicken in pan and bake at 375° for 30 minutes.
- Turn chicken over and bake for 20 minutes more.

Tip: If you don't want to cut up chicken, buy the pieces you want. It's much easier.

Lois Davis' Orange Chicken

1 (2½ pound) chicken, cut in serving pieces
1 (12 ounce) can orange soda
¼ cup soy sauce

- Place chicken pieces in foil-lined, 9 x 13-inch pan sprayed with non-stick cooking spray.
- Mix orange soda and soy sauce and pour over chicken.
- Bake at 350° for 1 hour or until chicken is tender.
- Baste chicken occasionally as it bakes.

Tip: If you don't want to cut up chicken, buy the pieces you want. It's much easier.

Lois Rohm's Crisp Chicken

8 boneless, skinless chicken breast halves
2 eggs, beaten
Crushed corn flakes

- Dip chicken in eggs and roll in crushed corn flakes until well coated.
- Spray baking sheet with non-stick cooking spray, place chicken on it and bake at 350° for about 1 hour.

Oven-Fried Chicken

1 (2 to 3 pound) chicken, cut in serving pieces
¼ (½ stick) butter, melted
1 cup seasoned breadcrumbs

- Wash and dry chicken.
- Coat each piece of chicken with melted butter and roll in breadcrumbs. Coat well.
- Bake in greased 9 x 13-inch pan at 350° for 50 minutes to 1 hour.

Tip: If you don't want to cut up chicken, buy your favorite pieces.

Ritzy-Baked Chicken

4 boneless, skinless chicken breast halves
1 cup sour cream
1 cup crushed Cheezits crackers

- Roll chicken breasts in sour cream and crushed crackers.
- Bake at 325° for 1 hour or until tender.

Mushroom-Onion Roast

1 (3 to 4 pound) chuck roast
1 (10 ounce) can cream of mushroom soup
½ package dry onion soup mix

- Brown or sear meat on all sides. (This step may be omitted, but roast tastes better if it is seared.)
- Place roast on 2 to 3 sheets foil, spread soup over meat and sprinkle with dry soup mix. Wrap roast tightly, place in pan and bake at 325° for 3 to 4 hours or until done.

Coffee-Beef Roast

1 (3 to 5 pound) beef roast
2 cups black coffee
1 cup vinegar

- Place roast in glass baking dish or pan. Pour vinegar over meat.
- Cover meat and refrigerate for 24 hours or longer and drain.
- Place roast in large skillet and brown on all sides. Pour black coffee over meat, add 2 cups water and cover. Simmer stove top for 4 to 6 hours (depending on size or roast). Add more water if needed.

Onion Roast

1 (3 pound) rump or chuck roast
1 (1 ounce) package dry onion soup mix
½ teaspoon of garlic powder

- Place beef roast on large sheet of foil. Sprinkle roast with soup mix and dash of garlic powder and seal foil.
- Place in large pan and bake at 325° for 1 hour 30 minutes or until tender (or bake at 200° for 8 to 9 hours, depending on size roast).

Rosebillie Horn's Old-Fashioned Roast Beef

3 pound beef roast
½ cup flour
1 to 2 sliced onions

- Dredge beef in flour, place in greased skillet and brown on all sides to seal in juices.
- Lay sliced onions on top of roast.
- Pour ½ cup water over roast, cover and bake at 300° for 2 hours 30 minutes.
- Remove cover and bake for 30 minutes longer.

Tip: After baking for 2 hours, you may add potatoes and carrots and bake for 1 hour longer.

Yankee Pot Roast

1 (4 to 5 pound) beef pot roast
2 (10 ounce) cans French onion soup
6 potatoes, peeled, quartered

- Brown meat on all sides in iron skillet or Dutch oven.
- Add soup, cover and cook on low heat on stove for 3 to 4 hours or until roast is fork-tender.
- Add potatoes after meat cooks for 2 hours and continue cooking until done.

Buttermilk-Baked Roast

1 (3 to 5 pound) beef roast
½ cup buttermilk
1 (1 ounce) package dry onion soup mix

- Trim off all visible fat, place foil on cookie sheet and roast on top.
- Drizzle buttermilk over meat and sprinkle soup mix over roast.
- Wrap up foil and bake at 275° for 5 hours or to desired doneness and drain.

Tip: To make buttermilk, mix 1 cup milk with 1 tablespoon lemon juice or vinegar and let milk rest for about 10 minutes.

Baked Pot Roast and Peppers

1 (3 to 4 pound) beef pot roast
1 (10 ounce) can beef consomme
1 green and 1 red bell pepper

- Brown roast on all sides in greased skillet.
- Place in roasting pan and pour consomme and 1 cup water evenly over beef.
- Cover tightly and bake at 325° for 1 hour. Reduce heat to 275°.
- Bake 4 hours longer or until done.
- Add bell peppers 20 minutes before roast is done.

Overnight Brisket

2 tablespoons liquid smoke
1 (3 to 4 pound) brisket
Garlic powder

- Rub 2 tablespoons liquid smoke on sides of brisket and sprinkle with garlic powder.
- Wrap tightly in foil and refrigerate overnight.
- Next day, sprinkle with more garlic powder and rewrap in foil.
- Bake in 9 x 13-inch dish (or whatever size is needed) at 275° for 6 hours or at 325° for 5 hours. Refrigerate overnight again.
- Next day, slice.

Tip: When you serve this as leftovers, pour barbecue sauce over it and reheat.

Marilyn Weaver's Brisket

Brisket:
1 (3 to 4 pound) brisket
Marilyn Weaver's Sauce:

Sauce For Brisket:
1 (8 ounce) bottle chili sauce
1 (12 ounce) can cola soda, not diet
1 (1 ounce) package dry onion soup mix

- To prepare brisket, place 3 to 4-pound brisket in roasting pan with lid.
- Pour sauce over it, cover and bake at 325° for 3 to 5 hours or for 30 minutes per pound until tender.
- Pour off sauce and serve in gravy bowl with brisket.
- To prepare sauce combine chili sauce, cola and onion soup mix. Makes 2½ cups sauce.

Barbecued Beef Brisket

4 pound brisket
1 (3½ ounce) bottle liquid smoke
6 to 8 ounce bottle barbecue sauce

- Place brisket in 9 x 13-inch baking pan, pour liquid smoke over meat and rub into brisket.
- Cover and chill overnight. Next day, bake covered at 275° for 5 hours. Remove from oven and slice.
- Pour barbecue sauce over brisket and reheat before serving.

Texas Brisket

1 (6 pound) boneless beef brisket
2 tablespoons worcestershire sauce
4 tablespoons bottle liquid smoke

- Place brisket in pan and pour sauce and liquid smoke over brisket.
- Cover and bake at 275° for 5 to 7 hours or until tender.

Party Brisket

1 (5 pound) beef brisket
1 (6 ounce) can frozen lemon juice concentrate, thawed
1 (1 ounce) package dry onion soup mix

- Trim off all visible fat from meat.
- Stir enough juice concentrate into soup mix to make paste.
- Place brisket in 9 x 13-inch pan or in roasting pan.
- Spread paste over meat and cover tightly with foil or lid. Bake at 250° for 5 to 6 hours or until fork-tender.

Husband's Favorite Flank Steak

1 (2 pound) beef flank steak
⅓ cup soy sauce
⅓ cup worcestershire sauce

- Score flank steak with sharp knife and place in glass baking dish.
- Combine soy sauce and worcestershire sauce and pour marinade over steak.
- Marinate steak in refrigerator for 2 to 4 hours. Turn steak several times.
- Remove steak from marinade and broil or grill to desired doneness.
- Turn with tongs and broil other side.
- Let steak rest 10 minutes before slicing. Slice diagonally across grain into thin strips.

South Seas Flank Steak

1 flank steak
¼ cup soy sauce
¼ cup pineapple juice

- Pour soy sauce and pineapple juice in shallow 9 x 13-inch dish.
- Lay flank steak in mixture and turn to coat both sides.
- Marinate 1 hour, turning every 15 minutes.
- Remove steak from marinade and broil or grill.

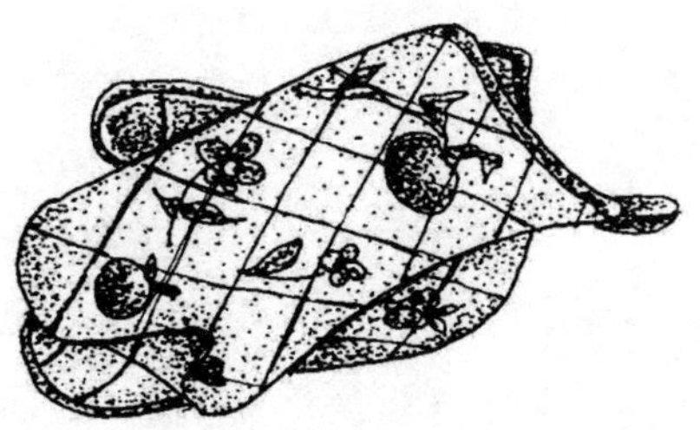

Mushroom Steak

1 (2 pound) round steak
1 (10 ounce) can cream of mushroom soup
1 (4 ounce) can sliced mushrooms, drained

- Place round steak in 9 x 13-inch pan lined with foil.
- Pour mushroom soup over steak and top with mushrooms.
- Cover with foil and bake at 350° for 1 hour.

Swiss Steak

2 pounds round steak, tenderized
1 onion, sliced
1 (15 ounce) can tomato sauce with onions and peppers

- Trim fat and pound steak thin.
- Place in greased 9 x 13-inch pan, top with onion slices and pour tomato sauce over it.
- Cover and bake at 350° for 1 hour 30 minutes. Uncover and bake for 15 minutes longer.
- Baste occasionally with tomato sauce and bake until tender.

Onita Copeland's Chicken-Fried Steak

1 (1 pound) minute or sirloin steak, cut in serving pieces
1 cup flour
1 to 2 eggs, beaten

- Trim fat and pound steak thin.
- Roll steaks in flour, dip in well beaten egg and roll in flour again.
- Fry in hot oil until brown.

Broiled T-Bone Steaks

4 T-bone steaks
½ teaspoon black pepper
1 teaspoon garlic powder or seasoned salt

- Make few diagonal cuts in fat around steak so it won't curl when broiling.
- Place steaks on broiler pan lined with foil. Broil 5 minutes on 1 side, turn and broil 5 minutes on other side.
- Continue cooking to desired doneness if steaks are too rare.
- Sprinkle with pepper and garlic powder.

Mock Filet Mignon

2 pounds ground round steak
1 (1 ounce) package dry onion soup mix
6 bacon slices

- Combine ground round and soup mix.
- Shape into 6 thick patties and wrap slice of bacon around each.
- Secure with wooden picks, place in 9 x 13-inch dish and bake at 450° for 15 to 20 minutes or broil on each side.

Speedy Spaghetti

1 (16 ounce) package spaghetti
1 pound ground beef
1 (20 ounce) jar chunky garden-style spaghetti sauce with extra tomatoes, garlic and onions

- Prepare spaghetti according to package directions.
- In saucepan, brown beef, crumble and drain. Stir spaghetti sauce into meat and heat thoroughly.
- Pour drained spaghetti into large platter and spread meat sauce over spaghetti or combine spaghetti and meat sauce and mix thoroughly.

Tip: Top spaghetti with 1 cup shredded cheddar cheese and heat at 350° until cheese melts.

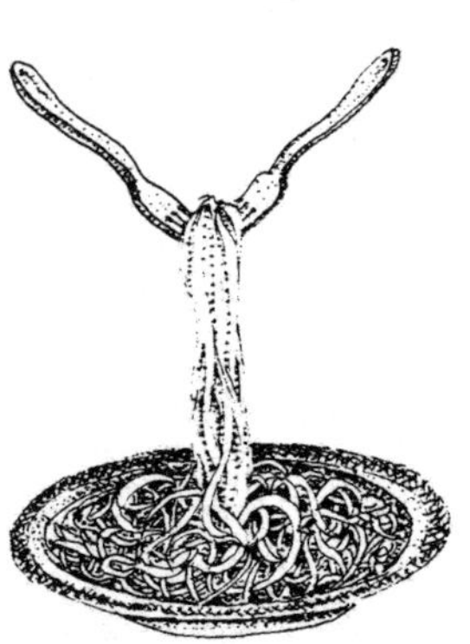

Onion Burgers

2 pounds ground beef
1 (1 ounce) package dry onion soup mix
½ cup water

- Combine beef with soup mix and water and mix well.
- Shape into 8 burgers and place in 9 x 13-inch baking dish.
- Cook uncovered at 350° for 15 minutes or until brown.
- Serve on hamburger buns.

Hamburger Stroganoff

1 pound ground beef or ground round
2 (10 ounce) cans cream of mushroom soup
1 (16 ounce) package noodles

- In skillet, brown beef, crumble and drain. Stir soup into meat and mix well.
- Cook for 10 minutes or until well heated and stir often.
- Boil noodles according to package directions and drain.
- Serve beef mixture over noodles.

Kids' Favorite Casserole

1 pound ground beef
2 tablespoons chopped onion
1 (15 ounce) can baked beans

- In saucepan, brown ground beef and onion together. Drain well.
- Stir in baked beans and cook until thoroughly heated.

Hobo Dinner

1 pound ground beef
4 onion slices
4 potatoes

- Shape beef into patties and place on foil.
- Slice potatoes ½-inch thick and top patties with 2 to 3 potato slices. Add slice of onion and season to taste.
- Wrap tightly inside foil and place in pan.
- Bake at 350° for 45 minutes.

Tip: Season beef patties with 1 teaspoon seasoned salt.

Hamburger-Potato Casserole

2 pounds ground beef
1 (10 ounce) can cream of mushroom soup
1 (1 pound) package tater tots

- Form ingredients into 3 layers.
- Press meat into greased 9 x 13-inch pan to make bottom layer, spread soup over meat and tater tots form third or top layer.
- Bake casserole at 350° for 45 to 55 minutes.

Tip: Potatoes could be the second layer, then top with soup.

Beef Tips and Noodles

1½ pounds stew meat, fat trimmed
2 (10 ounce) cans cream of onion soup, diluted
1 (8 ounce) package noodles

- Brown stew meat in greased skillet.
- When brown, add diluted soup with 1 cup water.
- Simmer for 3 hours and stir occasionally.
- Cook noodles according to package directions.
- Serve beef tips over noodles.

Cory Rigg's Barbecue Beef

1 pound ground beef or ground sirloin
½ cup packed brown sugar
1 (16 ounce) bottle barbeque sauce

- In skillet, brown meat. Crumble and drain.
- Stir in brown sugar and barbecue sauce.
- Cover, simmer for 15 minutes and stir often.
- Spoon onto heated hamburger buns.

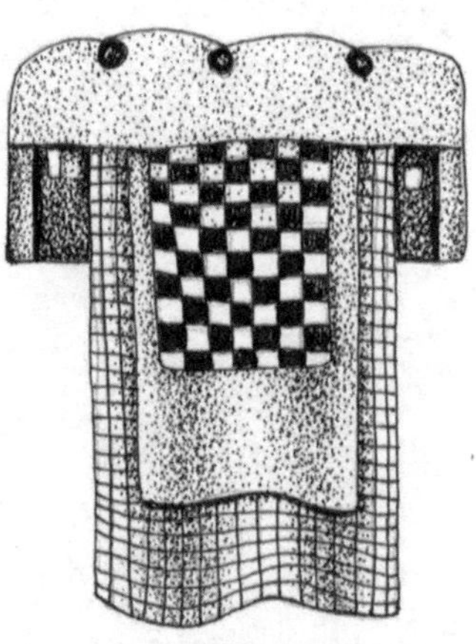

As-Easy-As-Fallin-Off-A-Log Chili

2 pounds ground beef or ground round
2 (1 ounce) packets chili seasoning
2 (32 ounce) jars spaghetti sauce with chunky tomatoes, onions, peppers

- In heavy skillet, brown meat.
- Drain and stir in chili seasoning.
- Add sauce and 1 cup water. Mix well and simmer for 30 minutes.

Tip: If you have to have beans in your chili, add 1 or 2 cans pinto beans and heat for 20 minutes longer.

Chili Casserole

2 (15 ounce) cans chili con carne
2 to 3 cups corn chips
1 cup shredded cheddar cheese

- Alternate layers of chili and corn chips in greased casserole dish.
- Top with cheese.
- Bake covered at 350° for 30 minutes.

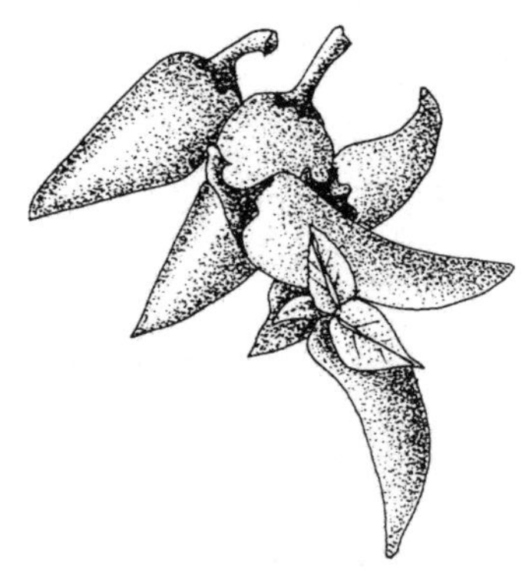

Juanita's Stuffed Green Peppers

4 green peppers
1 pound ground beef or ground round, browned, drained
1 (15 ounce) can Spanish rice

- Blanch or place green peppers into boiling water and cook for several minutes.
- Remove and dip into cold water to stop cooking process. (This brings out flavor and color of peppers.) Cool.
- Cut off tops of peppers and remove seeds and membranes.
- Stuff peppers with mixture of cooked meat and Spanish rice and bake at 350° for 20 minutes.

Tip: You may stuff peppers that have not been boiled or blanched. Place them in greased casserole and bake at 350° for 25 minutes. Add a little water to dish before baking peppers.

Spanish Meatloaf

1 pound ground beef
1 (16 ounce) can Spanish rice, drained
1 egg, beaten

- In bowl, combine all ingredients and mix well.
- Pour into greased loaf pan and bake at 350° for 1 hour.
- Drain off excess liquid.

Chili Pie

4 cups corn chips
2 (15 ounce) cans chili
1⅓ cups shredded cheddar cheese

- Place 1 cup corn chips on 4 serving plates and top with 1 cup hot chili on each.
- Sprinkle ⅓ cup cheese over chili and serve.

Chili and Tamales

1 (15 ounce) cans tamales
1 (15 ounce) cans chili without beans
½ cup shredded cheddar cheese

- Heat tamales and remove papers. Heat chili.
- Place 2 tamales on each serving plate and pour hot chili over tamales. Top with cheese.

No-Peek Stew

2 pounds beef stew meat, fat trimmed
1 (10 ounce) can cream of mushroom soup
1 (1 ounce) envelope dry onion soup mix

- In Dutch oven or roasting pan, combine all ingredients and mix well.
- Stir in 1 cup water, cover and bake at 325° for 2 hours 30 minutes.
- Do not peek! Serve over rice or noodles.

John Beuscher's Incredible Ribs

1 slab ribs
1 tablespoon seasoning salt
1 (8 ounce) bottle Italian dressing

- Place ribs, bone down, on grill in bottom layer of foil and "paint" ribs with dressing.
- Sprinkle with seasoning and cover top with foil.
- When fire is out on coals, place wrapped ribs on grill and cover.
- Close top vent until only a light is visible and cook for 6 hours, turning ribs every 2 hours.
- At hour 6, remove foil top and puncture bottom foil to drain.

Tip: If you want your ribs "wet", coat with barbecue sauce and cook 45 to 60 minutes more. Barbecue sauce should only be added at the last because the sugar will burn.

Margie Luben's Corned Beef Brisket

1 (3 to 4 pound) corned beef brisket
2 tablespoons prepared mustard
4 tablespoons brown sugar

- In pot of water, on top of stove, cook corned beef over low heat for 2 hours 30 minutes.
- Remove from pot, place in 9 x 13-inch roasting or broiler pan and poke holes in meat with fork.
- Mix mustard and brown sugar until creamy and paste forms.
- Spread mixture over entire brisket and bake at 350° for 1 hour 30 minutes or until tender.

Corned Beef and Cabbage

4 to 6 pound boneless corned beef
1 head cabbage, cored, quartered
6 potatoes

- Cover corned beef with cold water and bring to boil.
- Lower heat and simmer 4 hours or until tender.
- Drain most of water, add potatoes and cook for 20 minutes.
- Add cabbage and cook for about 12 minutes longer or until all ingredients are fork-tender.

Roast Leg of Lamb

1 (6 pound) leg of lamb
⅓ cup honey
6 tablespoons soy sauce, divided

- Trim fat off lamb and place on rack in shallow pan.
- Brush with honey and pour water into pan to depth of ¾-inch.
- Bake lamb at 450° for 30 minutes and then reduce heat to 350°.
- Pour half soy sauce over lamb and roast for 3 hours 30 minutes longer or 35 minutes per pound.
- Baste lamb every 30 minutes with remaining soy sauce or pan drippings.

Dijon Pork Chops

6 loin pork chops
½ cup packed brown sugar
2 teaspoons dijon-style mustard

- Arrange pork chops in greased baking dish.
- Combine sugar and mustard in small dish and mix well.
- Spread mixture on chops and bake covered at 350° for 45 minutes.
- Uncover and bake about 10 minutes longer or until brown.

Pork Chop Special

4 to 6 pork chops
½ cup rice, cooked
2 (10 ounce) cans cream of mushroom soup

- Brown pork chops on both sides and drain.
- Place cooked rice in bottom of greased baking dish and lay browned chops over rice.
- Pour soup over pork chops, cover and bake at 375° for 40 minutes.

Onion-Pork Chops

6 pork chops
1 (10 ounce) can condensed French onion soup
1 tablespoon prepared mustard

- Arrange pork chops in greased 9 x 13-inch baking dish.
- In bowl, combine soup and mustard and mix well. Pour over pork chops, cover and bake at 350° for 30 minutes.
- Uncover and bake another 15 to 20 minutes or until pork chops are brown. Serve over hot cooked rice.

Cranberry-Glazed Pork Roast

1 (6 pound) pork shoulder roast
1 (16 ounce) can whole cranberry sauce
¼ cup packed brown sugar

- Place pork on rack in roasting pan and roast at 325° for 3 hours or until fork-tender. (If using meat thermometer, it should register 185°.)
- Remove roast, pour off drippings and trim skin and fat. Return meat to pan.
- Mash cranberry sauce with fork, stir in brown sugar and mix well.
- Cut deep gashes in meat, brush generously with cranberry sauce and bake at 350° for about 30 minutes. Brush often with glaze.

Easy Pork Loin Roast

1 (1 ounce) envelope dry onion soup mix
1 (4 to 5 pound) pork loin roast
1 teaspoon dried rosemary

- Place large piece heavy-duty foil in 9 x 13-inch baking pan.
- Sprinkle soup in middle of foil, place roast on top of soup mix and sprinkle with dried rosemary.
- Fold foil over, seal securely and fold ends of foil.
- Bake at 300° for 3 hours 30 minutes to 4 hours or until done to your preference.

Pennsylvania Dutch Pork and Sauerkraut

1 (2½ pound) tenderloin of pork
2 tablespoons (¼ stick) butter
2 (15 ounce) cans sauerkraut

- Melt butter in heavy iron skillet or Dutch oven and brown pork on both sides.
- Cover and cook over low heat for 20 minutes. Add sauerkraut.
- Cover and continue to simmer for 1 hour or until tenderloin cooks thoroughly.

Tip: Serve with mashed potatoes and applesauce for an authentic Pennsylvania Dutch dinner.

Ham Jubilee

1 fully cooked smoked ham slice
¼ teaspoon ground cloves
1 (20 ounce) can cherry pie filling

- Place ham slice in greased 9 x 13-inch pan and sprinkle with cloves.
- Cover and bake at 350° for 30 minutes or until hot. Cut into serving pieces.
- Pour cherry pie filling into saucepan, heat and stir often.
- Spoon over ham and serve as an accompaniment.

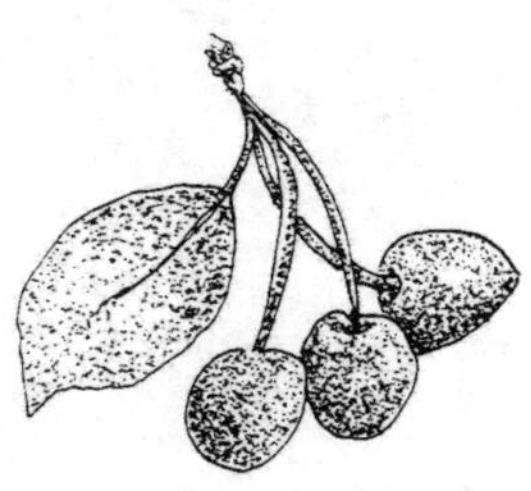

Honey Ham

1 (5 pound) boneless, fully cooked ham
¼ cup honey
½ cup packed brown sugar

- Score ham, wrap in foil and bake at 325° for 1 hour in broiler pan.
- Combine honey and brown sugar and mix well.
- Remove ham from oven, pull foil open and spread honey glaze over ham.
- Rewrap in foil and bake for 1 hour longer. Cool for 15 minutes before serving.

Judy McDonald Hutchinson's Ham and Red-Eye Gravy

4 slices country ham
Strong black coffee
Hot sauce

- Fry ham slices in heavy skillet and turn frequently.
- Remove ham slices and add coffee to skillet (in the amount of gravy desired).
- Simmer, stir and scrape pan.
- Add hot sauce to taste and serve with ham.

Ham and Limas

1 (10 ounce) package frozen, baby lima beans
1 center-cut ham slice
½ cup grated cheddar cheese

- Cook frozen beans according to package directions and drain.
- Place ham slice in shallow pan and broil 5 minutes on each side, about 3 inches from heat.
- Arrange beans over ham, sprinkle with shredded cheese and broil only until cheese melts and bubbles.

Hawaiian Ham Steaks

1 (8 ounce) can sliced pineapple with juice
2 tablespoons brown sugar
1 pound center-cut ham steak

- Pour ½-inch juice into skillet and stir in brown sugar. Make slashes in fat around steak to keep it from curling.
- Place ham in skillet with juice mixture and top with pineapple slices.
- Cook on medium low heat and turn twice.
- Cook until sauce becomes thick and serve with pineapple slice on each serving.

Broiled Ham and Pineapple

1 (1½ pound) fully cooked ham slice
1 (8 ounce) can sliced pineapple
Butter, softened

- Trim fat on ham. Diagonally slash out edge of fat at 1-inch intervals to prevent curling.
- Place ham on rack in broiler pan and broil 4-inches from heat for 5 minutes. Turn and broil 3 minutes on other side.
- Place drained pineapple slices on ham and brush with butter.
- Broil 2 minutes longer or until ham is light brown.

Apricot-Glazed Ham

1 (29 ounce) can apricots with syrup
¾ cup apricot preserves
1 (4 pound) baked, boneless ham

- Drain syrup from apricots and save fruit.
- Bring syrup to boil, reduce heat and simmer until liquid reduces to half, about 10 minutes.
- Remove from heat, stir in preserves and apricots and set aside.
- Bake ham at 325° for 2 hours and baste often with glaze during last hour of baking.
- Serve remainder with ham.

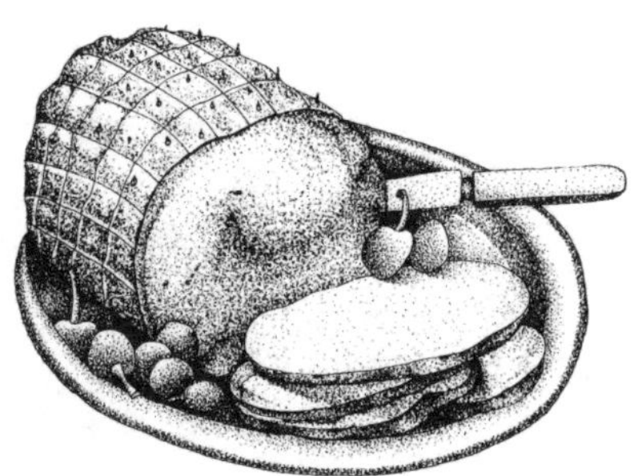

Ham and Noodles Romanoff

1 (7 ounce) box noodles romanoff mix
1½ cups cooked ham, cubed
1 (8 ounce) can cut green beans, drained

- Prepare noodles according to package directions, but increase milk to ⅔ cup.
- Stir in ham and green beans and bake in greased, covered 1½-quart casserole dish at 350° for 20 minutes.

Baked Orange Roughy

4 orange roughy fish filets
Butter, melted
Lemon-herb seasoning

- Cut dark spots out of fish and place on foil-lined cookie sheet.
- Brush fish with melted butter and sprinkle with lemon-herb seasoning.
- Bake at 400° for 5 to 8 minutes, turn over and brush other side of fish with butter.
- Sprinkle with seasoning and bake for 5 to 8 minutes longer or until flaky when tested with fork.

Tip: Placing fish on foil helps keep it moist. You can also butter the foil before placing filets on top.

Flounder Italiano

4 to 6 frozen flounder filets
1½ cups spaghetti sauce
½ cup shredded mozzarella cheese

- Place filets in greased 9 x 13-inch pan and pour spaghetti sauce over filets.
- Bake uncovered at 350° for about 30 minutes, sprinkle with cheese and bake 5 minutes longer or until cheese melts.

Salmon Casserole

1 (14 ounce) can salmon, drained
1 (10 ounce) can cream of mushroom soup
1 cup crushed potato chips

- Remove bone and skin from salmon.
- Arrange half salmon, soup and chips in layers in greased 8-inch baking dish.
- Repeat layers and end with chips on top.
- Bake at 350° for 20 minutes.

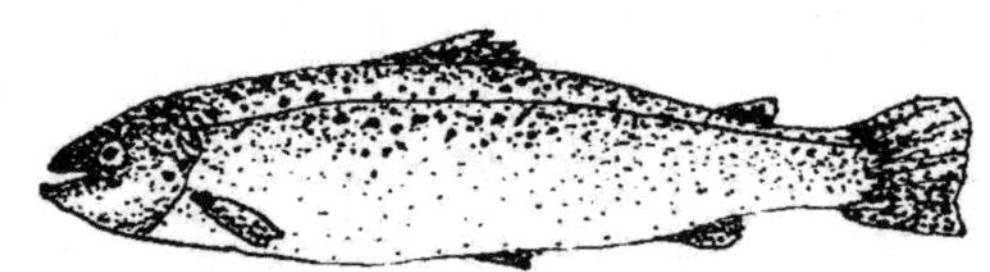

Salmon Loaf

1 (14 ounce) can salmon with liquid
2 eggs, beaten
1 cup matzo meal

- Remove bones and skin from salmon and chop.
- Combine salmon, eggs and meal and mix well.
- Pack in greased loaf pan and bake at 325° for 30 minutes or until done.

Chinese Tuna Bake

2 (6 ounce) cans tuna, well drained
1 (10 ounce) can cream of celery soup
1 (3 ounce) can Chinese fried noodles

- In bowl, combine tuna, soup and half can fried noodles.
- Mix well and pour into greased casserole dish.
- Bake at 350° for 25 minutes, remove from oven and top with remaining noodles.
- Bake for 10 minutes longer.

Sockeye or red salmon has a moderate fat content with firm, deep red flesh that is preferred for canning and widely available.

Tuna-Chip Casserole

2 cups crushed potato chips
2 (6 ounce) cans tuna fish, drained
2 (10 ounce) cans cream of mushroom soup

- Place 1 layer of crushed potato chips in greased casserole dish and top with layer of tuna.
- Repeat layers and pour mushroom soup over tuna.
- Bake at 350° for 25 minutes.

Grilled Tuna Steaks

4 (6 ounce) tuna steaks
½ cup lime juice
1 garlic clove, minced

- Combine lime juice and garlic in 8 x 8-inch baking dish.
- Add tuna, cover and marinate for 3 hours in refrigerator, turning occasionally.
- Drain, reserve marinade and grill over medium heat for 8 to 10 minutes on each side and baste often with marinade.

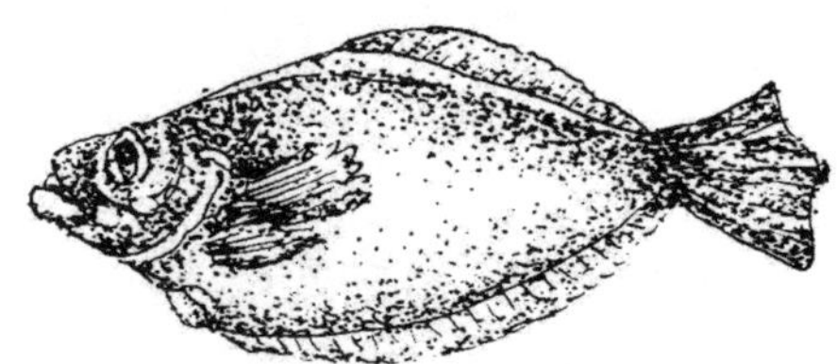

Creamed Tuna

1 (6 ounce) can tuna fish, drained
1 (10 ounce) can cream of mushroom soup
½ can milk

- In bowl, combine all ingredients and mix well.
- Heat thoroughly and serve over rice, toast, noodles or in patty shells.

Tuna Burgers

1 (6 ounce) can tuna fish, drained
1 beaten egg
½ cup crushed Cheezits crackers

- In bowl, combine all ingredients and mix well. Shape into patties.
- In sprayed, non-stick skillet, brown patties on both sides (or fry in a little vegetable oil).

Mother's Salmon Patties

1 (7 ounce) can pink salmon, rinsed, drained
1 egg, beaten
1 cup cracker crumbs

- In bowl, combine all ingredients and mix well. Shape mixture into patties
- In sprayed, non-stick skillet, brown patties on both sides (or fry in a little vegetable oil).

Bob Batterson's Fried Fish Filets

8 fish filets
1 cup biscuit mix
1 teaspoon seasoned salt

- Dip fish in biscuit mix.
- Sprinkle with seasoned salt and fry until golden brown on both sides.
- Allow 2 filets per person.

Haddock Parmigiana

4 (4 ounce) haddock filets, fresh or frozen
1 cup spaghetti sauce
4 mozzarella cheese slices

- Place haddock in greased baking dish.
- Pour spaghetti sauce over fish, cover both sides and top each with cheese slice.
- Bake at 375° for about 15 minutes or until cheese bubbles or fish flakes easily when tested with fork. Watch carefully.

South-of-the-Border Baked Cod

4 cod filets
Thick and chunky salsa
4 slices cheddar or Monterey Jack cheese

- Spray pan with non-stick cooking spray and place fish in pan.
- Spread salsa over fish and top with cheese slices.
- Bake at 350° until fish flakes when tested with fork.

Italian Cod Filets

4 cod filets
½ cup chopped onion
1 (15 ounce) can stewed tomatoes and peppers

- Place cod in non-stick sprayed baking pan.
- Layer onions and tomatoes over fish and bake at 350° for 30 minutes or until fish flakes when tested with fork.

Broiled Fish Filets

4 (5 to 7 ounce) fish filets
⅓ cup mayonnaise
3 tablespoons grated parmesan cheese

- Preheat broiler. Spread mayonnaise over each filet and sprinkle cheese on top of each.
- Place filets in broiler pan and broil 4 to 6 inches from heat for 5 to 8 minutes or until fish flakes easily when tested with a fork.

Sole Amandine

⅓ cup almonds, slivered
8 tablespoons butter, divided
1 (2 pound) filet of sole

- Saute almonds in 4 tablespoons butter. Add additional butter to almonds.
- Place fish in 9 x 13-inch glass baking dish and pour almond-butter mixture over fish.
- Bake uncovered at 350° for about 15 minutes or until fish flakes easily when tested with fork.

French Fish Filets

1 pound fish filets
¼ cup French salad dressing
½ cup cracker crumbs

- Dip filets in dressing, roll in crumbs and coat well.
- Place in 9 x 13-inch baking dish and bake at 350° for 10 minutes.
- Turn fish and cook 10 minutes longer or until fish is light brown.

Scalloped Oysters

1 pint fresh oysters
15 saltine crackers, crushed
2 cups milk

- Combine cracker crumbs and milk and mix well. Stir in oysters.
- Pour mixture into 9-inch greased baking pan and bake at 350° for 30 minutes.

❖❖❖

Cream of Coconut Cake

1 (18 ounce) box white cake mix
1 (3 ounce) can flaked coconut
1 (15 ounce) can cream of coconut

- Prepare cake mix according to package directions and add flaked coconut.
- Bake in greased, floured 9 x 13-inch cake pan according to package directions.
- Remove from oven when done and punch deep holes in top of cake with fork.
- Pour cream of coconut over cake and let cool for 5 minutes.

Carrot Cake

1 (18 ounce) box spice cake mix
2 cups shredded carrots
1 cup chopped walnuts or pecans

- Prepare cake mix according to package directions. Stir in carrots and nuts.
- Bake according to package directions in greased, floured 9 x 13-inch pan.
- Cool before frosting.

Frosting for Carrot Cake:

½ cup (1 stick) butter, softened
1 (8 ounce) package cream cheese, softened
1 (1 pound) box powdered sugar

- Combine butter and cream cheese and beat until creamy.
- Stir in powdered sugar and beat. Spread on carrot cake.

Fruit Cocktail Cake

1 (18 ounce) box yellow cake mix
3 eggs
1 (15 ounce) can fruit cocktail with juice

- In large bowl, combine all ingredients and mix well.
- Pour into greased, floured 9 x 13-inch pan and bake at 350° for 45 to 50 minutes.

Quick-Company Blueberry Torte

The pound cake name is derived from the traditional weight of its ingredients - 1 pound flour, 1 pound butter, 1 pound sugar, 1 pound eggs.

1 (20 ounce) pound cake
1 (21 ounce) can blueberry pie filling
1 (12 ounce) carton frozen whipped topping, thawed

- Slice pound cake lengthwise to make 4 layers.
- Spread pie filling between each layer and spread whipped topping over top and sides of cake.

Cake ingredients should be at room temperature before using. You'll get better volume.

Lemon Cheesecake

1 (8 ounce) packages cream cheese, softened
1 (3.4 ounce) package instant lemon pudding mix
1 graham cracker piecrust, baked

- In mixing bowl, beat cream cheese until creamy.
- Prepare pudding mix according to package directions and add to cream cheese mixture.
- Pour into baked piecrust and chill 2 to 4 hours.

Date-Nut Spice Cake

1 (18 ounce) box spice cake mix
1 cup chopped dates
½ cup chopped pecans

- Prepare cake mix according to package directions. Stir dates and pecans into batter.
- Bake in greased, floured 9 x 13-inch cake pan following package directions.

Tip: If you would like an icing on this cake, use Carrot Cake Frosting.

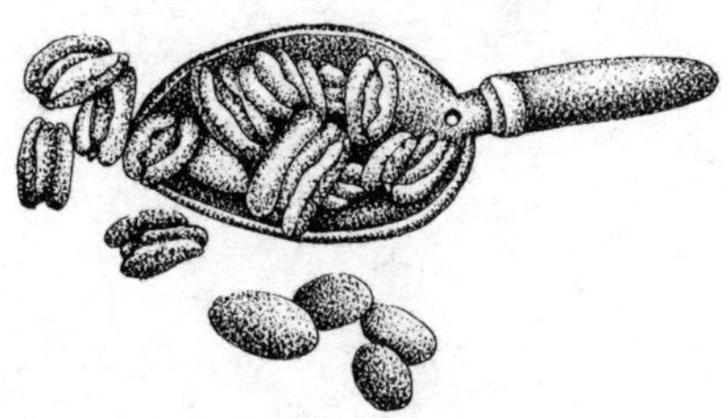

Strawberry Shortcake

1 (21 ounce) pound cake, cut in 12 slices
1 pint strawberries, sliced, sweetened
1 (8 ounce) container frozen whipped topping, thawed

- Place 6 cake slices on 6 dessert plates.
- Arrange half strawberries over cake slices and repeat layers.
- Top with whipped topping.

Pineapple Cake

1 (20 ounce) can crushed pineapple, drained
1 cup (2 sticks) butter, sliced
1 (18 ounce) box white or yellow cake mix

- Spread pineapple in greased 9 x 13-inch dish.
- Sprinkle dry cake mix over fruit and dot with slices of butter.
- Bake at 350° for about 35 minutes or until brown.

Tip: A dip of vanilla ice cream gives this a special taste.

Christmas Fruit Cake

1 (18 ounce) box spice cake mix
1¼ cups candied fruit, chopped
1 cup chopped pecan

- Prepare spice cake according to package directions.
- Stir in candied fruit and pecans.
- Bake according to package directions for bundt pan.

Black Forest Cake

1 (19 ounce) box brownie mix
1 (21 ounce) can cherry pie filling, divided
¼ cup almonds, sliced

- Prepare brownie mix according to package directions.
- Divide dough in half and spread over bottom of 2 greased, 8-inch round baking pans.
- Bake at 350° for 30 minutes. Cool in pans on wire racks for 10 minutes.
- Remove from pans and cool completely. Place 1 brownie layer on serving plate and spoon half cherry pie filling evenly top.
- Place second brownie layer over filling and top with remaining cherry pie filling. Sprinkle with almonds.

Chocolate-Applesauce Cake

1 (18 ounce) box chocolate cake mix
1 (16 ounce) can applesauce
½ to ¾ cup egg substitute (or 3 eggs)

- In mixing bowl, combine all ingredients and blend well.
- Pour into sprayed 9 x 13-inch baking dish and bake according to cake package directions.

Tip: If you would like icing on the cake, use 1 can prepared milk chocolate icing.

Angel Pudding Cake

1 loaf angel food cake, cubed
1 (4 ounce) package chocolate pudding mix
1 (8 ounce) package frozen whipped topping, thawed

- Arrange cake cubes in greased 9 x 13-inch pan or glass dish.
- Prepare pudding mix according to package directions and spread over cake cubes.
- Spread whipped topping over pudding.
- Refrigerate 6 hours and cut into squares to serve.

Apricot Cake

1 (18 ounce) box lemon cake mix
3 eggs, beaten slightly
1 (15 ounce) can apricots with juice, chopped

- In mixing bowl, combine all ingredients and mix well.
- Bake in greased, floured 9 x 13-inch pan at 350° for 30 to 35 minutes or until cake tests done.

Cherries-On-A-Cloud

1 (18 ounce) box angel food cake mix
1 (20 ounce) can cherry pie filling
1 (8 ounce) carton frozen whipped topping

- Prepare and bake cake mix according to package directions. Cool and slice.
- Place 1 cake slice on each dessert plate.
- Spoon cherries and whipped topping on top of each cake slice.

Tip: Use pre-baked, angel food cake from grocery store if you need to save time.

Angel-food cake is a light, puffy cake made without yeast but with several egg whites. The egg whites give the cake such an airy texture that its confection is light and sublime, "angel like" thus the name. The cake became known in the 1870's in America and began as a simple way of using leftover egg whites.

Children's Cake Cones

1 (9 ounce) package chocolate cake mix
1 (12 count) box ice cream cones (flat bottoms)
1 (12 ounce) cake frosting (your choice of flavors)

- Prepare cake batter according to package directions.
- Pour 3 tablespoons batter into ice cream cones to fill about half full.
- Set cones in muffin tins and bake at 350° for 25 to 30 minutes. (These should rise to top of cone).
- Cool and top with canned frosting.

Dick Hader's Maple Fudge

1½ cups dark corn syrup
6 cups sugar
3 (8 ounce) cartons whipping cream

- In large pan or skillet, combine all ingredients and mix well.
- Cook to soft-ball stage and remove from heat.
- In mixing bowl, beat with mixer until smooth and stiff.
- Pour onto pan and let set until firm. Cut into squares.

Marshmallow Fudge

1 (12 ounce) package semi-sweet chocolate chips
1 (14 ounce) can sweetened condensed milk
1 (8 ounce) package miniature marshmallows

- In double boiler, melt chocolate chips and stir until creamy. Remove from heat.
- Mix in milk and marshmallows and pour into buttered pan.
- Cool and refrigerate until firm. Cut into squares.

Peanut Butter Fudge

1 (12 ounce) package chocolate chips
1 (12 ounce) jar extra chunky peanut butter
1 (14 ounce) can sweetened condensed milk

- Melt chocolate chips and peanut butter on top of double boiler over hot water.
- Remove from heat and stir in milk.
- Pour into 8 x 8-inch pan lined with wax paper and let it set.

Magic Microwave Fudge

1 (12 ounce) package semi-sweet or milk chocolate chips
1 (14 ounce) can sweetened condensed milk
1 teaspoon vanilla

- Combine chocolate chips and milk in glass dish and microwave on HIGH for 3 minutes. Stir until chocolate melts and is smooth. Mix in vanilla.
- Spread mixture evenly into foil-lined 8-inch square pan and chill until firm. Cut into squares.

Chocolate-Covered Cherries

1 (6 ounce) package chocolate chips
2 tablespoons milk
1 (8 ounce) jar maraschino cherries with stems

- In double boiler or microwave, melt chocolate chips. Stir in milk.
- Pat dry cherries, dip into chocolate mixture and coat well.
- Lay cherries on cookie sheet lined with wax paper and cool until firm.

Tip: The chocolate chip-milk mixture may be doubled or tripled.

Christmas-Peppermint Candy

1 (20 ounce) package white chocolate or white almond bark
1 cup crushed peppermint sticks
1 cup toasted slivered almonds

- In double boiler, melt chocolate and stir until creamy. Remove from heat and stir in crushed peppermint sticks and slivered almonds.
- Pour on greased cookie sheet and let rest until firm.
- Cut into squares or break into pieces. Store in tightly covered container.

Pretzels-and-Peanuts Chocolate Candy

1 pound white chocolate
3 cups pretzel sticks
1 (8 ounce) package Spanish peanuts

- In double boiler, melt chocolate. Stir in pretzels and peanuts until they coat in chocolate.
- Spread in jelly-roll pan and let set until firm. Break into pieces.

Peanut Clusters

1 (12 ounce) package chocolate chips
1½ pounds almond bark
1 (9 ounce) package salted peanuts

- In double boiler, melt chocolate chips and almond bark and stir until creamy.
- Remove from heat and stir in peanuts.
- Drop by spoonfuls on wax paper. Set aside until firm or chill to firm.

Chinese Noodle Candy

1 (12 ounce) package chocolate chips
1 (3 ounce) can Chinese noodles
½ cup chopped pecans

- In double boiler, melt chocolate chips and stir until creamy.
- Remove from heat and stir in Chinese noodles and pecans until they coat in chocolate.
- Drop by spoonfuls on wax paper and set aside until firm.

Chocolate-Butterscotch Clusters

1 (6 ounce) package chocolate chips
1 (12 ounce) package butterscotch chips
1 (12 ounce) package Spanish peanuts, salted

- Combine chocolate and butterscotch chips in 2-quart glass dish.
- Microwave on MEDIUM power for 5 to 6 minutes or until they melt. Stir after 3 minutes and again after 5 or 6 minutes. Watch carefully for burning. (Some microwaves have higher power. If chips melt before time given, remove immediately.)
- Stir in peanuts and drop by teaspoonfuls on wax paper. Set aside until firm.
- Store in airtight container.

Chocolate Leaves

Leaves from yard
2 squares semi-sweet chocolate or ½ cup chocolate chips
1 teaspoon butter

- Wash and dry 2 dozen leaves of varying sizes. Ensure they are non-poisonous leaves.
- Melt 2 squares chocolate and 1 teaspoon butter and mix well.
- Using clean "watercolor-type" paintbrush, paint chocolate ⅛-inch thick on backs of leaves and cover well.
- Chill until chocolate is firm. Peel green leaves off chocolate leaves.
- Decorate cakes or tarts with chocolate leaves.

Peanut Butter Cookies

1 (14 ounce) can sweetened condensed milk
½ cup chunky peanut butter
½ cup chopped peanuts

- In bowl, combine and mix all ingredients.
- Drop by teaspoonfuls onto greased, floured cookie sheets.
- Bake at 375° to 400° for 7 to 9 minutes.

Honey-Wafer Cookies

3 egg whites
½ cup honey
1 cup graham cracker crumbs

- In mixing bowl, beat egg whites until stiff. Gradually add honey and mix well.
- Stir in graham cracker crumbs.
- Drop by teaspoonfuls onto well greased cookie sheets and bake at 300° for about 8 minutes.

Cookie Kisses

1 (18 ounce) refrigerated, chocolate chip cookie dough
⅓ cup flour
36 chocolate kisses, unwrapped

- Cut dough into 9 slices and cut each slice into 4 pieces.
- Place 1 piece of dough in each greased cup of mini-muffin pan and press with spoon coated in flour to form cups.
- Place 1 chocolate kiss in each cup and bake at 350° for 10 to 12 minutes.
- Let cookies cool in pan 15 minutes before removing to cool rack.

Forgotten Chocolate Chip Cookies

2 egg whites
⅔ cup sugar
1 cup chocolate chips

- Preheat oven to 350°.
- In mixing bowl, beat egg whites until frothy and gradually add sugar. Beat until stiff and fold in chocolate chips.
- Drop by teaspoonfuls onto greased cookie sheet and place in oven.
- Turn off heat and don't open door. Forget cookies until next day.

Chocolate Chip Cookies

2 cups finely crushed graham cracker crumbs
1 cup chocolate chips
1 (14 ounce) can sweetened condensed milk

- In bowl, combine all ingredients and mix well.
- Drop by teaspoonfuls onto greased cookie sheet and bake at 350° for 8 to 10 minutes.

Christmas Tree Cookies

1 pound butter
2¼ cups confectioners' sugar, divided
4½ cups flour

- In bowl, cream butter and add 2 cups sugar. Slowly add flour and combine well.
- Sprinkle board lightly with ¼ cup powdered sugar and roll out dough until very thin, about ⅛-inch thick.
- Cut dough with Christmas tree cookie cutters and bake on greased cookie sheets at 300° for 20 to 25 minutes.

Pecan Macaroons

2 cups finely ground pecans
2 eggs
1 cup sugar

- In blender or food processor, finely grind nuts and set aside.
- In bowl, beat eggs, stir in sugar and mix well. Add pecans and shape into balls.
- Place on greased cookie sheet and flatten balls with fork.
- Bake at 350° for 12 to 15 minutes or until light brown.

Don't throw out those cookie crumbs! Save them to use over ice cream or pudding. You can also freeze them to make cookie-crumb crusts for pies.

Chocolate Chip Macaroons

1 (14 ounce) can sweetened condensed milk
3 cups shredded coconut
½ cup chocolate chips

- In bowl, combine all ingredients and mix well.
- Drop by teaspoonfuls onto greased baking sheet 2 inches apart and bake at 350° for 15 minutes.
- Remove from pan immediately and cool on wax paper.

Cherry Macaroons

1 (14 ounce) can sweetened condensed milk
1 (14 ounce) package shredded coconut
½ cup candied chopped cherries

- In bowl, combine all ingredients and mix thoroughly.
- Drop by teaspoonfuls on greased cookie sheets and bake at 350° for about 10 minutes or until light brown.
- Cool slightly and remove from pan.

Tip: Place extra cherry halves in middle of each macaroon before baking.

Karen's Chocolate Peanut Butter Tarts

1 (18 ounce) roll refrigerated, ready-to-slice peanut butter cookie dough or chocolate chip cookie dough
2 (13 ounce) packages bite-size peanut butter cups
Butter

- Grease mini-muffin pan with butter or cooking spray. Slice cookie dough into 1-inch slices, then quarter slices.
- Lay 1 piece in each mini-muffin pan and bake at 350° for 8 minutes.
- While cookies are hot and puffed, gently push peanut butter cup into center of each cookie.
- Cool thoroughly before removing from tins. Keep refrigerated.

Chocolate-Orange Brownies

1 (15 ounce) package brownie mix
⅓ cup orange marmalade
⅓ cup chopped pecans

- Prepare brownie mix according to package directions. Stir in marmalade and pecans.
- Bake according to package directions in greased, floured jelly-roll pan.
- Cool and cut into 1-inch squares.

Tip: You may sprinkle additional pecans over top of batter before baking.

Chocolate Chip Brownies

1 (15 ounce) package fudge brownie mix
1 cup chopped pecans
1 (6 ounce) package chocolate chips

- Prepare brownie mixture according to package directions. Stir in pecans.
- Pour into greased, floured 9 x 13-inch pan and sprinkle with chocolate chips.
- Bake for 35 to 40 minutes or according to package directions.

Yield: 12 to 18 servings.

Butterscotch Bars

1 (12 ounce) package butterscotch morsels
1 cup chunky peanut butter
6 cups crispy rice cereal

- In large saucepan, combine butterscotch chips and peanut butter and stir over low heat until butterscotch morsels melt and mixture is smooth.
- Remove from heat and stir in cereal. Mix until cereal coats in butterscotch mixture.
- Press into buttered 9 x 13-inch pan. Chill until firm and cut into squares.

Ernie Massey's Haystacks

1 cup chow mein noodles
1 cup cashews
1 (12 ounce) package butterscotch chips

- Place noodles and cashews on cookie sheet pan in single layer.
- Toast noodles and cashews at 250° for 15 minutes and stir often.
- In saucepan, melt butterscotch chips. Remove from heat and stir in chow mein noodles and cashews until they coat well in butterscotch mixture.
- Drop in clusters by teaspoonfuls on wax paper and set aside until firm.

Chocolate Peanut Butter Cups

1 (21 ounce) package double-fudge brownie mix
2 eggs
2 (9 ounce) packages miniature peanut butter cups

- Preheat oven to 350°.
- Prepare brownie mix according to package directions using 2 eggs.
- Spoon into miniature foil cupcake liners and fill ¾ full.
- Place peanut butter cup in center of each and push into batter.
- Bake for 20 to 25 minutes or until cake tests done.

Butterscotch-Krispie Bars

1 (12 ounce) package butterscotch chips
1 cup creamy peanut butter
6 cups rice crispy cereal

- In saucepan, combine butterscotch chips and peanut butter. Heat and stir until smooth.
- Remove from heat and stir in cereal until it coats well with butterscotch mixture.
- Press into buttered 9 x 13-inch pan and chill until firm. Cut into bars.

Lucky Charm Bars

3 tablespoons butter, melted
3½ cups miniature marshmallows
5 cups Lucky Charms cereal

- Grease 9 x 9-inch pan.
- In large microwave-safe bowl, combine butter and marshmallows and microwave uncovered on HIGH for 1 to 3 minutes.
- Stir after each minute of cooking until mixture melts and is smooth. Add cereal and coat well with marshmallow mixture.
- Press into pan and set aside until firm. Cut into bars.

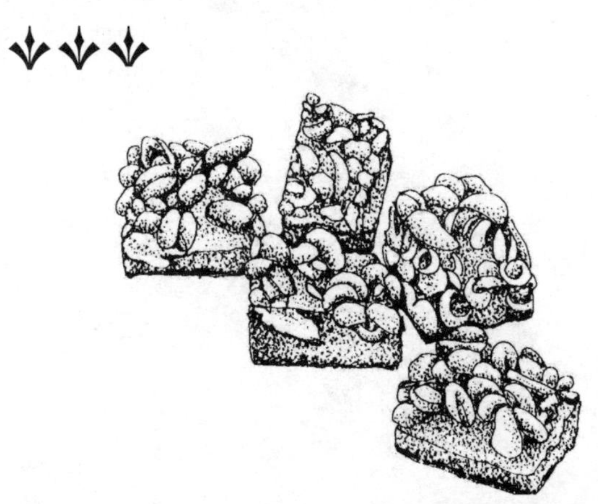

Milky Way Squares

4 (2 ounce) candy bars, chopped
½ cup butter
3 cups rice crispy cereal

- In saucepan or microwave-safe dish, combine candy and ½ cup butter. Stir until mixture melts and is smooth. Add cereal and coat well with mixture.
- Pat into greased 11 x 7-inch pan.
- Refrigerate until firm and cut into squares.

Mrs. Truman's Coconut Balls

Mrs. Truman served these at some White House gatherings.

1 (7 ounce) package shredded coconut
1 teaspoon vanilla
⅔ cup sweetened condensed milk

- In bowl, combine all ingredients and mix well.
- Shape into balls and bake on greased cookie sheets at 350° for 15 minutes.

Tip: If the shredded coconut has become dry, soak it in a little milk for several minutes before using. Drain well and blot on paper towels.

Gail Ward's Grandmother's Shortbread

2 cups (4 sticks) butter
1 cup sugar
4 cups flour

- In bowl, mix butter and sugar until creamy. Gradually add flour.
- Mix with your hands and knead 10 minutes until mixture holds together.
- Roll out ½-inch thick or pat down on breadboard and cut into 1-inch squares.
- Prick top with fork and bake on ungreased cookie sheet at 275° for 35 minutes or until light brown.

Easy Baklava

2 packages frozen patty shells
3 cups finely chopped pecans, divided
1 cup honey, warmed, divided

- Thaw frozen patty shells overnight in refrigerator.
- Line 8 x 8 x 2-inch cake pan with foil. Grease lightly and set aside.
- Stack 3 thawed patty shells, one on top of other.
- On lightly floured surface roll into 9-inch square. With knife, trim down to 8½-inch square and place in bottom of cake pan.
- Sprinkle with 1 cup chopped pecans and drizzle with ¼ cup honey. Repeat process 3 times, making top layer plain pastry (no nuts or honey on it).
- Mark pastry into diamond pattern with tip of knife.
- Bake at 425° for 20 to 25 minutes. Cool slightly in pan.
- Brush surface with last of honey, remove from pan and peel away foil.
- Cut into diamond shapes and serve with more honey.

Key Lime Pie

1 (6 ounce) can frozen limeade concentrate
1 (8 ounce) carton frozen whipped topping, thawed
1 (14 ounce) can sweetened condensed milk

- In bowl, combine all ingredients and mix well.
- Pour into prepared graham cracker crust or chocolate crumb crust.
- Refrigerate 2 hours or more before serving.

Frozen Lemonade Pie

1 (6 ounce) can frozen pink lemonade
1 (8 ounce) carton frozen whipped topping, thawed
1 (14 ounce) can sweetened condensed milk

- In bowl, combine all ingredients and mix well.
- Chill. Serve as pudding or pour into graham cracker piecrust and freeze.

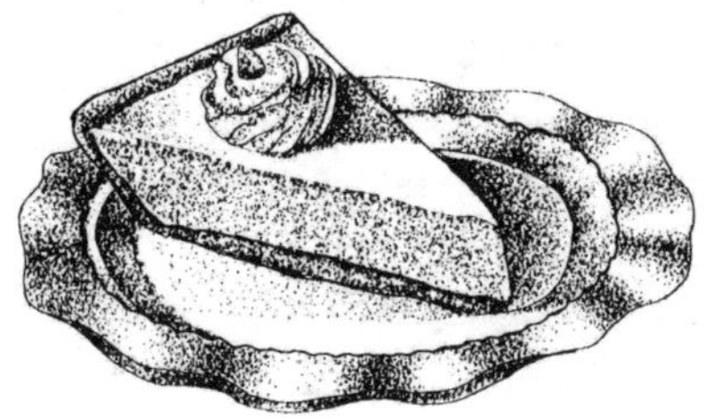

Coconut-Cream Pie

1 (3.4 ounce) package vanilla pie filling mix
1 (7 ounce) package shredded coconut
1 (9 inch) baked piecrust

- Prepare pudding as pie according to package directions.
- Cool and stir in coconut. Mix well and pour into baked piecrust.
- Refrigerate for 4 hours before serving.

Speedy Banana Pie

1 (3.4 ounce) box banana pudding
2 to 3 bananas, sliced
1 (8 inch) piecrust, baked

- Prepare pudding as pie according to package directions.
- Place banana slices in cooled crust and pour pudding over bananas.
- Garnish with banana slices and let stand 5 to 10 minutes.

Meringue For Speedy Banana Pie:

2 cups miniature marshmallows

- Sprinkle miniature marshmallows over top of pie and broil 2 to 3 minutes until they brown lightly and partially melt.

Brickle Chip Ice Cream Pie

½ gallon vanilla ice cream
1 (6 ounce) graham cracker crumb piecrust or chocolate piecrust
1 cup brickle bits, divided

- Spoon half of vanilla ice cream into piecrust and spread ⅔ cup brickle bits over ice cream.
- Top with other half of ice cream, sprinkle with remaining brickle chips and freeze.

Frozen Peanut Butter Pie

¾ cup chunky peanut butter
1 quart vanilla ice cream, softened
1 (6 ounce) graham cracker crust or chocolate crust

- In bowl, combine peanut butter and softened ice cream. Mix well.
- Pour into piecrust and freeze.

Missouri Mud Pie

1 (8 ounce) package chocolate wafers, divided
1 quart coffee ice cream, softened
1 jar chocolate sauce

- Arrange layer of chocolate wafers in bottom and along sides of 9-inch glass pie plate.
- Fill with ice cream and sprinkle additional crushed cookies over top.
- Freeze until firm, slice and serve.
- Drizzle chocolate sauce over each slice. Makes 9-inch pie.

Chocolate-Almond Pie

1 (8 ounce) chocolate-almond bar
1 (8 ounce) carton frozen whipped topping, thawed
1 (8-inch) graham cracker crust

- In double boiler, melt chocolate bar. Remove from heat and cool.
- Stir whipped topping into chocolate and pour into piecrust. Chill.

Tip: If you desire a garnish, use a potato peeler to shave chocolate curls from additional chocolate candy bar.

Strawberry Ice Cream Pie

1 (3 ounce) package strawberry gelatin
1 pint vanilla ice cream
1 pint fresh or frozen strawberries

- Prepare gelatin with 1 cup boiling water and mix well until gelatin dissolves.
- Stir in ice cream, then strawberries.
- Chill and serve as pudding or pour into prepared piecrust.

Cherry Cobbler

1 (20 ounce) can cherry pie filling
1 (18 ounce) box yellow or white cake mix
¾ cup (1½ sticks) butter, sliced

- Spread cherry pie filling on greased 9 x 13-inch baking dish and sprinkle with cake mix.
- Top with slices of butter and bake at 350° for about 35 minutes.
- Any pie filling or canned fruit may be substituted for cherries.

Don't throw away that butter wrap. Use it to grease the inside of your baking dish or pan. You won't waste butters and will feel so efficient!

Cherry-Chocolate Bundt Cake

1 (18 ounce) box chocolate cake mix
1 (21 ounce) can cherry pie filling
2 large eggs, beaten

- In mixing bowl, combine all ingredients and mix well.
- Lightly spray microwave-safe bundt pan with non-stick cooking spray.
- Pour batter into pan and microwave on HIGH for 4 minutes.
- Turn bundt pan ¼ turn and microwave additional 1 minute on HIGH or until cake tester comes out clean.

Yield: 12 slices.

Apricot Balls

½ pound dried apricots, minced
2 cups shredded coconut
½ (14 ounce) can sweetened condensed milk

- Combine and mix all ingredients. Chill overnight.
- Shape into balls and let rest in covered container 1 day before eating.

Oreo Cookie Ice Cream

½ gallon vanilla ice cream, softened
1 (12 ounce) container whipped topping
2 cups crushed Oreo cookies

- Combine all ingredients and mix well. Freeze in 9 x 13-inch pan.
- Cut into squares to serve.

Jan Ballard's Vanilla Ice Cream

2 (14 ounce) cans sweetened condensed milk
6 cups whole milk
2 teaspoons vanilla

- Combine all ingredients and mix well. Freeze in ice cream freezer according to freezer directions.

Yield: 1½ gallons.

Chocolate Ice Cream

1 (14 ounce) can sweetened condensed milk
1 (12 ounce) container frozen whipped topping, thawed
1 gallon chocolate milk, divided

- Fold condensed milk and whipped topping into 1-quart chocolate milk.
- Pour into 6-quart freezer container and add remaining chocolate milk.
- Freeze according to freezer directions.

Orange-Pineapple Sherbet

1 (20 ounce) can crushed pineapple with juice
1 (2 liter) bottle orange soda
2 (14 ounce) cans sweetened condensed milk

- Combine all ingredients and mix well. Freeze.

My Grandma's Banana Pudding Dessert

1 (5 ounce) package banana pudding
1 (12 ounce) box vanilla wafer cookies
4 to 6 bananas, sliced

- Prepare banana pudding according to package directions.
- Make cookie crust by placing whole vanilla wafers along bottom and sides of glass dish. Layer pudding, sliced bananas and cookies.
- Repeat layers until all ingredients are used.
- Refrigerate 2 to 4 hours to blend flavors.

Mocha Pudding

1 (16 ounce) almond candy bar
1 tablespoon instant coffee powder
1 (12 ounce) carton whipped topping

- Melt candy with coffee powder in double boiler over boiling water and mix often.
- Remove from heat and cool completely.
- Stir in whipped topping and serve in dessert dishes as pudding.

Tip: Pour into graham cracker crust to serve as pie. Refrigerate until firm.

S'Mores

Graham cracker squares
Chocolate squares
Marshmallows

- Place graham cracker squares on jelly-roll pan and top with squares of chocolate.
- Lightly melt marshmallows in oven or microwave.
- Pour hot marshmallow mixture over chocolate and place second cracker over top to form sandwich.

Fruit Pizza

1 (20 ounce) package refrigerated sugar cookie dough
3 cups whipped topping
2 to 3 cups assorted fresh fruit

- Press dough evenly into pizza pan and bake at 350° for 25 to 30 minutes or until brown.
- Cool completely in pan and spread layer of whipped topping over crust.
- Arrange fresh sliced fruit of your choice over cookie pizza

Pears Helene

1 pint vanilla ice
1 (15 ounce) can pear halves, drained
½ cup chocolate sauce

- In 4 glass dessert dishes, place 1 scoop ice cream and 2 pear halves.
- Drizzle chocolate sauce over pears and ice cream and serve.

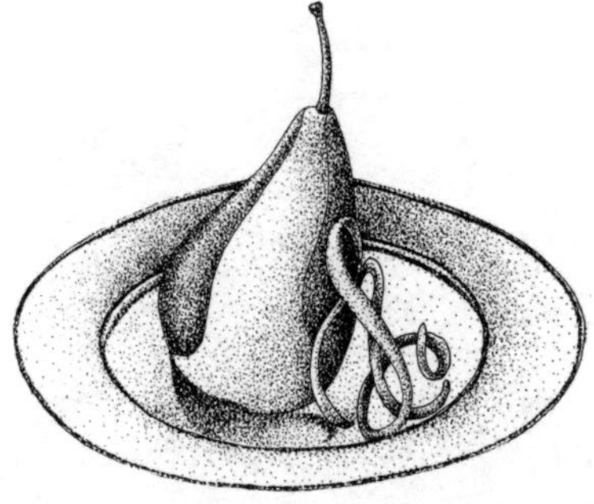

Mini Crusts

1 (3 ounce) package cream cheese, softened
½ cup (1 stick) butter, softened
1 cup flour

- In bowl, combine all ingredients and mix well. Chill dough.
- Shape into 24 balls, place in ungreased mini-muffin pan and press dough against bottom and sides.
- Bake at 350° until golden brown. Fill with pie filling of your choice.

Christmas Wreaths

½ cup (1 stick) butter
30 large marshmallows
3 cups corn flakes

- In saucepan, melt butter and marshmallows and stir until smooth. Remove from heat and stir in corn flakes. Add green food coloring to mixture to make "wreath" green.
- Drop by spoonfuls on wax paper to make circle.
- Form hole in middle with buttered fingers so these are shaped like wreaths.

Tip: Decorate, if desired, with cinnamon red-hot candies dotted on each wreath.

The Ultimate Cooking with 4 Ingredients

By Jean C. Coates

cookbook resources® LLC

The Ultimate Cooking with 4 Ingredients

Ist Printing – January 2002

2nd Printing – June 2002

3rd Printing – August 2003

4th Printing – October 2002

5th Printing – November 2002

6th Printing – February 2005

ISBN 1-931294-36-4 (hard bound)

ISBN 1-931294-37-2 (paper cover)

Library of Congress Number: 2002115116

Illustrations by Nancy Murphy Griffith

Edited, Designed, Published and Manufactured in the

United States of America by

Cookbook Resources, LLC

541 Doubletree Drive

Highland Village, Texas 75077

Toll free 866-229-2665

www.cookbookresources.com

Introduction

In our fast-paced, rush-here-and-there lives, a home-cooked meal may be considered a luxury. We live out of our cars, placing food orders on cell phones and going to drive-through windows for the night's meal and maybe the family sits down together to eat.

We hope to help families come back to the table and spend quality time while sharing good food to eat. The recipes in "**The Ultimate Cooking With 4 Ingredients"** are easy to prepare and ingredients are readily available. Most of them are already in your pantry.

Everyone in the family can cook out of **"The Ultimate Cooking With 4 Ingredients."** Mouth-watering meals are just minutes away and every minute we spend around the table enriches our lives and helps us grow stronger. Have a good time with this cookbook and don't hesitate to recruit some helpers.

It's a great time for all of us to come back to the table.

Jean C. Coates

Contents

The Ultimate Cooking with 4 Ingredients

Spicy Beef and Cheese Dip

1 (10 ounce) can tomatoes and green chilies
½ teaspoon garlic powder
2 (16 ounce) packages cubed, processed cheese
1 pound lean ground beef, browned, drained

- In large saucepan, combine tomatoes and green chilies, garlic and cheese. Heat on low until cheese melts.
- Add ground beef and mix well. Serve with tortilla chips.

Egg and Cheese Dip

5 hard-boiled eggs, mashed
1 cup mayonnaise
4 ounces shredded Monterey Jack cheese
½ teaspoon prepared mustard

- In bowl, combine all ingredients and mix well.
- Add salt to taste and refrigerate.
- Serve with wheat crackers.

Velvet Dip

2 (16 ounce) packages cubed Mexican processed cheese
2 cups mayonnaise
1 (4 ounce) jar chopped pimentos, drained
1 (7 ounce) can chopped green chilies

- Place cheese in saucepan and melt over low heat.
- Add remaining ingredients and mix well. Serve with chips.

Creamy Onion Dip

2 (8 ounce) packages cream cheese, softened
3 tablespoons lemon juice
1 (1 ounce) package dry onion soup mix
1 (8 ounce) carton sour cream

- With mixer, beat cream cheese until smooth. Add lemon juice and soup mix and blend well. Gradually fold in sour cream.
- Chill. Serve with chips, crackers or fresh vegetables.

Fiesta-Onion Dip

1 (1 ounce) package dry onion soup mix
1 (15 ounce) can Mexican stewed tomatoes
2 teaspoons chili powder
1 cup grated cheddar cheese

- In small saucepan, heat soup mix, tomatoes and chili powder. Bring to boil.
- Reduce heat and simmer for 20 minutes. Stir occasionally.
- Pour into serving bowl and sprinkle with cheese.
- Stir before serving and serve with chips.

Broccoli-Cheese Dip

1 (10 ounce) can broccoli cheese soup
1 (10 ounce) package frozen, chopped broccoli, thawed
½ cup sour cream
2 teaspoons of dijon-style mustard

- In saucepan, combine all ingredients and mix well. Heat, serve hot.

Hot Broccoli Dip

2 (16 ounce) packages cubed Mexican processed cheese
1 (10 ounce) can golden mushroom soup
1 (10 ounce) box frozen chopped broccoli, thawed
Chips

- In saucepan, melt cheese with soup. Stir in broccoli and heat thoroughly. Serve hot with chips.

Broccoli Dip

1 (10 ounce) package frozen, chopped broccoli, thawed
1 (10 ounce) can cream of chicken soup
3 cups grated cheddar cheese
1 (7 ounce) can chopped green chilies

- In saucepan, cook broccoli about 5 minutes in butter and about ½ teaspoon salt.
- Add soup, cheese and green chilies. Heat until cheese melts.

Tip: If chilies are not hot enough in dip, add several dashes of hot sauce.

Artichoke-Bacon Dip

1 (14 ounce) jar artichoke hearts, drained, chopped
1 cup mayonnaise
2 teaspoons worchestershire sauce
5 slices bacon, cooked crisp, crumbled

- In large bowl, combine all ingredients and mix well.
- Pour into buttered 8-inch baking dish and bake at 350° for 12 minutes. Serve hot with crackers.

Sassy Onion Dip

1 (8 ounce) package cream cheese, softened
1 (8 ounce) carton sour cream
½ cup chili sauce
1 (1 ounce) package dry onion soup mix

- Using mixer, beat cream cheese until fluffy.
- Add remaining ingredients and mix well.
- Cover and chill. Serve with strips of raw veggies.

Cottage Dip

1 (16 ounce) carton small-curd cottage cheese
1 (1 ounce) package dry onion soup mix
½ cup mayonnaise
½ teaspoon garlic powder

- In bowl, blend all ingredients and mix well.
- Chill and serve with chips, crackers or veggies.

Hot-to-Trot Dip

1 pound ground beef
2 (16 ounce) packages cubed, processed cheese
1½ cups salsa
Several drops hot sauce

- In skillet, brown ground beef and drain well.
- In saucepan, heat cheese and salsa until cheese melts. Add hot sauce.
- Combine meat and cheese mixtures. Serve hot with tortilla chips.

Five-Minute Dip

1 (8 ounce) package cream cheese, softened
1 cup mayonnaise
1 (1 ounce) package dry ranch-style salad dressing mix
½ onion, finely minced

- In mixing bowl, combine cream cheese and mayonnaise and beat until creamy.
- Stir in dressing mix and onion. Chill and serve with fresh veggies.

Horsey Shrimp Dip

1 (6 ounce) can tiny shrimp, chopped, drained
3 tablespoons cream-style horseradish
⅓ cup mayonnaise
½ teaspoon Cajun seasoning

- Combine all ingredients and mix well. Chill. Serve with crackers.

Spinach-Artichoke Dip

2 (10 ounce) boxes frozen spinach, thawed, drained
1 (14 ounce) jar marinated artichoke hearts, drained, finely chopped
1 cup mayonnaise
2 cups shredded mozzarella cheese

- Drain spinach with several layers of paper towels.
- Combine all ingredients and mix well.
- Cover and chill. Serve with chips.

Sombrero Dip

1 (15 ounce) can chili with no beans
½ teaspoon chili powder
¾ cup green chili sauce
1 (2½ ounce) can sliced black olives, drained

- In saucepan, combine chili and chili powder and warm over low heat. Stir in sauce and olives. Serve with chips.

Avocado Ole

3 large ripe avocados, mashed
1 tablespoon fresh lemon juice
1 (1 ounce) package dry onion soup mix
1 (8 ounce) carton sour cream

- In bowl, mix avocados with lemon juice and add soup mix and sour cream. (You may want to add a little salt.)
- Serve with chips or crackers.

Watercress To Do Dip

3 ripe avocados
1¼ cups snipped watercress
¾ cups mayonnaise
¼ teaspoon ground cumin seeds

- Peel and mash softened avocados and place in medium bowl.
- Add watercress, mayonnaise and cumin seeds and mix well. Add salt to taste. Cover and chill. Serve with chips.

Whiz Bang Dip

1 pound ground beef
¼ cup chopped onion
2 (16 ounce) packages cubed Mexican processed cheese
¾ cup mayonnaise salad dressing

- In skillet, brown meat and onion and drain well.
- Combine remaining ingredients and mix well.
- On low heat cook until cheese melts, stirring constantly.
- Serve with chips.

Pep-Pep-Pepperoni Dip

2 (8 ounce) packages cream cheese
1 (3.5 ounce) package pepperoni slices
1 (12 ounce) bottle chili sauce
1 bunch fresh green onions with tops, chopped

- In mixing bowl, beat cream cheese until creamy.
- Cut pepperoni slices into smaller chunks.
- Add pepperoni, chili sauce and green onions to cream cheese and mix well. Chill and serve with chips.

Picante Cream

1 (8 ounce) carton sour cream
½ teaspoon prepared mustard
¼ cup hot salsa
¼ teaspoon celery salt

- In bowl, combine all ingredients and mix well.
- Chill and serve with chips.

Dried Beef and Chips

1 (8 ounce) package cream cheese, softened
1 (8 ounce) carton sour cream
1 (3 ounce) package dried beef, cubed
½ cup finely chopped pecans

- In mixing bowl, combine cream cheese and sour cream and beat until creamy.
- Fold in dried beef chunks and pecans. Chill and serve with chips.

Pepper-Pot Bean Dip

1 (15 ounce) can refried beans
1 (16 ounce) package cubed Mexican processed cheese
½ cup (1 stick) butter
1 teaspoon garlic powder

- In large double boiler, combine all ingredients.
- Heat on low until cheese and butter melt. Stir often.
- Transfer to hot chafing dish and serve with tortilla chips.

Party Shrimp Dip

1 (8 ounce) package cream cheese, softened
½ cup mayonnaise
1 (6 ounce) can tiny, cooked shrimp, drained
¾ teaspoon Creole seasoning

- With mixer, blend cream cheese and mayonnaise.
- Stir in shrimp and seasoning and mix well.
- Chill and serve with chips.

Chunky Shrimp Dip

2 (6 ounce) cans shrimp, drained
2 cups mayonnaise
6 green onions, finely chopped
¾ cup chunky salsa

- In bowl, crumble shrimp and stir in remaining ingredients.
- Chill for 1 to 2 hours. Serve with crackers.

Tasty Tuna Dip

1 (6 ounce) can tuna in spring water, drained, flaked
1 (1 ounce) envelope Italian salad dressing mix
1 (8 ounce) carton sour cream
¼ cup chopped black olives, drained

- In bowl, combine all ingredients and blend well.
- Chill 8 hours. Serve with melba rounds.

Gitty-Up Crab Dip

1 (8 ounce) package cream cheese, softened
3 tablespoons salsa
2 tablespoons prepared horseradish
1 (6 ounce) can crabmeat, drained, flaked

- In mixing bowl, beat cream cheese until smooth and creamy.
- Add salsa and horseradish and mix well.
- Stir in crabmeat and chill. Serve with assorted crackers.

Hot, Rich Crab Dip

1 (10 ounce) can cheddar cheese soup
1 (16 ounce) package cubed Mexican processed cheese
1 (6 ounce) cans crabmeat, flaked, drained
1 (16 ounce) jar salsa

- In microwave-safe bowl, combine cheese soup and processed cheese.
- Microwave at 1-minute intervals until cheese melts.
- Add crabmeat and salsa and mix well. Serve hot with chips.

Unbelievable Crab Dip

1 (6 ounce) can white crabmeat, drained, flaked
1 (8 ounce) package cream cheese
½ cup (1 stick) butter
Chips or crackers

- In saucepan, combine crabmeat, cream cheese and butter.
- Heat and mix thoroughly.
- Transfer to chafing dish and serve with chips or crackers.

Crab Crackers

1 (6 ounce) can crabmeat, drained, flaked
1 (8 ounce) package cream cheese, softened
2 (10 ounce) cans cream of celery soup
1 (4 ounce) can chopped black olives

- In saucepan, combine all ingredients and mix until cheese melts.
- Serve hot with crackers. Add drops of hot sauce for extra zip.

Water Chestnut Dip

1 (8 ounce) can sliced water chestnuts, chopped
1 cup pecans, chopped
1 (16 ounce) carton sour cream
1 (1.8 ounce) envelope leek soup mix

- In large bowl, combine water chestnuts, pecans and sour cream. Mix well.
- Fold in leek soup mix and stir well. Chill. Serve with wheat crackers.

Cottage-Ham Dip

1 (16 ounce) carton small-curd cottage cheese, drained
2 (6 ounce) cans deviled ham
1 1 (ounce) package dry onion soup mix
½ cup sour cream

- Blend cottage cheese with blender or mixer.
- Add ham, soup mix and sour cream and mix well.

Speedy Chili Con Queso

1 (16 ounce) package cubed, processed cheese
½ cup milk
1 (12 ounce) jar salsa
Tortilla chips

- In saucepan or double boiler, combine cheese and milk and heat until cheese melts.
- Add about half salsa. Serve with tortilla chips.

Tip: Taste and add more salsa as needed for desired heat!

Border Queso

2 canned jalapeno peppers with 1 tablespoon liquid
1 (16 ounce) package cubed, processed cheese
1 (4 ounce) jar diced pimentos, drained
3 fresh green onions, chopped

- Seed jalapeno peppers and chop.
- Combine peppers, cheese, pimentos and onion in saucepan.
- Heat on stove, stirring constantly, until cheese melts. Stir in reserved liquid. Serve with tortilla chips.

Holy Guacamole

4 avocados, peeled
½ cup salsa
¼ cup sour cream
1 teaspoon salt

- Split avocados and remove seeds. Mash avocados with fork.
- Add salsa, sour cream and salt. Serve with tortilla chips.

Orange-Sour Cream Dip

1 (6 ounce) can frozen orange juice concentrate, thawed
1 (3.4 ounce) package vanilla instant pudding mix
1 cup milk
¼ cup sour cream

- In bowl, combine orange juice concentrate, pudding mix and milk.
- Stir with wire whisk until mixture blends and is smooth. Add in sour cream.
- Cover and chill at least 2 hours. Serve with fresh fruit.

Fruit Dip for Nectarines

1 (8 ounce) package cream cheese, softened
2 (7 ounce) cartons marshmallow cream
¼ teaspoon cinnamon
⅛ teaspoon ground ginger

- Combine all ingredients in mixing bowl and beat well using mixer.
- Chill and serve with unpeeled slices of nectarines or other fruit.

Cream Cheese Spread

1 (8 ounce) package cream cheese, softened
½ cup mayonnaise
1 (4 ounce) can chopped black olives
3 green onions, chopped very fine

- In bowl, blend cream cheese and mayonnaise until smooth.
- Add olives and onions. Chill and spread on slices of party rye bread.

Chicken-Cheese Spread

2 (8 ounce) packages cream cheese, softened
2 tablespoons white wine worchestershire
2 cups finely shredded, cooked chicken breasts
¼ cup almonds, chopped, toasted

- In mixing bowl, combine cream cheese and worchestershire and beat until creamy.
- Fold in shredded chicken and almonds.
- Spread on English muffin halves and toast but be careful not to burn.

Hot Artichoke Spread

1 (14 ounce) can artichoke hearts, drained, finely chopped
1 cup mayonnaise
1 cup grated parmesan cheese
1 package Italian salad dressing mix

- Remove tough outer leaves and chop artichoke hearts.
- Combine all ingredients in bowl and mix thoroughly.
- Pour into 9-inch square baking pan and bake at 350° for 20 minutes.
- Serve hot with assorted crackers.

Smoky Gouda Spread

¾ cup chopped walnuts
1 (8 ounce) smoked gouda cheese
1 (8 ounce) package cream cheese, softened
¼ cup sliced green onions

- Spread walnuts in shallow baking pan. Bake at 325° for 10 minutes or until they toast lightly. Cool and set aside.
- Trim and discard outer red edge of gouda cheese. Grate cheese.
- With mixer, combine cheeses, mix well and stir in walnuts and onions. Serve with apple wedges or crackers.

Ranch Cheese Ball

1 (1 ounce) package dry ranch-style salad dressing mix
2 (8 ounce) packages cream cheese, softened
¼ cup finely chopped pecans
1 (3 ounce) jar real bacon bits

- In mixing bowl, combine dressing mix and cream cheese with mixer and blend well.
- Roll into ball and then into pecans and bacon bits.
- Chill several hours before serving.

Beefy Cheese Balls

2 (8 ounce) packages cream cheese, softened
2 (2½ ounce) jars dried beef
1 bunch fresh green onions with tops, chopped
1 teaspoon cayenne pepper.

- In mixing bowl, beat cream cheese with mixer until smooth and creamy. Chop dried beef in food processor or blender.
- Combine all ingredients and form into ball and chill overnight. Serve with crackers.

Olive-Cheese Appetizers

1 cup pimento-stuffed olives, chopped
2 fresh green onions, finely chopped
1½ cups shredded Monterey Jack cheese
½ cup mayonnaise

- In large bowl, combine all ingredients and mix well.
- Spread mixture on English muffins and bake at 375° until bubbly.
- Cut muffins into quarters and serve hot.

Tuna Melt Appetizer

1 (10 ounce) package frozen spinach, drained
2 (6 ounce) cans white tuna in water, drained, flaked
¾ cup mayonnaise
1½ cups shredded mozzarella cheese, divided

- Drain spinach well with several paper towels.
- In bowl, combine all ingredients and mix well.
- Spoon into buttered pie plate and bake at 350° for 15 minutes. Remove from oven and sprinkle remaining cheese over top.
- Bake another 5 minutes. Serve with crackers.

Jack Quesadillas

¼ cup ricotta cheese, divided
6 (6-inch) corn tortillas
⅔ cup shredded Monterey Jack cheese, divided
1 (4 ounce) can diced green chilies, drained

- Spread about 1 tablespoon of ricotta over tortilla. Add 1 heaping tablespoon cheese and 1 tablespoon chilies. Place second tortilla on top. Repeat to make 2 more quesadillas.
- In heated skillet, add 1 quesadilla and cook 3 minutes on each side. Remove, cut into 4 wedges and repeat with remaining quesadillas. Serve warm with salsa.

✤✤✤✤

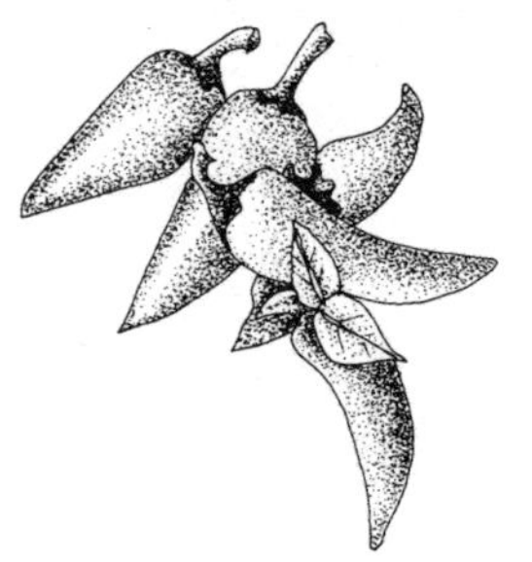

Great Balls of Fire

1 pound lean hot sausage
3 green onions, chopped
1 (4 ounce) can chopped tomatoes and green chilies
2 (16 ounce) packages cubed, processed cheese

- In large skillet, brown sausage and drain off fat.
- Add tomatoes and green chilies and mix.
- Add cheese to sausage mixture and cook on low heat until cheese melts.
- Serve hot in chafing dish with large chips.

Sausage Pinwheels

2½ cups biscuit mix
⅔ cup milk
1 (pound) package hot sausage at room temperature
1 green or red bell pepper, minced

- In medium bowl, combine biscuit mix and milk and mix well.
- Divide dough into 3 parts. Roll each piece of dough into thin rectangle.
- Crumble ⅓ sausage and minced bell pepper on each piece of dough and pat down.
- Roll up like jellyroll. Cover with foil and chill overnight. Slice into thin slices and bake at 375° for 15 to 20 minutes.

Bacon Nibblers

1 (1 pound) package sliced bacon
1½ cups packed brown sugar
1½ teaspoons prepared dry mustard
¼ teaspoon black pepper

- Cut slices of bacon in half. Combine remaining ingredients in shallow bowl.
- Dip half slices of bacon in brown sugar mixture and press down to coat well. Place on baking sheet with sides.
- Bake at 325° for 25 minutes, turning once, until bacon browns. Immediately remove with tongs to several layers of paper towels. Bacon will harden and can be broken in pieces.

Bacon-Oyster Bites

1 (5 ounce) can smoked oysters, drained, chopped
⅔ cup herb-seasoned stuffing mix
¼ cup water
8 slices bacon, halved, partially cooked

- In bowl, combine oysters, stuffing mix and water. Add 1 teaspoon water if mixture seems too dry.
- Form into balls, using about 1 tablespoon mixture for each. Wrap ½ slice bacon around each and secure with toothpick.
- Place on rack in baking pan. Cook at 350° for 25 to 30 minutes.

Hot Cocktail Squares

1 (4 ounce) can chopped green chilies
1 (3 ounce) jar bacon bits
1 (16 ounce) package shredded cheddar cheese
7 eggs

- In sprayed 7 x 11-inch baking dish, layer green chilies, bacon bits and cheese.
- Beat eggs with fork and season with a little salt and drops hot sauce.
- Pour over cheese mixture and bake covered at 350° for 25 minutes.
- Uncover and bake another 10 minutes. Serve warm.

Olive-Cheese Empanadas

1 cup pimiento-stuffed green olives or black olives, chopped, divided
1 cup finely shredded cheddar cheese
4 tablespoons mayonnaise
1 (15 ounce) package of 2 refrigerated piecrusts

- Preheat oven to 450°. In bowl, combine olives, cheese and mayonnaise.
- Use 3-inch biscuit cutter to cut piecrusts into 12 rounds. Place 1 teaspoon olive mixture in center of pastry round.
- Fold side of pastry to other side and press edges together to seal in olive mixture.
- Crimp edge to seal edges. If pastry begins to dry, it will not seal properly. Dip finger in water, lightly brush edges and seal.
- Place on baking sheet and bake 10 minutes or until golden brown.

Cinnamon Pecans

1 egg white
1 pound pecan halves
2 tablespoons cinnamon
¾ cup sugar

- Beat egg white slightly with fork. In bowl, combine pecan halves with egg white and mix well.
- Sprinkle with mixture of cinnamon and sugar and stir until it coats all pecans.
- Spread on baking sheet and bake at 325° for about 20 minutes.
- Cool and store in covered container.

Best Tropical Punch

1 (46 ounce) can pineapple juice
1 (46 ounce) can apricot nectar
3 (6 ounce) cans frozen limeade concentrate, thawed
3 quarts ginger ale, chilled

- Combine pineapple juice, apricot nectar and limeade and chill.
- When ready to serve, add ginger ale.

Perfect Party Punch

1 (12 ounce) can frozen limeade concentrate
1 (46 ounce) can pineapple juice, chilled
1 (46 ounce) apricot nectar, chilled
1 quart ginger ale, chilled

- Dilute limeade concentrate according to directions on can.
- Add pineapple juice and apricot nectar and stir well.
- When ready to serve, add ginger ale.

Great Fruit Punch

1 (46 ounce) can pineapple juice
2 (46 ounce) cans apple juice
3 quarts ginger ale
Fresh mint to garnish, optional

- Combine pineapple juice and apple juice and make ice ring with part of juice.
- Chill remaining juice and ginger ale.
- When ready to serve, combine juices and ginger ale and place ice ring in punch bowl.

Tip: If you don't have a round gelatin mold with hole in the middle, make ice ring with any type of gelatin mold.

Easiest Grape Punch

½ gallon ginger ale
Red seedless grapes
Sparkling white grape juice, chilled
Ice ring

- Make ice ring of ginger ale and seedless grapes.
- When ready to serve, pour sparkling white grape juice in punch bowl with ice ring.

Tip: If you don't have a round gelatin mold with hole in the middle, make ice ring with any type of gelatin mold.

Tip: Sparkling white grape juice is great just by itself!

Ruby Red Punch

1 (46 ounce) can pineapple-grapefruit juice
½ cup sugar
¼ cup cinnamon candies
1 quart ginger ale, chilled

- In large saucepan, combine pineapple-grapefruit juice, sugar and candies. Bring to boil and stir until candies dissolve.
- Cool until time to serve, stirring occasionally, to completely dissolve candies. Add ginger ale just before serving.

Cranberry-Ginger Ale Punch

2 (28 ounce) bottles ginger ale, chilled
1 (48 ounce) can pineapple juice, chilled
1 quart cranberry juice, chilled
1 quart pineapple sherbet, broken up

- Pour all ingredients in punch bowl and serve.

Creamy Strawberry Punch

1 (10 ounce) package frozen strawberries, thawed
½ gallon strawberry ice cream, softened
2 (2 liter) bottles ginger ale, chilled
Fresh strawberries, optional

- Process frozen strawberries through blender.
- Combine strawberries, chunks of ice cream and ginger ale in punch bowl.
- Stir and serve immediately. Garnish with fresh strawberries.

Mocha Cream Punch

4 cups brewed coffee
¼ cup sugar
4 cups milk
4 cups chocolate ice cream, softened

- In container, combine coffee and sugar and stir until sugar dissolves. Chill 2 hours.
- Just before serving, pour into small punch bowl.
- Add milk and mix well. Top with scoops of ice cream and stir well.

Sparkling Pink Punch

3 (6 ounce) cans frozen pink lemonade concentrate
1 (750 ml) bottle pink sparkling wine
3 (2 liter) bottles lemon-lime carbonated beverage, divided
Lime slices to garnish, optional

- Stir all ingredients, except 1 bottle carbonated beverage, in airtight container, cover and freeze 8 hours or until firm.
- Let stand at room temperature 10 minutes and place in punch bowl.
- Add remaining 1 bottle carbonated beverage and stir until slushy.

Strawberry Fizz

2 (10 ounce) boxes frozen strawberries, thawed
2 (6 ounce) cans frozen pink lemonade concentrate
2 (2 liter) bottles ginger ale, chilled
Fresh strawberries, optional

- Process frozen strawberries through blender.
- Pour lemonade into punch bowl and stir in strawberries.
- Add chilled ginger ale and stir well. Garnish with fresh strawberries.

Tip: If you want an ice mold to go in the punch bowl, pour ginger ale in a ring mold or gelatin mold and freeze.

Party-Hardy Punch

1 (46 ounce) can pineapple juice
1 (46 ounce) can apple juice
3 quarts ginger ale, chilled
Pineapple chunks, optional

- Combine pineapple and apple juice in very large plastic container, any container large enough to hold both juices or use 2 plastic pitchers. Freeze both juices.
- When ready to serve, place pineapple and apple juice in punch bowl and add chilled ginger ale. Stir to mix and garnish with pineapple chunks.

Cranberry-Lemon Punch

2 quarts cranberry juice
1 (6 ounce) can lemonade concentrate, thawed
⅔ cup maraschino cherry juice
2 liters lemon-lime soda, chilled

- Combine all ingredients.

Tip: If you have time, an ice ring made out of cranberry juice, lemon slices and maraschino cherries would be nice.

Pina Colada Punch

1 (46 ounce) can pineapple juice, chilled
1 (20 ounce) can crushed pineapple with juice
1 (15 ounce) can cream of coconut
1 (32 ounce) bottle 7-Up, chilled

- Combine all ingredients and serve over ice cubes.

White Wine Punch

2 quarts ginger ale, chilled
2 (12 ounce) cans frozen limeade concentrate
4 limeade cans white wine, chilled
Lime slices

- Make ice ring with as much ginger ale as necessary.
- Combine limeade, white wine and remaining ginger ale in punch bowl.
- Serve with ice ring and lime slices.

Sparkling Wine Punch

6 oranges, unpeeled, thinly sliced
1 cup sugar
2 (750 ml) bottles dry white wine
3 (750 ml) bottles sparkling wine, chilled

- Place orange slices in large plastic or glass container and sprinkle with sugar.
- Add white wine, cover and chill at least 8 hours.
- Stir in sparkling wine.

Champagne Punch

1 (750 ml) bottle champagne, chilled
1 (32 ounce) bottle ginger ale, chilled
1 (6 ounce) can frozen orange juice concentrate
Orange slices, optional

- Mix all ingredients in punch bowl. Serve chilled and garnish with orange slices.

Apple-Party Punch

3 cups sparkling apple cider
2 cups apple juice
1 cup pineapple juice
½ cup brandy

- Combine all ingredients and freeze 8 hours.
- Remove punch from freezer 30 minutes before serving.
- Place in small punch bowl and break into chunks. Stir until slushy.

Amaretto Cooler

1¼ cups amaretto
2 quarts cold orange juice
1 (15 ounce) bottle club soda, chilled
Orange slices, optional

- Combine all ingredients and stir well. Garnish with orange slices and serve over ice.

Kahlua Frosty

1 cup kahlua
1 pint vanilla ice cream
1 cup half-and-half cream
¼ teaspoon almond extract

- In blender, combine all ingredients and 1 heaping cup ice cubes.
- Blend until smooth. Serve immediately.

Holiday Egg Nog

1 gallon egg nog
1 pint whipping cream
1 quart brandy
½ gallon ice cream, softened

- Mix all ingredients.
- Serve in individual cups, sprinkle with nutmeg and serve immediately.

Amaretto

3 cups sugar
1 pint vodka
3 tablespoons almond extract
1 tablespoon vanilla

- Combine sugar and 2¼ cups water in large pan. Bring mixture to boil.
- Reduce heat. Simmer 5 minutes and stir occasionally.
- Remove from stove and add remaining ingredients.
- Stir to mix. Store in airtight jar.

Tip: Use real vanilla, not the imitation. It really makes a difference with this drink.

Mexican Coffee

1 ounce kahlua
1 cup hot, black coffee
Ground cinnamon
Sweetened whipped cream

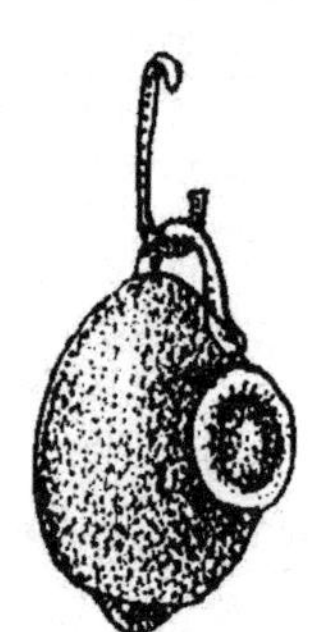

- Pour kahlua and coffee into tall mug.
- Sprinkle with cinnamon and stir.
- Top with whipped cream.

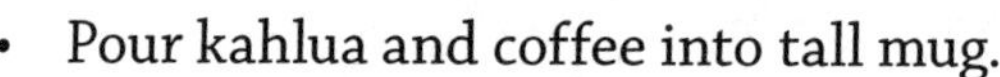

Tip: If you need a shortcut, substitute frozen whipped topping.

Strawberry Smoothie

2 bananas, peeled, sliced
1 pint fresh strawberries, quartered
1 (8 ounce) container strawberry yogurt
¼ cup orange juice

- Place all ingredients in blender and process until smooth.

Chocolate-Mint Fizz

¼ cup crème de menthe
¼ cup creme de cocoa
1 pint vanilla ice cream
1 pint chocolate ice cream

- Place liqueurs into blender container.
- Add ice cream gradually and blend until smooth after each addition.
- Pour into glasses and serve immediately.

Creamy Rich Biscuits

2 cups flour
3 teaspoons baking powder
½ teaspoon salt
1 (8 ounce) carton whipping cream

- Combine flour, baking powder and salt.
- In mixing bowl, beat whipping cream only until it holds its shape.
- Combine flour mixture and cream and mix with fork. Put dough on lightly floured board and knead it for about 1 minute.
- Pat dough to ¾-inch thickness. Cut out biscuits with small biscuit cutter.
- Place on baking sheet and bake at 375° for about 12 minutes or until light brown.

Quick, Creamy Biscuits

2½ cups biscuit mix
1 teaspoon
½ pint whipping cream
1 (8 ounce) bottle butter spray

- Mix biscuit mix, sugar and cream. Knead on floured board.
- Pat out to ½-inch thickness and cut out with small biscuit cutter.
- Bake at 375° for 12 to 15 minutes or until light brown. Spray with butter spray.

Refrigerator Biscuits

1 (8 ounce) package cream cheese, softened
½ cup (1 stick) butter, softened
1 cup self-rising flour
1 teaspoon sugar

- Beat cream cheese and butter at medium speed with mixer for 2 minutes. Gradually add flour and sugar. Beat at low speed until they blend.
- Spoon dough into miniature muffin pans, filling ⅔ full or chill dough for up to 3 days. Bake at 375° for 15 minutes or until brown.

Garlic Biscuits

5 cups biscuit mix
1 cup shredded cheddar cheese
1 (14 ounce) can chicken broth with roasted garlic
½ teaspoon garlic, minced

- Mix all ingredients to form soft dough. Drop by heaping spoonfuls onto greased baking sheet. Bake at 425° for 10 minutes until brown.

Sausage-Cheese Biscuits

1 (8 ounce) package grated cheddar cheese
1 pound hot bulk pork sausage
2 cups biscuit mix
¾ cup milk

- Combine cheese, sausage and biscuit mix.
- Drop on ungreased baking sheet.
- Bake at 400° until light brown. Serve hot.

French-Onion Biscuits

2 cups biscuit mix
¼ cup milk
1 (8 ounce) container French-onion dip
2 tablespoons finely minced green onion

- Mix all ingredients until soft dough forms. Drop dough onto greased cookie sheet.
- Bake at 400° for about 10 minutes or until light brown.

Ginger-Raisin Muffins

1 (16 ounce) box gingerbread mix
1¼ cups lukewarm water
1 egg
2 (1½ ounce) boxes seedless raisins

- Combine gingerbread mix, water and egg and mix well. Stir in raisins.
- Pour into greased muffin tins filled half full.
- Bake at 350° for 20 minutes or when tested done with toothpick.

Filled Muffins

1(16 ounce) box blueberry muffin mix
1 egg
⅓ cup red raspberry jam
¼ cup sliced almonds

- Rinse blueberries and drain.
- In bowl, combine muffin mix, egg and ½ cup water. Stir until moist and break up any lumps in mix.
- Place paper liners in 8 muffin cups. Fill cups half full of batter.
- Combine raspberry jam with blueberries. Spoon mixture on top of batter. Cover with remaining batter and sprinkle almonds over batter.
- Bake at 375° for about 18 minutes or until light brown.

Blueberry-Orange Muffins

1 (16 ounce) package blueberry muffin mix
2 egg whites
½ cup orange juice
Orange marmalade

- Wash blueberries with cold water and drain.
- Stir muffin mix, egg whites and orange juice and break up any lumps. Fold blueberries gently into batter.
- Pour into muffin tins (with paper liners) about half full.
- Bake at 370° for 18 to 20 minutes or until toothpick inserted in center comes out clean.
- Top with orange marmalade spooned over top of hot muffins.

Cheese Bread

1 (16 ounce) package shredded, sharp cheddar cheese
1 cup mayonnaise
1 package ranch-style dressing mix
10 (1-inch) slices French bread

- Combine cheese, mayonnaise and dressing mix.
- Spread on bread slices and heat in oven until brown.

Crunchy Breadsticks

1 package hot dog buns
1 cup (2 sticks) butter, melted
Garlic powder
Paprika

- Take each half bun and slice in half lengthwise.
- Use pastry brush to butter all breadsticks and sprinkle light amount of garlic powder and a couple of sprinkles paprika.
- Place on baking sheet and bake at 225° for about 45 minutes.

Corn Sticks

2 cups biscuit mix
1 (8 ounce) can cream-style corn
Melted butter
2 tablespoons minced green onion

- Mix biscuit mix, green onions and cream-style corn.
- Place dough on floured surface and cut into 3 x 1-inch strips. Roll in melted butter.
- Bake at 400° 15 minutes.

Breadsticks

1½ cups shredded Monterey Jack cheese
¼ cup poppy seeds
2 tablespoons dry onion soup mix
2 (11 ounce) cans breadstick dough

- Spread cheese evenly in 9 x 13-inch baking dish. Sprinkle poppy seeds and soup mix evenly over cheese.
- Separate breadstick dough into sticks. Stretch strips slightly until each strip is about 12 inches long.
- Place strips one at a time into cheese mixture. Turn to coat all sides.
- Cut into 3 or 4-inch strips. Place on baking sheet and bake at 375° for about 12 minutes.

Bacon-Cheese French Bread

1 (16 ounce) loaf unsliced French bread
5 slices bacon, cooked, crumbled
8 ounces mozzarella cheese, shredded
½ cup (1 stick) butter, melted

- Slice loaf of bread into 1-inch slices. Place sliced loaf on large piece of aluminum foil.
- Combine bacon and cheese. Sprinkle bacon and cheese in between slices of bread.
- Drizzle butter over loaf and let some drip in between slices. Wrap loaf tightly in foil.
- Bake at 350° for 20 minutes or until thoroughly heated. Serve hot.

Honey-Cinnamon Butter

1 cup (2 sticks) butter
½ cup honey
1 teaspoon ground cinnamon
Breakfast breads

- Combine all ingredients in mixing bowl and beat until smooth.

Tip: Serve with muffins, toast, French toast or pancakes. Refrigerate any leftovers.

Orange Butter

⅔ cup butter, softened
¼ cup frozen orange juice concentrate, thawed
1 (16 ounce) box powdered sugar
1 teaspoon dried orange peel

- Blend all ingredients in mixer. Store in refrigerator.

Ambrosia Spread

1 (11 ounce) can mandarin orange sections, drained
1 (8 ounce) container soft cream cheese with pineapple, softened
¼ cup flaked coconut, toasted
¼ cup slivered almonds, chopped, toasted

- Chop orange sections and set aside.
- Combine cheese, coconut and almonds and blend well. Gently fold in orange sections. Chill. Use as a spread for breads or dip for fruits.

Strawberry Butter

1 (10 ounce) package frozen strawberries with juice
1 cup (2 sticks) unsalted butter, softened
1 cup powdered sugar
Breakfast breads

- Place all ingredients in food processor or mixer and process until they mix well.
- Spread on breakfast breads and serve.

Tip: Strawberry butter is delicious on biscuits, muffins or breads.

Breakfast Wake-Up

12 eggs
2 (7 ounce) cans chopped green chilies with juice
2 (16 ounce) packages shredded cheddar cheese
Salsa, optional

- Drain green chilies and save juice.
- In separate bowl, beat eggs with juice of green chilies and add a little salt and pepper.
- Spray 9 x 13-inch pan and spread half cheese on bottom of pan and layer chilies over this. Top with remaining cheese.
- Pour eggs over top and bake uncovered at 350° for 45 minutes.

Mexican Eggs

4 corn tortillas
4 eggs
1 cup green chile salsa
4 ounces grated longhorn cheese

- Dip tortillas in heated oil in skillet and remove quickly. Set tortillas on baking pan to keep warm.
- In skillet, fry eggs in a little butter until whites are set. Place fried egg on each tortilla.
- Heat salsa and spoon over each egg. Sprinkle grated cheese on top.
- Place baking pan under broiler just until cheese melts. Serve hot.

Breakfast Tacos

4 eggs
4 flour tortillas
1 cup chopped, cooked ham
1 cup grated cheddar cheese

- Scramble eggs in skillet.
- Lay tortillas flat and spoon eggs over 4 tortillas.
- Sprinkle with ham and cheese. Roll up to enclose filling.
- Place tacos in microwave safe dish. Microwave for about 30 seconds or until cheese melts. Serve immediately.

Light and Crispy Waffles

2 cups biscuit mix
1 egg
½ cup oil
1 ⅓ cups club soda

- Preheat waffle iron.
- Combine all ingredients in mixing bowl and stir by hand.
- Pour just enough batter to cover waffle iron.

Tip: To have waffles for a "company weekend", make up all waffles in advance. Freeze separately on cookie sheet and place in large plastic bags. To heat, warm at 350° for about 10 minutes.

Praline Toast

½ cup (1 stick) butter, softened
1 cup packed brown sugar
½ cup finely chopped pecans
Bread slices

- Combine butter, sugar and pecans.
- Spread on bread slices.
- Toast in broiler until brown and bubbly.

Cinnamon Toast

⅔ cup sugar
1 heaping tablespoon cinnamon
Bread
Butter, softened

- Make cinnamon-sugar by mixing sugar with cinnamon. Place in large salt or sugar shaker.
- Place bread on baking sheet and toast top by broiling in oven until light brown.
- Remove baking sheet and spread soft butter on toasted side. Sprinkle with cinnamon mixture.
- Return to oven and broil until tops are bubbly. Watch closely because sugar burns easily.

Sunrise Tacos

4 eggs, scrambled
½ cup grated cheddar cheese, divided
½ cup salsa, divided
2 flour tortillas

- For each taco, spread half scrambled eggs, ¼ cup cheese and ¼ cup salsa on tortilla and roll up.

Cheese Enchiladas

12 corn tortillas
1 (8 ounce) package shredded cheddar cheese, divided
½ cup chopped onion, divided
2 (10 ounce) cans enchilada sauce

- Wrap tortillas in slightly damp paper towel. Put between 2 salad plates and microwave on HIGH for 45 seconds.
- Place ⅓ cup cheese, sprinkle onions on each tortilla and roll up. Place seam side down in 9 x 13-inch baking dish. Repeat with remaining tortillas.
- Pour enchilada sauce over enchiladas and sprinkle with remaining cheese and onions.
- Cover and microwave on MEDIUM-HIGH for 5 to 6 minutes.

Pineapple-Brunch Slices

1 cup cooked ground ham
1 teaspoon mustard
2 tablespoons mayonnaise
5 slices pineapple, drained

- Combine ham, mustard and mayonnaise and mix well.
- Spread on pineapple slices.
- Bake in ungreased baking pan at 375° for about 15 minutes or until it heats thoroughly.

Chile Rellenos

2 (7 ounce) cans chopped green chilies, drained
1 (16 ounce) package shredded Monterey Jack cheese
4 eggs, beaten
½ cup milk

- In 7 x 11-inch baking dish, layer half green chilies, half cheese, then remaining green chilies and cheese.
- Combine eggs, milk and a little salt and pepper in small bowl and mix well.
- Pour over layers of cheese and green chilies.
- Bake uncovered at 350° for 30 minutes or until light brown and set.
- Cool for 5 minutes before cutting into squares.

Peach Bake

2 (15 ounce) cans peach halves, drained
1 cup packed brown sugar
1 cup round, buttery cracker crumbs
½ cup (1 stick) butter, melted

- Butter 2-quart casserole and layer peaches, sugar and cracker crumbs until all ingredients are used.
- Pour melted butter over casserole.
- Bake at 325° for 35 minutes or until cracker crumbs are slightly brown. Serve hot or at room temperature.

Bacon-Cheese Stromboli

1 (10 ounce) tube refrigerated pizza dough
¾ cup shredded cheddar cheese
¾ cup shredded mozzarella cheese
6 bacon strips, cooked, crumbled

- On ungreased baking sheet, roll dough into 12-inch circle.
- On one-half of dough, sprinkle cheeses and bacon to within ½-inch of edge.
- Fold dough over filling and pinch edges to seal.
- Bake at 400° for about 10 minutes or until golden. Serve with salsa.

Tip: Cut in pie slices to serve.

Honey-Butter Spread

Wonderful with hot biscuits!

½ cup (1 stick) butter, softened
¼ cup honey
2 tablespoons lemon juice
1 tablespoon brown sugar

- With hand mixer, cream butter until fluffy and add honey in fine stream.
- Add lemon juice and brown sugar and stir until all ingredients blend evenly.
- Chill until ready to serve.

Pineapple Coffee Cake

1 (18 ounce) box butter cake mix
½ cup oil
4 eggs, slightly beaten
1 (20 ounce) can pineapple pie filling

- In mixer, combine cake mix, oil and eggs and beat until they blend well.
- Pour batter into greased, floured 9 x 13-inch baking pan. Bake at 350° for 45 to 50 minutes. Test with toothpick to make sure cake is done.
- With knife, punch holes in cake about 2 inches apart. Spread pineapple pie filling over cake while cake is still hot.

Spicy Tomato Soup

2 (10 ounce) cans tomato soup
1 (16 ounce) can Mexican stewed tomatoes
Sour cream
½ pound bacon, fried, drained, crumbled

- In saucepan, combine soup and stewed tomatoes and heat.
- To serve, place dollop of sour cream on each bowl of soup and sprinkle crumbled bacon over sour cream.

Swiss-Vegetable Soup

1 (1.5 ounce package) package dry vegetable soup mix
3 cups water
1 cup half-and-half cream
1½ cups shredded Swiss cheese

- Combine vegetable soup mix and water in saucepan and boil.
- Lower heat and simmer about 10 minutes.
- Add half-and-half cream and cheese and serve hot.

Supper Gumbo

1 (10 ounce) can condensed pepper pot soup
1 (10 ounce) can condensed chicken gumbo soup
1 (6 ounce) can white crabmeat, flaked
1 (6 ounce) can tiny shrimp

- Combine all ingredients and include 1½ soup cans water.
- Cover and simmer for 15 minutes.

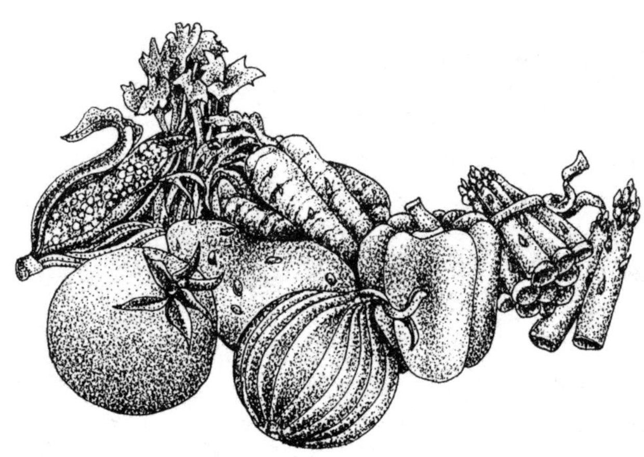

Bacon-Potato Soup

2 (14 ounce) cans chicken broth seasoned with garlic
2 potatoes, peeled, cubed
1 onion finely chopped
6 strips bacon, cooked, crumbled

- In large saucepan, combine broth, potatoes and onion. Bring to a boil, reduce heat to medium high and boil about 10 minutes or until potatoes are tender.
- Season with pepper.
- Ladle into bowls and sprinkle with crumbled bacon.

Tomato-French Onion Soup

1 (10 ounce) can tomato bisque soup
2 (10 ounce) cans French-onion soup
Grated parmesan cheese
Croutons

- In saucepan combine soups with 2 soup cans water. Heat thoroughly.
- Serve in bowls topped with croutons and sprinkle of cheese.

Speedy Taco Soup

1 (12 ounce) can chicken with liquid
1 (14 ounce) can chicken broth
1 (16 ounce) jar mild thick and chunky salsa
1 (15 ounce) can ranch-style beans

- In large saucepan combine chicken, broth, salsa and beans.
- Bring to boil, reduce heat and simmer 15 minutes.

New England Clam Chowder

1 (10 ounce) can New England clam chowder
1 (10 ounce) can cream of celery soup
1 (10 ounce) can cream of potato soup
½ cup whole milk

- Combine all ingredients in saucepan.
- Heat and stir.

Cream Cheese Sandwiches

2 (8 ounce) packages cream cheese, softened
1 (4 ounce) can black olives, chopped
¾ cups finely chopped pecans
Pumpernickel rye bread

- Beat cream cheese until creamy. Fold in olives and pecans.
- Trim crusts on bread. Spread cream cheese on bread.
- Slice sandwich into 3 finger strips.

Luncheon Sandwich

1 loaf thinly sliced, sandwich bread
1 cup (2 sticks) butter, softened
1 (5 ounce) jar cheese spread, softened
½ teaspoon worcestershire sauce

- Trim crust on bread.
- With mixer, beat butter and cheese spread until smooth and creamy and adding worcestershire sauce.
- Spread mixture on 3 slices bread to make triple-decker sandwich.
- Place fourth slice bread on top. Cut into finger sandwiches.

Tip: These sandwiches may be served cold or warmed at 300° for 5 or 10 minutes.

Cream Cheese Tea Sandwiches

1 (8 ounce) package cream cheese, softened
½ pound bacon, fried, finely chopped
12 to 14 slices whole wheat bread
1 (12 ounce) package bean sprouts

- With mixer, beat cream cheese until smooth. Add finely chopped bacon (or chop cream cheese and bacon together in food processor).
- On 6 to 8 slices bread, spread bacon-cream cheese mixture. Add layer of bean sprouts.
- On other 6 to 8 slices, spread either mayonnaise or butter and place on top of bean sprouts making 6 or 8 sandwiches.
- With sharp knife remove crust and cut each sandwich in 3 finger shapes. Refrigerate.

Beefy-Cream Cheese Spread

2 (8 ounce) packages cream cheese, softened
1 (2½ ounce) jar dried beef, finely chopped
1 bunch fresh green onions with tops, chopped
¾ cup mayonnaise, 1 teaspoon seasoned pepper

- Combine all ingredients until mixture spreads smoothly.
- Trim crust of whole wheat bread and spread cream cheese mixture on bread.
- Top with another slice of bread and slice into 3 strips or 4 quarters.

Party Sandwiches

1 cup bacon, cooked, crumbled
½ cup ripe olives, coarsely chopped
½ cup chopped pecans
1¼ cups mayonnaise

- Mix all ingredients and spread on thin sliced white bread.
- Cut sandwiches into 3 strips.

Watercress-Tea Sandwiches

1 small bunch watercress
5 hard-boiled eggs, peeled
6 tablespoons mayonnaise
1 tablespoon dijon-style mustard

- Trim half watercress stems and save rest for garnish.
- In food processor, coarsely chop eggs and add mayonnaise, mustard and a little salt. Process until smooth.
- Fold in chopped watercress and chill.
- Trim crusts and add mixture on thinly sliced white bread. Cut into finger sandwiches.

Green Chile Grilled Cheese

4 slices bread
4 slices cheddar cheese
1 (4 ounce) can chopped green chilies, drained
3 tablespoons butter, softened

- On 2 slices bread, place 1 slice cheese on each bread slice. Sprinkle with green chilies.
- Top with 2 remaining slices cheese and remaining 2 slices bread.
- Butter outside of sandwiches.
- In large skillet over medium heat brown sandwiches on both sides until golden brown and cheese melts.

Confetti Sandwiches

1 tablespoon lemon juice
1 (8 ounce) package cream cheese, softened
½ cup grated carrots
¼ cup each grated cucumber, purple onion and bell pepper

- Combine lemon juice with cream cheese and add enough mayonnaise to make cheese into spreading consistency.
- Fold in grated vegetables, spread on bread for sandwiches refrigerate.

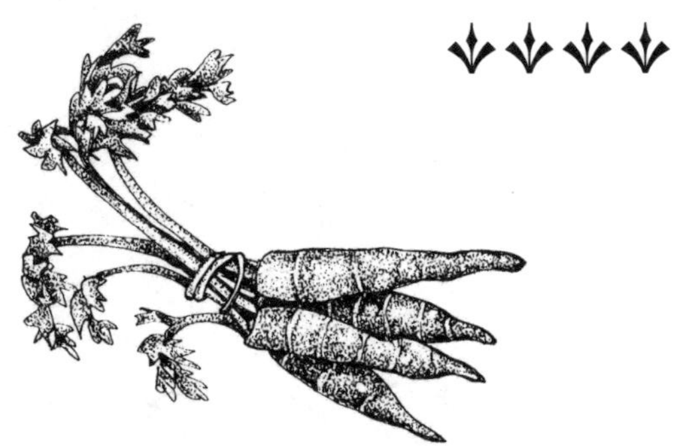

Hot Bunwiches

8 hamburger buns
8 slices Swiss cheese
8 slices ham, 8 slices turkey
8 slices American cheese

- Lay out all 8 buns. On bottom bun, place slices of Swiss cheese, ham, turkey and American cheese.
- Place top bun over American cheese.
- Wrap each bunwich individually in foil and place in freezer.
- When ready to serve, take out of freezer 2 to 3 hours before serving.
- Heat at 325° for about 30 minutes and serve hot.

Reubens on a Bun

1 (1 pound) packaged smoked frankfurter
8 hot dog buns
1 (8 ounce) can sauerkraut, well drained
Caraway seeds

- Pierce each frankfurter and place into split buns.
- Arrange 2 tablespoons sauerkraut over each frank. Sprinkle with caraway seed.
- Place in 9 x 13-inch shallow pan and drizzle with Thousand Island dressing.
- Heat just until hot dogs are thoroughly hot.

Italian-Sausage Sandwiches

1 pound sweet Italian sausage, cooked, casing removed
1 red bell pepper, chopped
1 onion, chopped
1 ⅔ cups Italian-style spaghetti sauce

- In skillet over medium heat, cook sausage, bell pepper and onion until sausage browns and is no longer pink.
- Stir in spaghetti sauce and heat until boiling. Simmer for 5 minutes, stirring constantly.
- Pour mixture over split hoagie rolls.

Pizza Burger

1 pound lean ground beef
½ teaspoon salt
½ cup pizza sauce
4 slices mozzarella cheese

- Combine beef, salt and half pizza sauce.
- Mold into 4 patties and pan-fry over medium heat for 5 to 6 minutes on each side.
- Just before burgers are done, top each with 1 spoonful pizza sauce and 1 slice cheese.
- Serve on hamburger bun.

Marshmallow Sandwiches

1 (7 ounce) jar marshmallow cream
Chunky peanut butter
White bread or whole wheat bread
Vanilla wafers, optional

- On 1 slice bread, spread marshmallow cream.
- On second slice bread, spread peanut butter.
- Put marshmallow and peanut butter sides together.

Ranch Cheeseburgers

1 packet ranch-style salad dressing mix
1 pound lean ground beef
1 cup shredded cheddar cheese
4 large hamburger buns, toasted

- Combine dressing mix with beef and cheese.
- Shape into 4 patties.
- Cook on charcoal grill until thoroughly cooked and browned.

Barking Dogs

10 wieners
5 slices cheese
10 corn tortillas
Oil

- Slice wieners lengthwise and halfway through.
- Cut each cheese slice in half and place inside each wiener.
- Wrap tortillas around wiener and secure with toothpick.
- Heat several inches of oil in frying pan. Fry dogs in oil until tortilla is crisp. Serve hot.

Cheese Doggies

Sliced frankfurters
Cheddar cheese slices
Bacon slices
Hot dog buns

- Use 1 bacon slice for each frankfurter. Place bacon on paper towel or paper plate, cover with paper towel and microwave for 45 seconds or until almost crisp.
- Cut lengthwise pocket in frankfurter and stuff with 1 strip cheese.
- Wrap bacon around doggie and secure with toothpick.
- Place in split hot dog bun and microwave for about 30 seconds or until hot dog is warm.

Dog Wrap

8 wieners
8 slices cheese
1 (8 ounce) package refrigerated crescent rolls
Mustard

- Split wieners lengthwise and fill with folded cheese slice.
- Wrap in crescent dough roll and bake at 375° for about 12 minutes.
- Serve with mustard.

Hot and Sweet Mustard

4 ounces dry mustard
1 cup vinegar
3 eggs
1 cup sugar

- Soak dry mustard in vinegar overnight.
- Beat eggs and sugar and add to vinegar-mustard mixture.
- In top of double boiler, cook over low heat for about 15 minutes, stirring constantly. Mixture will resemble custard consistency. Pour immediately into jars. Store in refrigerator. Serve with ham.

Tip: This is great to keep in the refrigerator for ham sandwiches.

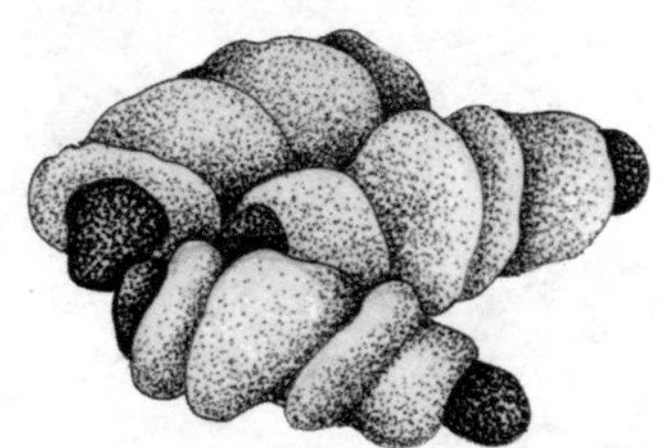

Avocado Butter

2 large avocados, peeled
2 tablespoons lime juice
1 pound butter, softened
¼ teaspoon ginger

- Combine all ingredients in electric blender or food processor. Blend until smooth.
- Serve on crackers or make party sandwiches on white or rye bread.

Red and Green Salad

2 (10 ounce) packages fresh spinach
1 quart fresh strawberries, halved
½ cup slivered almonds, toasted
Poppy seed dressing

- Tear spinach into smaller pieces and add strawberries and almonds.
- Chill until ready to serve.
- Toss with poppy seed dressing.

Oriental-Spinach Salad

1 (10 ounce) package fresh spinach
1 (16 ounce) can bean sprouts, drained
8 slices bacon, cooked crisp, drained
1 (11 ounce) can water chestnuts, chopped

- Combine spinach and bean sprouts.
- When ready to serve, add crumbled bacon and toss with vinaigrette dressing made from 3 parts olive oil and 1 part red wine vinegar.

Swiss Salad

1 large head romaine lettuce
1 bunch fresh green onions with tops, chopped
1 (8 ounce) package of shredded Swiss cheese
½ cup toasted sunflower seeds

- Tear lettuce into bite-size pieces.
- Add onions, cheese, sunflower seeds and toss.
- Serve with vinaigrette dressing.

Vinaigrette for Swiss Salad:

⅔ cup oil
⅓ cup red wine vinegar
1 tablespoon seasoned salt
1 teaspoon sugar

- Mix all ingredients and chill.

Broccoli-Pepperoni Salad

1 pound bunch broccoli
½ pound fresh mushrooms, sliced
6 ounces Swiss cheese, diced
1 (3 ounce) package sliced pepperoni, chopped

- Cut off broccoli flowerets and combine broccoli, mushrooms, cheese and pepperoni.
- Toss with Italian dressing.
- Chill at least 8 hours before serving.

Sunshine Salad

2 (15 ounce) cans mexi-corn, drained
2 (15 ounce) cans peas, drained
1 (15 ounce) can kidney beans, rinsed, drained
1 (8 ounce) bottle Italian dressing

- In large bowl, combine corn, peas and beans.
- Pour salad dressing over vegetables and chill several hours.

Salads don't only have to consist of greens. Use any of the dozens of fresh vegetables available in your area or region. Depending upon the season, mix broccoli, cauliflower, celery, peppers, corn, cucumbers, fennel, green beans, jicama, or turnips. Peel if necessary, chop dice or shred.

Bean and Onion Salad

1 (15 ounce) can whole green beans
1 (15 ounce) can yellow wax beans
½ cup finely chopped red onion
¼ cup slivered almonds

- Combine all ingredients and mix with dressing recipe below.

Dressing for Bean and Onion Salad:

¼ cup oil
1 tablespoon white vinegar
1 teaspoon sugar
2 teaspoons dijon-style mustard

- Combine all ingredients adding ½ teaspoon salt and ½ teaspoon black pepper.
- Pour over bean and onion salad.
- Chill at least 1 hour before serving.

Be sure to dress salad greens just before serving to avoid salad becoming soggy. Don't overdress your salads. Too much dressing weighs down the ingredients and masks their delicious flavors. The dressing should highlight the salad and not overpower its ingredients.

Spinach-Bacon Salad

1 (10 ounce) package fresh spinach
3 hard-boiled eggs, chopped
8 mushroom caps, sliced
1 (11 ounce) can water chestnuts, chopped

- Mix all ingredients and serve with hot bacon dressing.

Hot Bacon Dressing for Spinach-Bacon Salad:

½ pound bacon, chopped
1 cup sugar
1 ⅓ cups white vinegar
5 teaspoons corn starch

- To make dressing fry bacon until crisp, drain and leave bacon drippings in skillet.
- Add sugar and vinegar to skillet and stir well. Add 1 cup water and bring to a boil.
- Mix corn starch with ⅔ cup water and stir until it dissolves. Pour cornstarch mixture into skillet with dressing.
- Return to a boil and simmer for 5 minutes. Remove from heat and toss salad with warm bacon dressing.

Stop! Don't throw away your leftover tossed salad next time. Recycle it into a soup by pureeing it, then adding broth and chopped vegetables to it.

Cucumber Salad

1 (3 ounce) package lime gelatin
2 medium cucumbers
1 tablespoon minced onion
½ cup mayonnaise, ½ cup sour cream

- Dissolve gelatin in ¾ cup boiling water and mix well. Bring to room temperature.
- Slice cucumber in half and remove seeds. Grate cucumber and add to cooled gelatin with onion, mayonnaise and sour cream.
- Pour into square dish. Chill until set.

Broccoli Salad

5 cups cut broccoli, florets
1 sweet red bell pepper, julienned
1 cup chopped celery
8 to 12 ounces Monterey Jack cheese, cubed

- Combine all ingredients and mix well.
- Toss with Italian or your favorite dressing. Chill.

Save on salad cleanup time by refridgerating the cleaned salad greens in a large plastic bag. Right before serving, pour dressing over the greens, seal the bag, and toss. Arrange the dressed salad on individual serving plates. Fast, simple and easy!

Green and White Salad

1 (16 ounce) package frozen green peas, thawed, uncooked
1 head cauliflower, cut into bite-size pieces
1 (8 ounce) carton sour cream
1 envelope dry ranch-style salad dressing

- In large bowl, combine peas and cauliflower.
- Combine sour cream and salad dressing.
- Toss with vegetables and chill.

Color-Coded Salad

1 (16 ounce) package tri-colored macaroni, cooked, drained
1 red bell pepper, julienned
1 cup chopped zucchini
1 cup broccoli florets

- Combine all ingredients.
- Toss with about 1 cup Caesar salad dressing and chill.

A good salad has good contract and balance of textures, colors and flavors. Mix crunchy ingredients with soft, tangy flavors – mild or slightly sweet. Add bright colors with those more muted. The results will be pleasing to the eye and good tasting to your palate!

Holiday Salad

1 (15 ounce) can whole cranberry sauce
1 (15 ounce) can crushed pineapple, drained
2 (15 ounce) cans fruit cocktail, drained
1 (8 ounce) carton sour cream

- Combine all ingredients and freeze in cranberry can and another can of equal size.
- When ready to serve, cut upper end of can and push salad out. Slice and serve on lettuce leaf.

Watergate Salad

1 (20 ounce) can crushed pineapple with juice
2 (3.4 ounce) packages pistachio instant pudding mix
¾ cup chopped pecans
1 (12 ounce) carton whipped topping

- Mix pineapple with instant pudding mix until it thickens slightly. Add pecans.
- When mixed well, fold in whipped topping.
- Pour into pretty crystal bowl and chill.

Keep your salads crisper longer by chilling the salad plates or serving bowl.

Cherry-Cranberry Salad

1 (6 ounce) package cherry gelatin
1 cup boiling water
1 (20 ounce) can cherry pie filling
1 (16 ounce) can whole cranberry sauce

- In mixing bowl, combine cherry gelatin and boiling water and mix until gelatin dissolves.
- Mix pie filling and cranberry sauce into gelatin.
- Pour into 7 x 11-inch dish and chill.

Tropical-Mango Salad

2 (15 ounce) cans mangoes with juice
1 (6 ounce) package orange gelatin
1 (8 ounce) package cream cheese, softened
½ (8 ounce) carton whipped topping

- Place mango slices on dinner plate and cut slices in bite-size pieces. Place 1½ cups mango juice (add water to make 1½ cups) in saucepan and bring to boiling point.
- Pour over gelatin in mixing bowl and mix well.
- Add cream cheese and start mixer very slowly. Gradually increase speed until cream cheese mixes into gelatin. Pour in mango pieces.
- Place in refrigerator until it congeals slightly. Fold in whipped topping.
- Pour into 7 x 11-inch dish and chill.

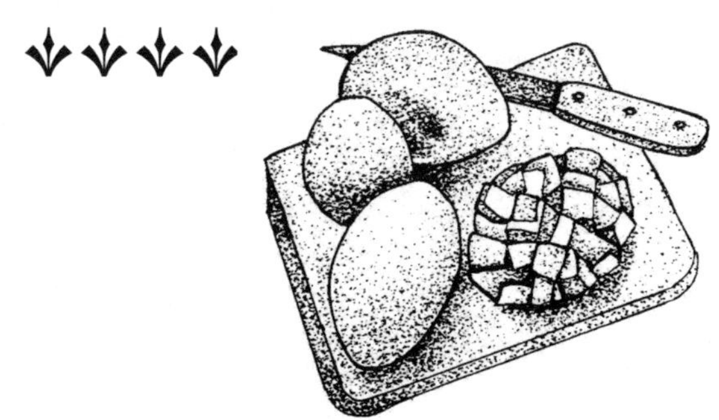

Cream Cheese-Mango Salad

2 (15 ounce) cans mangoes
1 (6 ounce) package lemon gelatin
2 (8 ounces) cream cheese, softened
1 (8 ounce) can crushed pineapple with juice

- Drain juice from mangoes. Combine juice and enough water to make ¾ cup liquid. Bring to boil and add gelatin. Stir until it dissolves.
- In mixing bowl, cream mangoes and cream cheese. Fold in pineapple.
- Mix into hot gelatin and pour into muffin tins or mold.

Salad Supreme

1 (6 ounce) package orange gelatin
1 (8 ounce) package cream cheese, softened
2 (15 ounce) cans mangoes with juice
2 (10 ounce) cans mandarin oranges, drained

- Place gelatin in mixing bowl and pour ¾ cup boiling water over gelatin and mix well. Let partially cool and add cream cheese.
- At very slow speed at first, beat in cream cheese until it mixes.
- Fold in mangoes and mandarin oranges. Pour into 8-cup molds.
- Chill several hours.

Add flavor to a recipe by substituting other liquids for all or part of the water called for in gelatin mixes.

Never let gelatin over-boil or you'll destroy its setting capabilities

Stained-Glass Fruit Salad

2 (20 ounce) cans peach pie filling
3 bananas, sliced
1 (16 ounce) package frozen unsweetened strawberries, drained
1 (20 ounce) can pineapple tidbits, drained

- Drain all fruits except peach pie filling.
- Mix all fruits, chill and place in pretty crystal bowl.
- Chill overnight.

Tip: If you like, use 1 can peach pie filling and 1 can apricot pie filling.

Orange Glow

1 (6 ounce) package orange gelatin
1 cup finely grated carrots
1 (15 ounce) can crushed pineapple with juice
¾ cup chopped pecans

- Mix gelatin in 1 cup boiling water and mix well.
- Add carrots, pineapple and pecans.
- Pour into 7 x 11-inch glass dish. Chill until congealed.

Glazed-Fruit Salad

2 (11 ounce) cans mandarin oranges, drained
1 (15 ounce) can pineapple chunks, drained
3 bananas, sliced
1 (18 ounce) carton creamy glaze for bananas

- In large bowl combine fruit and glaze.
- Toss to coat fruit.
- Serve immediately.

Applesauce Salad

2 cups applesauce
1 (6 ounce) package lime gelatin
2 (12 ounce) cans lemon-lime carbonated drink
1 (8 ounce) can crushed pineapple, drained

- Heat applesauce in large saucepan.
- Add gelatin to hot applesauce and stir until it dissolves. Add lemon lime drink and pineapple.
- Pour into 8-inch mold and chill.

When in a hurry for a dish to set, only mix enough hot liquid into the gelatin to dissolve it (¼ cup should be enough), then use ice water or other liquid for the balance.

Fruit pieces will not sink in a gelatin mixture if you wait until it is partially set (like the consistency of egg whites) before stirring them in.

Cinnamon-Apple Salad

1 cup cinnamon red hot candies
1 (6 ounce) package cherry gelatin
1 (16 ounce) jar applesauce
1 cup chopped pecans

- Heat cinnamon red hots in 1¼ cups boiling water until candy melts.
- While mixture is still hot, pour over gelatin and mix well. Add applesauce and chopped pecans and mix well.
- Pour into 7 x 11-inch glass dish and chill until firm. When serving, cut in squares.

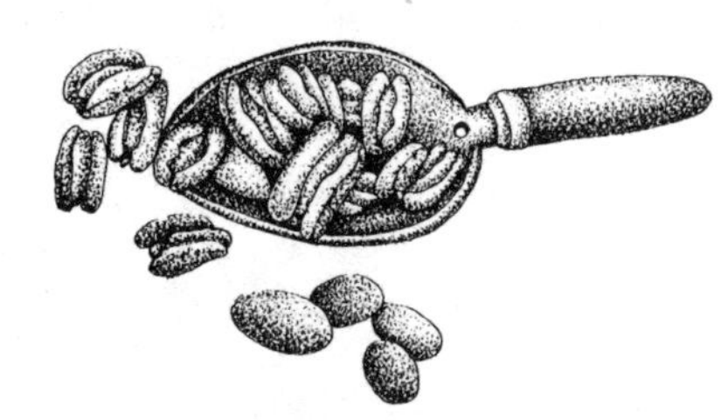

Cranberry Mousse

1 (15 ounce) can jellied cranberry sauce
1 (8 ounce) can crushed pineapple, drained
1 (8 ounce) carton sour cream
1 tablespoon mayonnaise

- In saucepan place cranberry sauce and crushed pineapple. Cook until cranberry sauce liquefies.
- Fold in sour cream and mayonnaise.
- Pour into molds or muffin tins and freeze.

Nutty Cranberry Relish

1 pound fresh cranberries
2¼ cups sugar
1 cup chopped pecans, toasted
1 cup orange marmalade

- Wash and drain cranberries and mix with sugar. Place in 1-quart baking dish. Cover dish and bake at 350° for 1 hour.
- Add marmalade and pecans to cranberry mixture.
- Mix well and pour into container. Chill before serving.

Pear Mousse

2 (15 ounce) cans sliced pears with juice
1 (6 ounce) package lemon gelatin
1 (8 ounce) package cream cheese, softened
1 (8 ounce) carton whipped topping

- Drain pears and reserve juice. Heat juice and add water to equal ¾ cup. Heat juice to boiling point. Add gelatin. Mix well and cool.
- Place pears and cream cheese in blender and blend until smooth. Place into large bowl and fold in cooled, but not congealed, gelatin mixture and whipped topping. Mix until smooth.
- Pour into individual dessert dishes. Cover with piece of plastic wrap and chill.

Broccoli-Chicken Salad

3 to 4 boneless, skinless chicken breasts, cooked, cubed
2 cups fresh broccoli florets
1 sweet red bell pepper, seeded, chopped
1 cup chopped celery

- Combine chicken, broccoli, bell pepper and celery.
- Toss with honey-mustard dressing and chill.

Savory Chicken Salad

4 boneless, skinless chicken breasts, cooked
1 cup chopped celery
1 red bell pepper, seeded, chopped
⅔ cup slivered almonds, toasted

- Slice chicken breasts into long thin strips.
- Combine chicken, celery, bell pepper and almonds. Toss and chill.

Tip: For dressing use flavored mayonnaise (½ cup mayonnaise with 1 tablespoon lemon juice).

You can use leftover meat, fish or poultry as a base for a main course salad next day. Just add salad greens, chopped veggies, croutons and a favorite dressing. Wow! Another meal in minutes.

Apple-Walnut Chicken Salad

3 to 4 boneless, skinless chicken breasts, cooked, cubed
2 tart green apples, peeled, chopped
½ cup chopped pitted dates
1 cup finely chopped celery

- Mix all ingredients and toss with dressing.

Dressing for Apple-Walnut Chicken Salad

½ cup chopped, toasted walnuts
⅓ cup sour cream
⅓ cup mayonnaise
1 tablespoon lemon juice

- Toast walnuts in a 300° oven for 10 minutes.
- Mix sour cream, mayonnaise and lemon juice.
- Mix with walnuts.
- Pour over chicken salad and toss and chill.

A time-saving idea when preparing salads is to mix the dressing right in the salad bowl. When it's almost time to serve, just add the salad ingredients and toss.

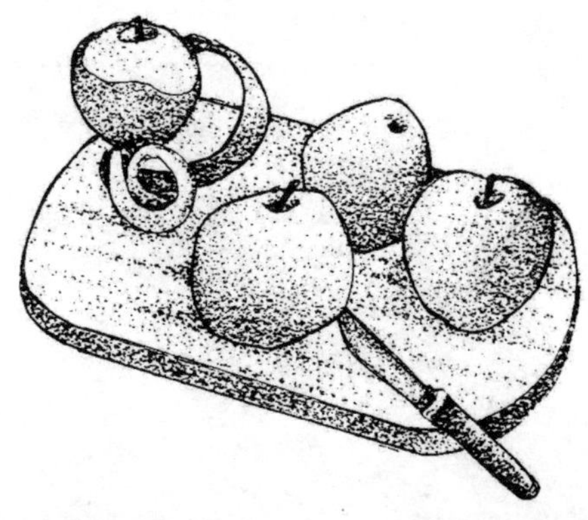

Posh Squash

8 medium yellow squash, sliced
½ green bell pepper, seeded, chopped
1 small onion, chopped
1 (8 ounce) package cubed Mexican processed cheese

- Combine squash and onion in large saucepan and just barely cover with water. Cook just until tender, about 10 to 15 minutes.
- Drain and add cheese. Stir until cheese melts and pour into buttered 2-quart baking dish. Bake at 350° for 15 minutes.

Baked Squash

5 cups squash, cooked, drained
¾ cup grated Monterey Jack cheese
1 (10 ounce) can cream of chicken soup
1 (16 ounce) box herb dressing mix

- Place cooked squash in mixing bowl and season with salt to taste.
- Add cheese and soup and blend well. Mix dressing according to package directions.
- Place half dressing in 9 x 13-inch greased baking dish. Spoon squash mixture on top and sprinkle remaining dressing on top.
- Bake uncovered at 375° for 30 minutes.

You can save time by chopping enough vegetables or herbs (like bell peppers, carrots, onions, and parsley) to use for two separate meals. Cover the vegetables and refrigerate the batch to be used for the next day's meal.

Sunny Yellow Squash

6 to 8 medium yellow squash
1 (8 ounce) package cream cheese, softened, cubed
2 tablespoons butter
1 teaspoon sugar

- In saucepan, cut up squash, add a little water and boil until tender. Drain. Add cream cheese, butter, sugar and a little salt and pepper.
- Cook over low heat and stir until cream cheese melts.

Italian Corn

1 (16 ounce) package frozen whole kernel corn
2 slices bacon, cooked, diced
1 onion, chopped
1 (16 ounce) can Italian stewed tomatoes

- Place all ingredients in 2-quart size pan.
- Cook until most liquid in tomatoes cooks out. Add a little salt and pepper and serve hot.

Corn Au Gratin

3 (15 ounce) cans mexi-corn, drained
1 (4 ounce) can sliced mushrooms, drained
1 (10 ounce) can cream of mushroom soup
1 cup shredded cheddar cheese

- Mix all ingredients in saucepan and heat slowly until cheese melts. Serve hot.

Wild West Corn

3 (15 ounce) cans whole kernel corn, drained
1 (10 ounce) can tomatoes and green chilies, drained
1 (8 ounce) package shredded Monterey Jack cheese
1 cup cheese cracker crumbs

- In large bowl, combine corn, tomatoes and green chilies and cheese and mix well.
- Pour into buttered 2½-quart baking dish.
- Sprinkle cracker crumbs over casserole. Bake uncovered at 350° for 25 minutes.

Corn Pudding

1 (8 ounce) package corn muffin mix
1 (15 ounce) can cream-style corn
½ cup sour cream
3 eggs, slightly beaten

- Combine all ingredients and pour into buttered 2-quart baking dish.
- Bake uncovered at 350° for about 35 minutes.

You can highlight a vegetable's natural sweetness and reduce its starchy flavor by adding ½ to 1 teaspoon sugar to cooked vegetables such as carrots, corn and peas.

Stewed-Tomato Casserole

2 (15 ounce) cans Mexican-style stewed tomatoes
2 onions, sliced
1¼ cups cracker crumbs
1 cup shredded cheddar cheese

- In 2-quart casserole layer tomatoes, onions, cracker crumbs and cheese and repeat layers.
- Sprinkle a little salt and pepper. Bake at 350° for 45 minutes.

Tasty Black-Eyed Peas

2 (10 ounce) packages frozen black-eyed peas
1¼ cups chopped green pepper
¾ cup chopped onion
1 (15 ounce) can Mexican stewed tomatoes with liquid

- Cook black-eyes peas according to package directions and drain.
- Saute green pepper and onion in 3 tablespoons butter. Add peas, tomatoes and a little salt and pepper. Cook over low heat until hot and stir often.

Did you know? Many of the "baby vegetable" varieties in our supermarkets today are either early-harvested youngsters or specially developed mini (yet mature) vegetables.

Black-Eyed Peas and Okra

3 (15 ounce) cans black-eyed peas, drained
¾ cup shredded ham
1 onion, chopped
1 pound small fresh, whole okra pods

- In large saucepan, combine peas, ham and onion and bring to a boil.
- Place all okra on top of pea-onion mixture and do not stir.
- Bring to a boil again, lower heat and simmer about 5 to 10 minutes or until okra is tender. Serve hot.

Brown-Sugar Carrots

2 (15 ounce) cans carrots
¼ cup (½ stick) butter
3 tablespoons brown sugar
1 teaspoon brown ginger

- Drain carrots but reserve 2 tablespoons liquid.
- Combine 2 tablespoons liquid with butter, brown sugar and ginger. Heat thoroughly.
- Add carrots, stirring gently, and cook 3 minutes. Serve hot.

Creamy Cabbage Bake

1 head cabbage, shredded
1 (10 ounce) can cream of celery soup
⅔ cup milk
1 (8 ounce) package shredded cheddar cheese

- Place cabbage in 2-quart buttered baking dish.
- Pour celery soup diluted with milk over top of cabbage. Bake covered at 325° for 30 minutes.
- Remove from oven, sprinkle with cheese and bake uncovered another 5 minutes.

Cheesy Onion Casserole

5 sweet onions, sliced
½ cup (1 stick) butter
1 cup shredded cheddar cheese
22 saltine crackers, crushed

- Saute onion in butter until soft.
- In buttered 2-quart casserole, layer half onions, half cheese, half crackers and repeat layers.
- Bake at 325° for 35 minutes.

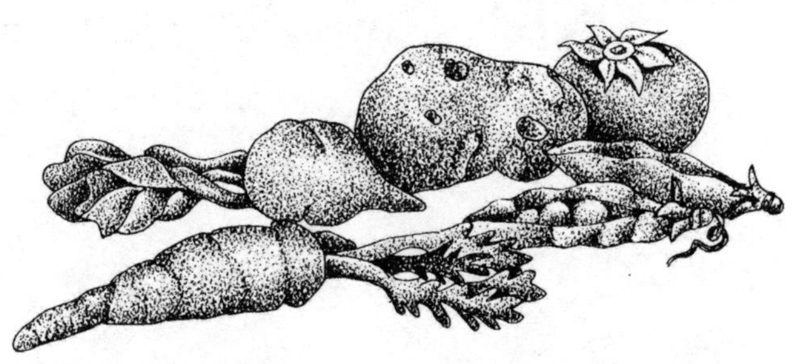

Creamed-Spinach Bake

1 (16 ounce) package frozen chopped spinach
2 (3 ounce) packages cream cheese, softened
3 tablespoons butter
1 cup Italian-style seasoned breadcrumbs

- In saucepan, cook spinach with ¾ cup water for 6 minutes and drain. Add cream cheese and butter to spinach. Heat until cream cheese and butter melt and mix well with spinach.
- Pour into greased 2-quart baking dish. Sprinkle a little salt over spinach and cover with breadcrumbs.
- Bake uncovered at 350° for 15 to 20 minutes.

Asparagus Bake

2 (15 ounce) cans cut asparagus spears with liquid
3 hard-boiled eggs, chopped
½ cup chopped pecans
1 (10 ounce) can cream of asparagus soup

- Arrange asparagus spears in buttered 2-quart baking dish.
- Top with eggs and pecans.
- Heat asparagus soup and add liquid from asparagus spears.
- Spoon over eggs and pecans.
- Bake covered at 350° for 25 minutes.

Herbed Spinach

2 (16 ounce) packages frozen chopped spinach
1 (8 ounce) package cream cheese, softened
¼ cup (½ stick) butter, melted
1 (6 ounce) package herbed stuffing

- Cook spinach according to package directions. Drain and add cream cheese and half butter. Season with a little salt and pepper.
- Pour into buttered casserole dish. Spread herb stuffing on top and drizzle with remaining butter.
- Bake at 350° for 25 minutes.

Spinach Bake

2 (8 ounce) packages cream cheese, softened
1 (10½ ounce) can cream of chicken soup
2 (16 ounce) packages frozen chopped spinach, thawed, well drained
1 cup crushed round, buttery crackers

- In mixing bowl, beat cream cheese until smooth. Add soup and mix well.
- Stir in spinach. Spoon into well greased 3-quart baking dish.
- Sprinkle cracker crumbs over top of casserole.
- Bake uncovered at 325° for 35 minutes.

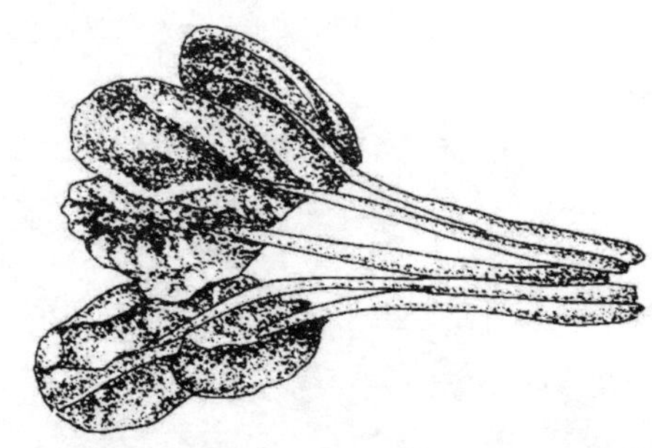

Crunchy Green Beans

3 (15 ounce) cans whole green beans
2 (10 ounce) cans cream of mushroom soup
2 (11 ounce) cans water chestnuts, drained, chopped
2 (2.8 ounce) cans french-fried onion rings

- Combine green beans, mushroom soup, water chestnuts, ½ teaspoon salt and a little pepper.
- Pour into 2-quart casserole.
- Bake covered at 350° for 30 minutes.
- Remove casserole from oven and sprinkle onion rings over top and bake 10 minutes longer.

Souper Cauliflower

1 (16 ounce) package frozen cauliflower, cooked, drained
1 (10 ounce) can cream of celery soup
¼ cup milk
1 cup shredded cheddar cheese

- Place cauliflower in 2-quart greased baking dish.
- In saucepan, combine soup, milk and cheese and heat just enough to mix well. Pour over cauliflower.
- Bake at 350° for 15 minutes.

Tip: Be sure not to overcook frozen vegetables.

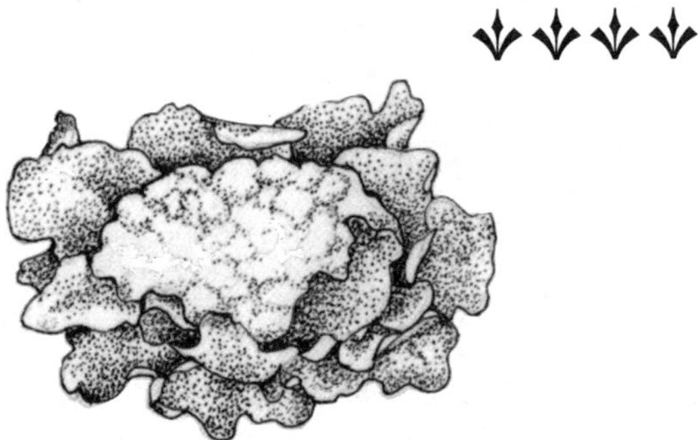

Best Cauliflower

1 (16 ounce) package frozen cauliflower
1 (8 ounce) carton sour cream
1½ cups grated American or cheddar cheese
4 teaspoons sesame seeds, toasted

- Cook cauliflower according to package directions. Be sure not to overcook
- Drain and place half cauliflower in 2-quart baking dish. Sprinkle a little salt and pepper on cauliflower. Spread half sour cream and half cheese, top with 2 teaspoons sesame seed and repeat layers.
- Bake at 350° for about 15 to 20 minutes.

Creamy Vegetable Casserole

1 (16 ounce) package frozen broccoli, carrots and cauliflower
1 (10 ounce) can cream of mushroom soup
1 (8 ounce) carton spreadable garden-vegetable cream cheese
1 cup seasoned croutons

- Cook vegetables according to package directions, drain and place in large bowl.
- In saucepan, place soup and cream cheese and heat just enough to mix easily.
- Pour into vegetable mixture and mix well.
- Pour into 2-quart baking dish. Sprinkle with croutons. Bake uncovered at 375° for 25 minutes or until bubbly.

Tip: Be sure not to overcook frozen vegetables

Potatoes With A Zip

1 (32 ounce) bag frozen hash brown potatoes
1 (16 ounce) package cubed, processed cheese
2 cups mayonnaise
1 (7 ounce) can green chilies

- In large bowl, combine all ingredients and mix well.
- Spoon into buttered 9 x 13-inch baking dish. Cover and bake at 325° for 1 hour. Stir twice during baking to prevent burning.

Creamy Potato Bake

6 to 8 baked potatoes
1 (8 ounce) carton sour cream
1 (8 ounce) package cream cheese, softened
1½ cups shredded cheddar cheese

- Cut potatoes in half lengthwise. Scoop meat out of potatoes and place in mixing bowl.
- Add salt to taste, sour cream and cream cheese and whip until all mix well. Spoon mashed potatoes back into potato skins and place in hot oven until potatoes reheat. Sprinkle cheddar cheese on top of potatoes.

Baked Potato Toppers

1 cup grated cheddar cheese
½ cup sour cream
¼ cup (½ stick) butter, softened
4 tablespoons chopped green onions

- Mix all ingredients and serve on baked potato.

Loaded Baked Potatoes

6 medium to large potatoes
1 (1 pound) hot sausage
1 (16 ounce) package cubed, processed cheese
1 (10 ounce) can tomatoes and green chilies, drained

- Wrap potatoes in foil and bake at 375° for 1 hour or until done.
- Brown sausage and drain. Add cheese to sausage and heat until cheese melts.
- Add tomatoes and green chilies.
- Serve sausage-cheese mixture over baked potatoes.

Vegetable-Stuffed Potatoes

2 (10 ounce) cans fiesta nacho cheese soup
1 (16 ounce) bag frozen assorted vegetables, cooked, drained
8 large potatoes, baked
Black pepper

- In saucepan, heat nacho cheese and vegetables.
- Cut lengthwise slice in top of each potato.
- Slightly mash pulp in each potato.
- Spoon sauce mixture on each potato. Sprinkle with black pepper.

Broccoli Potatoes

5 baking potatoes
Butter
1 (9 ounce) package frozen broccoli and cheese sauce
Paprika to garnish, optional

- Bake potatoes at 400° for 1 hour. (Potatoes are thoroughly cooked when center is soft.)
- Just before serving, slit each potato lengthwise.
- Fluff potato up with fork and add butter.
- Heat broccoli and cheese sauce in saucepan and pour over each potato.

Company Potatoes

5 potatoes, peeled, sliced
2 (8 ounce) cartons whipping cream
2 tablespoons dijon-style mustard
½ cup grated parmesan cheese

- In greased 9 x 13-inch baking dish, layer potatoes and a little salt and pepper.
- In saucepan, combine cream, mustard, 2 tablespoons butter and a little garlic powder and heat to boiling. Pour over potatoes.
- Cover and bake at 350° for 1 hour.
- Uncover and top with parmesan cheese.
- Bake 10 minutes longer or until potatoes are tender.

Ranch-Mashed Potatoes

4 cups instant, unsalted mashed potatoes, prepared
1 packet ranch-style dressing mix
¼ cup (½ stick) butter
½ cup sour cream

- Combine all ingredients in saucepan.
- Heat on low until potatoes are thoroughly heated.

Carnival Couscous

1 (5.7 ounce) box herbed-chicken couscous
¼ cup (½ stick) butter
1 red bell pepper, 1 yellow squash, cut in tiny pieces
¾ fresh broccoli florets, finely chopped

- Cook couscous according to package directions, but leave out butter.
- With butter in saucepan, saute bell pepper, squash and broccoli and cook about 10 minutes or until vegetables are almost tender.
- Combine couscous and vegetables. Serve hot.

Chop extra vegetables to use for next day's meal. Just cover the vegetables and refrigerate the batch. Use for tomorrow's meal.

Potato Puff

3 eggs, separated
2 cups instant mashed potatoes, prepared, hot
½ cup sour cream
2 teaspoons dried parsley

- Beat egg whites until stiff but still moist and set aside.
- Beat yolks until smooth and add to potato mixture.
- Fold in beaten egg whites, sour cream, parsley, teaspoon seasoned salt and ½ teaspoon white pepper.
- Pour into buttered 2-quart casserole.
- Bake uncovered at 350° for 45 minutes.

Potato Souffle

2 ⅔ cups instant mashed potatoes
2 eggs, beaten
1 cup shredded cheddar cheese
1 (3 ounce) can french-fried onion rings

- Prepare mashed potato mix according to package directions.
- Add eggs, cheese and stir until blended.
- Spoon mixture into lightly greased 2-quart dish. Sprinkle with onion rings.
- Bake uncovered at 325° for 25 minutes.

Ham-Baked Potatoes

4 potatoes, baked
1 cup diced, cooked ham
1(10 ounce) can cream of mushroom soup
1 cup shredded cheddar cheese

- Place hot potatoes on microwave-safe plate. Cut in half lengthwise.
- Fluff up potatoes with fork. Top each potato with one-quarter ham.
- In saucepan, heat soup with ¼ cup water and heat just until it is easy to spread.
- Spoon soup over potatoes and top with cheese.
- Microwave on HIGH for 4 minutes or until hot.

Broccoli-Topped Potatoes

4 hot baked potatoes, halved
1 cup diced, cooked ham
1 (10 ounce) can cream of broccoli soup
½ cup shredded cheddar cheese

- Place hot baked potatoes on microwave-safe plate.
- Carefully fluff up potatoes with fork. Top each potato with ham.
- Stir soup in can until smooth.
- Spoon soup over potatoes and top with cheese.
- Microwave on HIGH for 4 minutes.

Sweet Potatoes and Pecans

2 (17 ounce) cans sweet potatoes, drained, divided
1½ cups packed brown sugar
¼ cup (½ stick) butter, melted
1 cup chopped pecans

- Slice half sweet potatoes and place in buttered, 2-quart baking dish.
- Mix brown sugar, butter and pecans and sprinkle half mixture over sweet potatoes. Repeat layer.
- Bake uncovered at 350° for 30 minutes.

Baked Rice

2 cups uncooked rice
½ cup (1 stick) butter, melted
1 (10 ounce) can cream of celery soup
1 (10 ounce) can cream of onion soup

- Combine rice, butter, soups and 1½ cups water.
- Pour into buttered 3-quart baking dish.
- Bake at 350° covered for 1 hour.

Did you know? Add a teaspoon or two of lemon juice in the cooking water to make cooked rice whiter.

Broccoli and Wild Rice

2 (10 ounce) packages frozen chopped broccoli
1 (6 ounce) box long grain and wild rice
1 (8 ounce) jar processed cheese spread
1 (10 ounce) can cream of chicken soup

- Cook broccoli and rice according to package directions.
- Combine all ingredients and pour into buttered 2-quart casserole dish.
- Bake at 350° for 25 to 30 minutes or until bubbly.

Mushroom Rice

1 (5.9 ounce) package chicken Rice-a-Roni
1 (4 ounce) can sliced mushrooms, drained
⅓ cup slivered almonds
1 (8 ounce) carton sour cream

- Prepare rice according to package directions.
- Fold in mushrooms and sour cream. Place in 3-quart greased casserole.
- Bake covered at 350° for 25 to 30 minutes.

One or two teaspoons of vegetable oil added to the cooking water will keep rice from boiling over. It will also keep the rice grains separated.

Spinach Fettuccine

1 (6 ounce) can tomato paste
1 (5 ounce) can evaporated milk
½ cup (1 stick) butter
1 (12 ounce) package spinach fettuccine

- In saucepan, combine tomato paste, milk and heat until butter melts.
- Season with a little salt and pepper.
- Cook fettuccine according to package directions. Serve sauce over fettuccine.

Tip: No need to break the fettuccine into shorter pieces. Once set in boiling water, it will soften down in to pan.

Special Macaroni and Cheese

1 (8 ounce) package small macaroni shells
1 (15 ounce) can stewed tomatoes
1 (8 ounce) package cubed, processed cheese
3 tablespoons butter, melted

- Cook shells according to package directions and drain.
- In large bowl, combine shells, tomatoes, cheese cubes and butter.
- Pour into 2-quart buttered baking dish.
- Bake covered at 350° for 35 minutes.

Bacon-Wrapped Chicken

6 boneless, skinless chicken breast halves
1 (8 ounce) carton whipped, cream cheese with onion and chives
Butter
6 bacon strips

- Flatten chicken to ½-inch thickness. Spread 3 tablespoons cream cheese over each.
- Dot with butter and a little salt and roll up. Wrap each with bacon strip.
- Place seam side down in greased 9 x 13-inch baking dish.
- Bake, uncovered, at 375° for 40 to 45 minutes or until juices run clear.
- To brown, broil 6 inches from heat for about 3 minutes or until bacon is crisp.

Saucy Chicken

5 to 6 boneless, skinless chicken breast halves
2 cups thick and chunky salsa
⅓ cup packed light brown sugar
1½ tablespoons dijon-style mustard

- Place chicken breasts in greased 9 x 13-inch baking dish.
- Combine salsa, sugar and mustard and pour over chicken.
- Cover and bake at 350° for 45 minutes.
- Serve over rice.

Spicy Chicken and Rice

3 cups cooked, sliced chicken
2 cups cooked brown rice
1 (10 ounce) can fiesta nacho cheese soup
1 (10 ounce) can chopped tomatoes and green chilies

- Combine chicken, rice, cheese soup, tomatoes and green chilies and mix well.
- Spoon mixture into buttered 3-quart baking dish.
- Cook covered at 350° for 45 minutes.

Chile Pepper Chicken

5 boneless, skinless chicken breast halves
1 envelope hot and spicy recipe coating mixture
1 (4 ounce) can chopped green chilies
Chunky salsa

- Dredge chicken in coating mixture and place in greased 9 x 13-inch baking dish.
- Bake at 375° for 25 minutes.
- Remove from oven and spread green chilies over chicken breasts and return to oven for 5 minutes.
- Serve with salsa over each chicken breast.

Catalina Chicken

6 to 8 boneless, skinless chicken breast halves
1 (8 ounce) bottle Catalina dressing
1 teaspoon black pepper
1½ cups crushed cracker crumbs

- Marinate chicken breasts in Catalina dressing for 3 to 4 hours and discard marinade.
- Combine pepper and cracker crumbs.
- Dip each chicken breast in crumbs and place in large, greased baking dish.
- Bake uncovered at 350° for 1 hour.

Cola Chicken

4 to 6 boneless, skinless chicken breast halves
1 cup ketchup
1 cup cola
2 tablespoons worcestershire sauce

- Place chicken in 9 x 13-inch casserole dish. Sprinkle with salt and pepper.
- Mix ketchup, cola and worcestershire and pour over chicken.
- Cover and bake at 350° for 50 minutes.

Asparagus Chicken

1 package hollandaise sauce mix
2 large boneless, skinless chicken breasts, cut into strips
1 tablespoon lemon juice
1 (15 ounce) can asparagus spears

- Prepare hollandaise sauce according to package directions.
- In large skillet with a little oil, cook chicken strips for 12 to 15 minutes or until brown, stirring occasionally.
- Add hollandaise sauce and lemon juice.
- Cover and cook another 10 minutes, stirring occasionally. Serve over hot cooked noodles.
- When ready to serve, place chicken strips over noodles and add heated asparagus spears.

Wine and Chicken

6 to 8 boneless, skinless chicken breast halves
1 (10 ounce) can cream of mushroom soup
1 (10 ounce) can cream of onion soup
1 cup white wine

- In skillet brown chicken in a little bit of oil. Place in 9 x 13-inch baking dish.
- Combine soups and wine and pour over chicken.
- Bake covered at 325° for 35 minutes.
- Uncover and bake another 25 minutes.

Lemonade Chicken

6 boneless, skinless chicken breast halves
1 (6 ounce) can frozen lemonade, thawed
⅓ cup soy sauce
1 teaspoon garlic powder

- Place chicken in greased 9 x 13-inch baking dish.
- Combine lemonade, soy sauce and garlic powder and pour over chicken.
- Cover with foil and bake at 350° for 45 minutes.
- Uncover, pour juices over chicken and cook another 10 minutes uncovered.

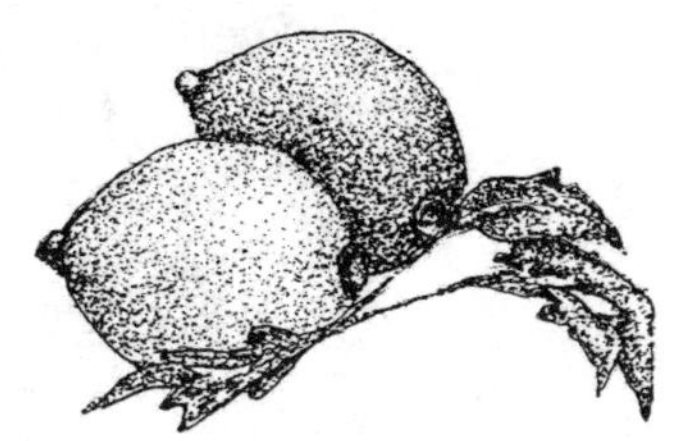

Mozzarella Cutlets

4 boneless, skinless chicken breast halves
1 cup Italian seasoned, dry breadcrumbs
1 cup prepared spaghetti sauce
4 slices mozzarella cheese

- Pound each chicken breast to flatten slightly.
- Coat well in breadcrumbs. Arrange chicken breasts in greased 9 x 13-inch baking dish.
- Place quarter of sauce over each portion. Place 1 slice cheese over each and garnish with remaining breadcrumbs.
- Bake uncovered at 350° for 45 minutes.

Sunday Chicken

5 to 6 boneless, skinless chicken breast halves
½ cup sour cream
¼ cup soy sauce
1 (10 ounce) can French-onion soup

- Place chicken in greased 9 x 13-inch baking dish.
- In saucepan, combine sour cream, soy sauce and soup and heat just enough to mix well. Pour over chicken breasts.
- Bake covered at 350° for 55 minutes.

Chicken and Beef

1 (4 ounce) jar sliced dried beef, separated
6 strips bacon
6 boneless, skinless chicken breast halves
1(10 ounce) can cream of chicken soup

- Place dried beef in greased 9 x 13-inch baking dish.
- Wrap bacon strip around each chicken breast and place over beef.
- In saucepan heat chicken soup and ¼ cup water just until it can be poured over chicken.
- Bake covered at 325° for 1 hour 10 minutes.

Chicken and Noodles

1 package chicken-flavored, instant ramen noodles
1 (16 ounce) package frozen broccoli, cauliflower and carrots
⅔ cup sweet and sour sauce
3 boneless, skinless chicken breast halves, cooked

- Reserve seasoning packet from noodles. In saucepan, cook noodles and vegetables in 2 cups boiling water for 3 minutes, stirring occasionally and drain.
- Combine noodle-vegetable mixture with seasoning packet, sweet and sour sauce and a little salt and pepper. (You may want to add 1 tablespoon soy sauce.)
- Cut chicken in strips, add chicken to noodle mixture and heat thoroughly.

Chicken Parmesan

1½ cups biscuit mix
⅔ cup grated parmesan cheese
6 to 8 boneless, skinless chicken breast halves
½ cup (1 stick) butter, melted

- In shallow bowl, combine biscuit mix and parmesan cheese.
- Dip chicken in butter and in biscuit-cheese mixture.
- Place in large, buttered baking dish.
- Bake uncovered at 325° for 1 hour or until light brown.

Chicken Bake

8 boneless, skinless chicken breast halves
8 slices Swiss cheese
1 (10 ounce) can cream of chicken soup
1 (8 ounce) box chicken stuffing mix

- Flatten each chicken breast with rolling pin and place in greased 9 x 13-inch baking dish.
- Place cheese slice over chicken. Combine chicken soup and ½ cup water and pour over chicken.
- Mix stuffing mix according to package directions and sprinkle over chicken. Bake uncovered at 325° for 1 hour.

Chicken Quesadillas

3 boneless, skinless chicken breasts, cubed
1 (10 ounce) can cheddar cheese soup
⅔ cup chunky salsa
10 flour tortillas

- Cook chicken in skillet until juices evaporate; stir often.
- Add soup and salsa and heat thoroughly.
- Spread about ⅓ cup soup mixture on half tortilla to within ½ inch of edge. Moisten edge with water, fold over and seal. Place on 2 baking sheets.
- Bake at 400° for 5 to 6 minutes.

Chicken Oriental

1 (6 ounce) jar sweet and sour sauce
1 envelope dry onion soup mix
1 (16 ounce) can whole cranberry sauce
6 to 8 boneless, skinless chicken breast halves

- In bowl combine sweet and sour sauce, onion soup mix and cranberry sauce.
- Place chicken breasts in sprayed 9 x 13-inch shallow baking dish.
- Pour cranberry mixture over chicken breasts.
- Bake covered at 325° for 30 minutes.
- Uncover and bake 25 minutes longer.

Fried Chicken Breasts

4 boneless, skinned chicken breast halves
20 saltine crackers, crushed
2 eggs, beaten
¼ teaspoon black pepper

- Pound chicken breasts to ¼-inch thickness.
- Combine eggs, pepper and 2 tablespoons water.
- Dip chicken in egg mixture and crushed crackers and coat well.
- Deep fry until golden brown and drain well.

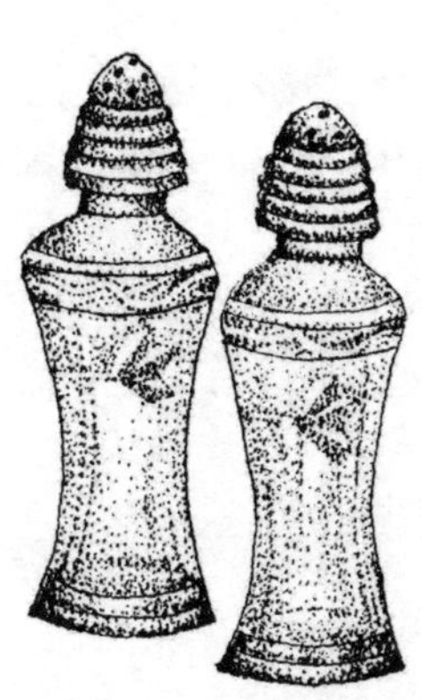

Company Chicken

2 chickens, quartered
2 (10 ounce) cans cream of mushroom soup
1 pint sour cream
1 cup sherry

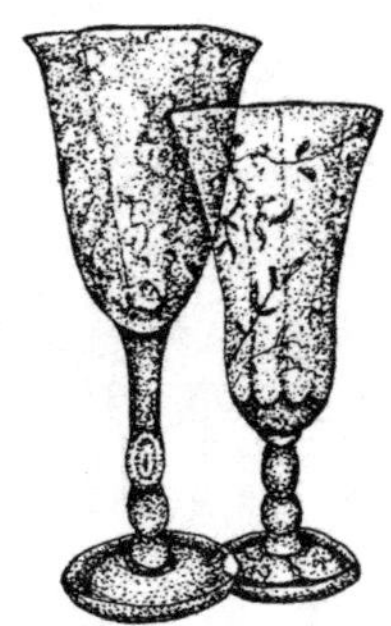

- Place chickens in large shallow baking dish.
- In saucepan, combine soup, sour cream and sherry. Pour mixture over chicken. (You might sprinkle a little paprika on top.)
- Bake covered at 300° for 1 hour 15 minutes.

Tip: This good served with rice.

Sweet 'N Spicy Chicken

1 pound boneless, skinless chicken breast halves
3 tablespoons taco seasoning
1 (11 ounce) jar chunky salsa
1 cup peach preserves

- Cut chicken into ½-inch cubes. Place chicken in large resealable plastic bag, add taco seasoning and toss to coat.
- In skillet, brown chicken in a little oil.
- Combine salsa and preserves. Stir into skillet.
- Bring to a boil. Reduce heat, cover and simmer until juices run clear.

Tip: Serve over rice or noodles.

✤✤✤✤

Sweet and Sour Chicken

2 to 3 pounds chicken pieces
Oil
1 package dry onion soup mix
1 (6 ounce) can frozen orange juice concentrate, thawed

- In skillet, brown chicken in a little oil. Place chicken in 9 x 13-inch baking dish.
- In small bowl, combine onion soup mix, orange juice and ⅔ cup water and stir well. Pour over chicken.
- Bake uncovered at 350° for 50 minutes.

Adobe Chicken

2 cups cooked brown rice
1 (10 ounce) can chopped tomatoes and green chilies, drained
3 cups chopped cooked chicken
1 (8 ounce) package shredded Monterey Jack cheese, divided

- Combine rice, tomatoes, green chilies, chicken and half Jack cheese.
- Spoon into buttered, 7 x 11-inch baking dish. Cook covered at 325° for 30 minutes.
- Uncover, sprinkle remaining cheese over casserole and return to oven for 5 minutes.

Smothered Steak

1 (2 pound) round steak
1 (10 ounce) can golden mushroom soup
1 (1 ounce) package dry onion soup mix
⅔ cup milk

- Cut steak into serving-size pieces and place in well greased 9 x 13-inch baking pan.
- In saucepan mix soup, dry onion soup and milk. Heat just enough to be able to mix well. Pour over steak.
- Seal with foil. Bake at 325° for 1 hour.

Steak-Bake Italiano

2 pounds lean round steak
2 teaspoons Italian seasoning
1 teaspoon garlic salt
2 (15 ounce) cans stewed tomatoes

- Cut steak into serving-size pieces and brown in skillet.
- Place in 9 x 13-inch baking dish.
- Combine Italian seasoning, garlic salt and stewed tomatoes. Pour over steak pieces.
- Cover and bake at 325° for 1 hour.

Southwestern Steak

½ pound tenderized round steak
1 (15 ounce) can Mexican stewed tomatoes
¾ cup salsa
2 teaspoons beef bouillon

- Cut beef into serving-size pieces and dredge in flour.
- In skillet, brown steak in a little oil.
- Mix tomatoes, salsa and beef bouillon and pour over steak.
- Cover and bake at 325° for 1 hour.

Baked Onion-Mushroom Steak

1½ pounds (½-inch thick) round steak
Salt and pepper
1 (10 ounce) can cream of mushroom soup
1 envelope dry onion soup mix

- Place steak in greased 9 x 13-inch baking dish. Sprinkle with salt and pepper.
- Pour mushroom soup and ½ cup water over steak and sprinkle with onion soup mix.
- Cover and bake at 325° for 2 hours.

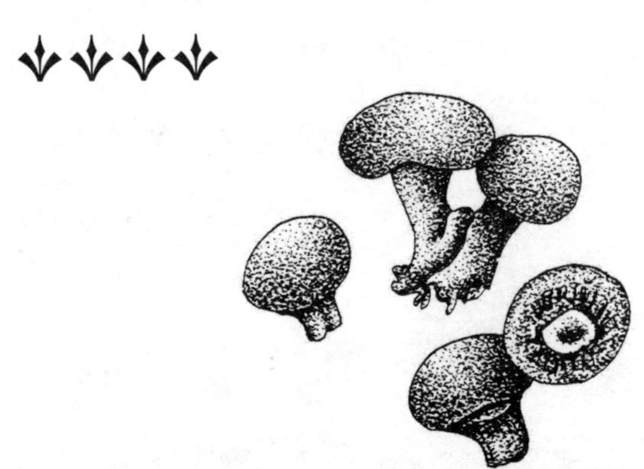

Casserole Supper

1 pound lean ground beef
¼ cup uncooked white rice
1 (10 ounce) can French-onion soup
1 can french-fried onion rings

- Brown ground beef, drain and place in buttered 7 x 11-inch baking dish.
- Add rice, onion soup and ½ cup water.
- Cover and bake at 325° for 40 minutes.
- Uncover, sprinkle onion rings over top and return to oven for 10 minutes.

Pepper Steak

Seasoning salt
1 (1¼ pound) sirloin steak, cut in strips
1 (16 ounce) package frozen bell pepper and onion strips, thawed
1 (16 ounce) package cubed Mexican processed cheese

- Sprinkle steak with seasoned salt.
- Coat large skillet with non-stick vegetable spray. Cook steak strips about 10 minutes or until no longer pink. Remove steak from skillet and set aside.
- Stir in vegetables and ½ cup water. Simmer vegetables about 5 minutes until all liquid cooks out.
- Add processed cheese. Turn heat to medium low until cheese melts. Stir in steak and serve over hot cooked rice.

Beef and Broccoli

1 pound beef sirloin steak
1 onion, chopped
1 (10 ounce) can cream of broccoli soup
1 (10 ounce) package frozen chopped broccoli, thawed

- Slice beef across grain into very thin strips. In large skillet brown steak strips and onion in a little oil and stir several times.
- Reduce heat and simmer 10 minutes. Stir in soup and broccoli and heat.
- When ready to serve, spoon beef mixture over hot, cooked noodles.

Easy Roast

1 (4 pound) rump roast
1 (10 ounce) can cream of mushroom soup
1 envelope dry onion soup mix
½ cup white wine

- Place roast in roaster.
- Combine mushroom soup, onion soup mix and white wine and ⅓ cup water. Pour over roast.
- Cover roast with foil and bake at 325° for about 3 to 4 hours.

Tip: Remove toast from the refrigerator 2 to 3 hours before cooking. Cook roast fast side up so melting will baste meat during cooking.

Rump Roast

1 (3 to 4 pound) boneless rump roast
4 medium potatoes, peeled, cut into pieces
2 onions, quartered
1 (10 ounce) can golden mushroom soup

- Place roast in roaster, season with seasoned salt and pepper and cover.
- Bake at 350° for about 1 hour.
- Uncover and add potatoes and onions and continue cooking for 1 more hour.
- In saucepan combine soup and ½ cup water. Heat just enough to pour over roast and vegetables.
- Place roaster back in oven just until soup is hot.

Onion-Beef Bake

3 pounds lean ground beef
1 package dry onion soup mix
½ cup water
2 (10 ounce) cans condensed French-onion soup

- Combine beef, soup mix and water. Stir well and shape into patties about ½-inch thick.
- Cook in large skillet and brown on both sides.
- Move patties to 9 x 13-inch baking dish. Pour soup over patties.
- Cover and bake at 350° for about 35 minutes.

A Wicked Meatloaf

1 (7 ounce) package stuffing mix plus seasoning packet
1 egg
½ cup salsa
1½ pounds lean ground beef

- In bowl combine stuffing mix, seasoning, egg, salsa and ⅓ cup water and mix well.
- Add ground beef to stuffing mixture.
- Spoon into 9 x 5-inch loaf pan.
- Bake at 350° for 1 hour.

Tip: Place meatloaf ingredients in a large, ziplock plastic bag, seal and squish contents together until they mix well if you don't want to get your hands messy mixing meatloaf.

Smothered Beef Patties

1½ pounds ground beef
½ cup chili sauce
½ cup buttery cracker crumbs
1 (14 ounce) can beef bouillon

- Combine beef, chili sauce and cracker crumbs and form into 5 or 6 patties.
- In skillet, brown patties and pour beef bouillon over patties. Bring to a boil.
- Reduce heat, cover and simmer for about 40 minutes.

Savory Herb Meat Loaf

1 pound ground round beef, browned
2 (10 ounce) cans soup: 1 cream of mushroom soup and 1 cream of celery soup
1 package dry savory-herb-with-garlic onion soup mix
1 cup cooked rice

- Mix all ingredients.
- Place into 9 x 13-inch baking dish and form loaf.
- Bake at 350° for 50 minutes.

Mexican Casserole

1 (13 ounce) bag tortilla chips, divided
2 pounds lean ground beef
1 (10 ounce) can Mexican stewed tomatoes
1 (8 ounce) package shredded Mexican 4-cheese blend

- Partially crush half bag chips and place in bottom of buttered 9 x 13-inch baking dish.
- Brown ground beef and drain.
- Add stewed tomatoes and cheese and mix well. Sprinkle finely crushed chips over top of casserole.
- Bake uncovered at 350° for 40 minutes.

When purchasing ground beef, remember that fat greatly contributes to its flavor. The lower the fat content, the drier it will be once cooked.

Avoid meat that smells bad, is dry and brown around the edges or is discolored. Always cook ground meat fully to insure food safety and guard against bacteria.

Beef Patties in Creamy Onion Sauce

1½ pounds lean ground beef
⅓ cup salsa
⅓ cup butter cracker crumbs
1 (10 ounce) can cream of onion soup

- Combine beef, salsa and cracker crumbs and form into 5 to 6 patties. Brown in skillet and reduce heat.
- Add ¼ cup water and simmer for 15 minutes. In saucepan combine onion soup and ½ cup water or milk, heat and mix.
- Pour over beef patties. Serve over hot, cooked noodles.

Next-Day Beef

1 (5 to 6 pound) trimmed beef brisket
1 packet dry onion soup mix
1 (10 ounce) bottle Heinz 57 sauce
1 (12 ounce) bottle barbecue sauce

- Place brisket, cut side up, in roasting pan.
- In bowl, combine onion soup mix, Heinz 57 sauce and barbecue sauce. Pour over brisket.
- Cover and cook at 325° for 4 to 5 hours or until tender. Remove brisket from pan and pour off drippings. Chill both, separately, overnight.
- The next day, trim all fat from meat, slice and reheat. Skim fat off drippings and reheat. Serve sauce over brisket.

Easy Breezy Brisket

1 (4 to 5 pound) brisket
1 envelope dry onion soup mix
2 tablespoons worcestershire
1 cup red wine

- Place brisket in shallow baking pan and sprinkle onion soup over brisket.
- Pour worcestershire and red wine in pan.
- Cover and bake at 325° for 5 to 6 hours.

Slow Cookin', Good Tastin' Brisket

½ cup liquid hickory-flavored smoke
1 (4 to 5 pound) beef brisket
1 (5 ounce) bottle worcestershire
¾ cup barbecue sauce

- Pour liquid smoke over brisket. Cover and refrigerate overnight.
- Drain and pour worcestershire sauce over brisket.
- Cover and bake at 275° for 6 to 7 hours.
- Cover with barbeque sauce. Bake uncovered for another 30 minutes. Slice very thin across grain.

Giddy-Up Pork Chops

6 boneless pork chops
½ cup salsa
½ cup honey or packed brown sugar
1 teaspoon soy sauce

- Brown pork chops in oven-proof pan.
- Combine salsa, honey or brown sugar and soy sauce and heat for 20 to 30 seconds in microwave oven.
- Pour salsa mixture over pork chops, cover and bake at 325° for about 45 minutes or until pork chops are tender.

Pork Chops in Cream Gravy

4 (¼-inch thick) pork chops,
Flour
Oil
2¼ cups whole milk

- Dip chops in flour with a little salt and pepper. Brown pork chops on both sides in a little oil. Remove chops from skillet.
- Add about 2 tablespoons flour to skillet, brown lightly and stir in a little salt and pepper.
- Slowly stir in milk to make gravy. Return chops to skillet with gravy.
- Cover and simmer on low burner for about 40 minutes.

Tip: Serve over rice or noodles.

Chops and Stuffing

1 (6 ounce) box savory herb stuffing mix
6 center-cut pork chops
Oil
3 onions, halved

- Make stuffing according to package directions and set aside.
- Fry pork chops in skillet with a little oil. Brown chops on both sides and place in greased 9 x 13-inch baking dish.
- Divide stuffing and onions among pork chops and mound on top of each.
- Cover and bake at 350° for about 30 minutes.

Apple-Pork Chops

4 butter-flied pork chops
2 apples, peeled
2 teaspoons butter
2 tablespoons brown sugar

- Place pork chops in non-stick sprayed shallow baking dish. Season with salt and pepper.
- Cover and bake at 350° for 30 minutes. Uncover and place peeled and cored apple halves on top of pork chops.
- Add a little butter and a little brown sugar on each apple.
- Bake for another 15 minutes.

Baked Pork Chops

¾ cup ketchup
¾ cup packed brown sugar
¼ cup lemon juice
4 butter-flied pork chops

- Combine ketchup, ½ cup water, brown sugar and lemon juice.
- Place pork chops in 7 x 11-inch buttered baking dish and pour sauce over pork chops.
- Bake covered at 325° for 50 minutes.

Spicy Pork Chops

4 to 6 pork chops
1 large onion
1 bell pepper
1 (10 ounce) can diced tomatoes and green chilies

- Brown pork chops in skillet with a little oil.
- Spray casserole dish with nonstick spray. Place chops in dish.
- Cut onion and bell pepper into large chunks and place on chops. Pour tomato and green chilies over chops and sprinkle 1 teaspoon salt over casserole.
- Bake covered at 350° for 45 minutes.

When selecting pork, look for meat that is pale pink with a small amount of marbeling and white fat (not yellow). The darker pink the flesh appears, the older the animal.

Sweet and Sour Spareribs

4 pounds pork spareribs
1 (6 ounce) can lemonade concentrate
½ teaspoon garlic salt
⅓ cup soy sauce

- Place ribs, meaty side down in shallow roasting pan. Cook covered at 350° for 40 minutes.
- Remove cover, drain fat and return ribs to oven. Bake 30 minutes more. Drain fat again.
- Combine remaining ingredients and brush on ribs.
- Reduce temperature to 325° degrees. Cover and bake for 1 more hour or until tender, brushing occasionally with sauce.

Saucy Pork Chops

4 (½-inch thick) pork chops
1 tablespoon oil
1 (10 ounce) can cream of onion soup
2 tablespoons soy sauce

- In skillet, brown pork chops in oil, cook about 15 minutes and drain.
- Add soup and soy sauce. Heat to a boil.
- Return chops to pan. Reduce heat to low. Cover and simmer about 20 minutes.

Store fresh pork in the refrigerator as long as it's used within 6 hours or purchase. Otherwise, remove its packaging and loosely wrap it in wax paper. Store in the coldest part of the refrigerator for up to 2 days. Ground pork and pork sausage shouldn't be stored for more than 2 days.

Honey-Ham Slice

⅓ cup orange juice
⅓ cup honey
1 teaspoon prepared mustard
1 (1-inch thick) slice fully cooked ham

- Combine orange juice, honey and mustard in saucepan and cook slowly for 10 minutes, stirring occasionally.
- Place ham in broiling pan about 3 inches from heat. Brush with orange glaze.
- Broil 8 minutes on first side. Turn ham slice over. Brush with glaze again and broil another 6 to 8 minutes.

Orange-Pork Chops

6 to 8 medium thick pork chops
¼ cup (½ stick) butter
2¼ cups orange juice
2 tablespoons orange marmalade

- Brown both sides of pork chops in butter in hot skillet and add salt and pepper.
- Pour orange juice over chops. Cover and simmer until done, about 1 hour. (Time will vary with thickness of pork chops.) Add more orange juice if necessary.
- During last few minutes of cooking add the 2 tablespoons orange marmalade.

Tip: This makes delicious gravy to serve over rice.

Hawaiian Pork

1 (2 pound) lean pork tenderloin, cut in 1-inch cubes
1 (15 ounce) can pineapple chunks with juice
1 (12 ounce) bottle chili sauce
1 teaspoon ground ginger

- In skillet, season pork cubes with salt and pepper.
- Combine meat, pineapple with juice, chili sauce and ginger.
- Simmer covered for 1 hour 30 minutes.

Tip: This is great served over rice.

Supper In A Dish

2 bags instant rice in a bag
1½ cups cubed, cooked ham
1½ cups shredded cheddar cheese
1 (8 ounce) can green peas

- Prepare rice according to package directions.
- In large bowl, combine rice, ham, cheese and peas.
- Pour into 3-quart baking dish and bake at 350° for 15 to 20 minutes.

If you want succulent chops, choose those that are about 1 inch thick. Thinner chops will tend to dry out no matter how careful you are about cooking them.

Cranberry Sauce

1 (14 ounce) carton strawberry glaze
1 (12 ounce) package frozen cranberries
½ cup orange juice
Sugar

- In saucepan combine glaze, cranberries and juice. Heat to boiling.
- Reduce heat and simmer 10 minutes or until cranberries pop, stirring often.
- Refrigerate several hours before serving.
- Cool and taste. Add sugar if necessary.

Tip: Serve with pork or ham.

Peach-Pineapple Baked Ham

1 (3 to 4) pound boneless smoked ham
4 tablespoons dijon-style mustard, divided
1 cup peach preserves
1 cup pineapple preserves

- Preheat oven to 325°. Spread 2 tablespoons mustard on ham.
- Place ham in prepared, shallow baking pan and bake for 20 minutes.
- Combine remaining 2 tablespoons mustard and both preserves and heat in microwave oven for 20 seconds (or in small saucepan at low heat for 2 to 3 minutes).
- Pour over ham and bake for about 15 minutes.

Orange Spareribs

4 to 5 pounds pork spareribs
1 (6 ounce) can orange juice concentrate, thawed
½ teaspoon garlic salt
⅔ cup honey

- Place ribs, meaty side down in shallow roasting pan. Bake at 350° for 30 minutes. Drain off fat and turn ribs. Bake 30 minutes more.
- Combine remaining ingredients and brush on ribs. Reduce temperature to 325°.
- Cover pan, bake 1 hour 30 minutes or until tender and brush with sauce several times.

Plum Peachy Pork Roast

1 (4 to 5 pound) boneless pork loin roast
1 (12 ounce) jar plum jelly
½ cup peach preserves
½ teaspoon ginger

- Place roast in shallow baking pan and bake at 325° for about 35 minutes. Turn roast to brown other side and bake another 35 minutes.
- In saucepan heat jelly, peach preserves and ginger.
- Brush roast generously with preserve mixture after it is done.
- Bake another 15 minutes and baste again.

Tenderloin With Apricot Sauce

3 pounds pork tenderloin
1 cup jar apricot preserves
⅓ cup lemon juice, ⅓ cup ketchup
1 tablespoon soy sauce

- Place tenderloins in roasting pan.
- Combine preserves, lemon juice, ketchup and soy sauce.
- Pour over pork and bake covered at 325° for 1 hour 20 minutes. Baste once during cooking.

Tip: Serve over white rice.

Pork Picante

1 pound pork tenderloin, cubed
2 tablespoons taco seasoning
1 cup chunky salsa
⅓ cup peach preserves

- Toss pork with taco seasoning and brown with a little oil in skillet.
- Stir in salsa and preserves. Bring to a boil.
- Lower heat and simmer 10 minutes.

Tip: Pour over hot cooked rice.

Broiled Lemon-Garlic Shrimp

1 pound shrimp, peeled, veined
1 teaspoon garlic salt
2 tablespoons lemon juice
2 tablespoons butter

- Place shrimp in shallow baking pan.
- Sprinkle with garlic salt and lemon juice and dot with butter.
- Broil on 1 side for 3 minutes.
- Turn and broil 3 minutes more.

Tip: If shrimp are large, split them down middle and spread them out like a butterfly, then season.

Beer-Batter Shrimp

1 (12 ounce) can beer
1 cup flour
2 teaspoons garlic powder
1 pound shrimp, peeled, veined

- Make batter by mixing beer, flour and garlic powder and stirring to creamy consistency.
- Dip shrimp into batter to cover and deep-fry in hot oil.

Creamed Shrimp Over Rice

3 (10 ounce) cans frozen cream of shrimp soup
1 pint sour cream
1½ teaspoons curry powder
2 (5 ounce) cans veined shrimp

- Combine all ingredients in top of double boiler.
- Heat, stirring constantly, but do not boil.

Tip: Serve over hot, cooked rice.

Crab Mornay

2 (6 ounce) cans crabmeat, drained
1 cup cream of mushroom soup
½ cup shredded Swiss cheese
½ cup seasoned breadcrumbs

- Preheat oven to 350°.
- Combine crabmeat, soup and cheese.
- Pour into prepared 1½-quart casserole dish and sprinkle with breadcrumbs.
- Bake uncovered for 30 minutes or until soup bubbles and breadcrumbs are light brown.

Seafood Delight

1 (6 ounce) can shrimp, drained
1 (6 ounce) can crabmeat, drained, flaked
1 (10 ounce) can corn or potato chowder
2 to 3 cups seasoned breadcrumbs, divided

- Preheat oven to 350°. Mix shrimp, crabmeat, chowder and ⅓ cup breadcrumbs.
- Place in prepared 1½-quart casserole dish. Sprinkle with remaining breadcrumbs.
- Bake for 30 minutes or until casserole bubbles and breadcrumbs are light brown.

Tuna Noodles

1 (8 ounce) package wide noodles, cooked, drained
2 (6 ounce) cans white tuna, drained
1 can cream of chicken soup plus ¾ cup milk
¾ cup chopped black olives

- Place half noodles in 2-quart buttered casserole.
- In saucepan, combine tuna, soup, milk and olives. Heat just enough to mix well.
- Pour half soup mixture over noodles and repeat layers.
- Cover and bake at 300° for about 20 minutes.

Home-Fried Fish

1½ pounds haddock, sole or cod
1 egg beaten
2 tablespoons milk
2 cups corn flake crumbs

- Cut fish into serving-size pieces.
- Combine egg and milk. Dip fish in egg mixture and coat with crushed corn flakes on both sides.
- Fry in thin layer of oil in skillet until brown on both sides.

Crispy Flounder

⅓ cup mayonnaise
1 pound flounder fillets
1 cup seasoned breadcrumbs
¼ cup grated parmesan cheese

- Place mayonnaise in small dish. Coat fish with mayonnaise and dip in crumbs to coat well.
- Arrange in shallow baking dish. Bake uncovered at 375° for 25 minutes.

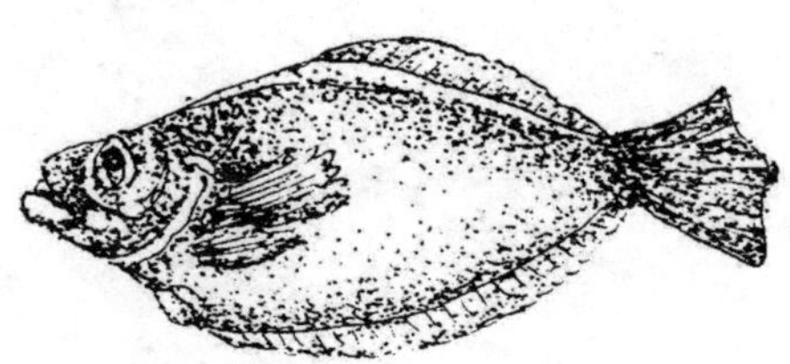

Chips and Fish

3 to 4 fish fillets, rinsed, dried
1 cup mayonnaise
2 tablespoons fresh lime juice and lime wedges
1½ cups crushed corn chips

- Preheat oven to 425°. Mix mayonnaise and lime juice. Spread on both sides of fish fillets.
- Place crushed corn chips on wax paper and dredge both sides of fish in chips. Shake off excess chips.
- Place fillets on foil-covered baking sheet and bake for 15 minutes or until fish flakes. Serve with lime wedges.

Orange Roughy With Peppers

1½ pounds orange roughy
2 red bell peppers, cut into julienne strips
1 teaspoon dried thyme leaves
¾ teaspoon seasoned salt

- Cut fish into serving-size pieces.
- Heat a little oil in skillet. Layer bell pepper and seasoning. Place fish on top.
- Turn burner on high until fish is hot enough to begin cooking.
- Lower heat, cover and cook fish for 15 to 20 minutes or until fish flakes easily.

Baked Oysters

1 cup oysters, drained, rinsed
2 cups cracker crumbs
¼ cup (½ stick) butter, melted
½ cup milk

- Make alternate layers of oysters, cracker crumbs and butter in 7 x 11-inch baking dish.
- Pour warmed milk over layers and add lots of salt and pepper.
- Bake at 350° for about 35 minutes.

Salmon Patties

1 (15 ounce) can pink salmon with juice
1 egg
½ cup cracker crumbs
1 teaspoon baking powder

- Pour off juice from salmon and set aside. Remove bones and skin.
- Stir in egg and cracker crumbs with salmon.
- In small bowl add baking powder to ¼ cup salmon juice. Mixture will foam. After foaming add to salmon mixture.
- Drop by teaspoons in hot oil in skillet. Brown lightly on both sides. Serve hot.

Black Forest Cake

1 (18 ounce) box devil's food cake mix
1 (20 ounce) can cherry pie filling
1 (3.4 ounce) package vanilla instant pudding
1 (8 ounce) carton whipped topping

- Bake cake according to package directions in greased, floured 9 x 13-inch baking pan. While cake is still warm, poke top with fork and spread cherry pie filling over cake.
- While cake cools, prepare the pudding using 1 cup milk. Fold in whipped topping.
- Spread pudding and whipped topping mixture over cake, carefully covering cherry pie filling. Refrigerate.

Pecan Cake

1 (18 ounce) box butter pecan cake mix
½ cup (1 stick) butter, melted
1 egg
1 cup chopped pecans

- Combine cake mix, ¾ cup water, butter and egg and mix well. Stir in pecans. Pour into 9 x 13-inch baking dish.
- Check with toothpick to make sure cake is done.

Topping for Pecan Cake:

1 (8 ounce) package cream cheese, softened
2 eggs
1 (1 pound) box powdered sugar

- With mixer, combine cream cheese, eggs and powdered sugar. Pour over cake mixture.
- Bake at 350° for 40 minutes.

Oreo Cake

1 (18 ounce) package white cake mix
⅓ cup oil
4 egg whites
1¼ cup coarsely chopped Oreo cookies

- In mixing bowl, combine cake mix, oil, 1¼ cups water and egg whites. Blend on low speed until moist. Beat 2 minutes at high speed.
- Gently fold in coarsely chopped cookies. Pour batter into 2 greased, floured 8-inch round cake pans.
- Bake at 350° for 25 to 30 minutes or until toothpick inserted in center comes out clean.
- Cool for 15 minutes and then remove from pan. Cool completely and frost.

Frosting for Oreo Cake:

4¼ cups powdered sugar
1 cup (2 sticks) butter, softened
1 cup shortening
1 teaspoon almond flavoring

- With mixer combine all ingredients and beat until creamy.
- Ice first layer of cake and place second layer on top; ice top and sides.
- Sprinkle with extra crushed Oreo cookies on top.

Tip: Do not use butter-flavored shortening.

O'Shaughnessy's Special

1 (10 ounce) pound cake loaf
1 (15 ounce) can crushed pineapple with juice
1 (3.4 ounce) box pistachio pudding mix
1 (8 ounce) carton whipped topping

- Slice cake horizontally and make 3 layers.
- Combine pineapple and pudding and beat until mixture begins to thicken. Fold in whipped topping and blend well. (You may add a few drops of green food coloring if you would like the cake to be a brighter green.)
- Spread on each layer and on top. Refrigerate.

Carnival Cake

1 (18 ounce) box white cake mix
2 (10 ounce) box frozen sweetened strawberries with juice
1 (3.4 ounce) package instant vanilla pudding
1 (8 ounce) carton whipped topping

- Make cake mix according to package directions. Pour into greased 9 x 13-inch baking dish. Bake according to package directions.
- When cool, poke holes with knife in top of cake and pour strawberries over top.
- Make instant pudding using 1¼ cups milk. When that is set, pour over strawberries. Cover cake with whipped topping and refrigerate.

Miracle Cake

1 (18 ounce) lemon cake mix
3 eggs
⅓ cup oil
1 (20 ounce) can crushed pineapple with juice

- In mixing bowl, combine all ingredients, blend on low speed and beat on medium for 2 minutes.
- Pour batter into greased, floured 9 x 13-inch baking dish.
- Bake at 350° for 30 to 35 minutes until cake tests done with toothpick.

Miracle Cake Topping:

1 (14 ounce) can sweetened condensed milk
¼ cup lemon juice
1 (8 ounce) carton whipped topping

- Blend all ingredients and mix well. Spread over cake and refrigerate.

Pink Lady Cake

1 (18 ounce) box strawberry cake mix
3 eggs
1 teaspoon lemon extract
1 (20 ounce) can strawberry pie filling

- In mixing bowl, beat cake mix, eggs and lemon extract.
- Fold in pie filling.
- Pour in greased, floured 9 x 13-baking pan.
- Bake at 350° for 30 to 35 minutes. Test with toothpick to make sure that cake is done.

Tip: Add a prepared vanilla icing or whipped topping.

Pound Cake Deluxe

1 (10 inch) round bakery pound cake
1 (20 ounce) can crushed pineapple with juice
1 (5 ounce) package coconut instant pudding mix
1 (8 ounce) carton whipped topping

- Slice cake horizontally to make 3 layers.
- Mix pineapple, pudding and whipped topping and blend well.
- Spread on each layer and top of cake. Coconut may be sprinkled on top layer. Refrigerate.

Strawberry Trifle

1 (5 ounce) package French vanilla instant pudding mix
1 (10 ounce) loaf pound cake
2 cups fresh strawberries, sliced
½ cup sherry

- Make pudding according to package directions.
- Place layer of pound cake slices in bottom of 8-inch crystal bowl. Sprinkle with ¼ cup sherry. Add layer of strawberries. Next, layer half pudding. Repeat these layers. Refrigerate overnight or several hours.
- Before serving, top with whipped topping.

Emergency Cheesecake

1 (8 ounce) package cream cheese, softened
1 (14 ounce) can sweetened condensed milk
½ cup lemon juice
1 teaspoon vanilla

- Blend all ingredients in mixer.
- Pour into graham cracker crust and refrigerate.

Tip: Add cherry pie filling if you want a topping.

Chocolate-Orange Cake

1 (16 ounce) loaf frozen pound cake, thawed
1 (12 ounce) jar orange marmalade
1 (16 ounce) can ready-to-spread chocolate fudge frosting

- Cut cake horizontally to make 3 layers.
- Place 1 layer on cake platter. Spread with half marmalade.
- Place second layer over first and spread on remaining marmalade.
- Top with third cake layer, spread frosting liberally on top and sides of cake and refrigerate.

Strawberry Delight

1 (6 ounce) package strawberry gelatin
2 (10 ounce) packages frozen strawberries with juice
1 (8 ounce) carton whipped topping
1 (12 ounce) prepared angel food cake

- Dissolve strawberry gelatin in 1 cup boiling water and mix well. Add strawberries.
- Chill in refrigerator until partially set and fold in whipped topping.
- Break angel food cake into large bite-size pieces and layer cake and gelatin mixture, one half at a time, in 9 x 13-inch shallow dish. Refrigerate and cut in squares to serve.

Easy Pineapple Cake

2 cups sugar
2 cups flour
1 (20 ounce) can crushed pineapple with juice
1 teaspoon baking soda

- Combine all cake ingredients and mix by hand.
- Pour into greased, floured 9 x 13-inch baking pan.
- Bake at 350° for 30 to 35 minutes.

Icing for Easy Pineapple Cake:

1 (8 ounce) package cream cheese, softened
½ cup (1 stick) butter, melted
1 cup powdered sugar
1 cup chopped pecans

- Combine cream cheese, butter and powdered sugar and beat with mixer.
- Add chopped pecans and pour over HOT cake.

Fruit Cocktail Crepes

4 (15 ounce) can fruit cocktail, thoroughly drained
1 cup packed brown sugar
2 cups (4 sticks) butter, divided
3 (8 inch) packages flour tortillas

- Preheat oven to 325°. In small saucepan over low heat, stir constantly brown sugar and ⅓ cup butter until sugar melts and mixes well.
- Use remaining butter and brush flour tortillas on both sides. (If each tortilla is not soft enough to roll without breaking, heat 2 to 3 at a time wrapped in damp paper towel for 30 seconds in microwave oven.)
- For each crepe, place 2 teaspoons sugar mixture and 1 tablespoon drained fruit cocktail in middle of each tortilla.
- Roll each tortilla and place, seam side down, in 11 x 7 x 2-inch baking pan. Spread remaining sugar mixture on top.
- Bake covered 10 to 15 minutes or until sugar mixture bubbles.

Angel Glaze

1 cup confectioners' powdered sugar
1 tablespoon hot water
2 tablespoons light corn syrup
¼ teaspoon vanilla

- Mix all ingredients and stir until well blended with creamy texture. Glaze should pour slowly and stay on cake long enough to soak in.
- If glaze runs down side of cake, thicken mixture with a little more powdered sugar.
- Use on any cake that needs light icing or topping of something sweet.

Macadamia Candy

2 (3 ounce) jars macadamia nuts
1 (20 ounce) package white almond bark
¾ cup flaked coconut
½ teaspoon vanilla extract

- Heat dry skillet and toast nuts until slightly golden. (Some brands of macadamia nuts are already toasted.) Set aside.
- In double boiler, melt 12 squares almond bark.
- As soon as almond bark melts, pour in all ingredients and stir well.
- Place wax paper on cookie sheet, pour candy on wax paper and spread out. Refrigerate 30 minutes to set. Break into pieces.

Diamond Fudge

1 (6 ounce) package semi-sweet chocolate morsels
1 cup creamy peanut butter
½ cup (1 stick) butter
1 cup powdered sugar

- Cook chocolate morsels, peanut butter and butter in saucepan over low heat, stirring constantly, just until mixture melts and is smooth. Remove from heat.
- Add powdered sugar and stir until smooth.
- Spoon into buttered 8-inch square pan and chill until firm. Cut into squares.

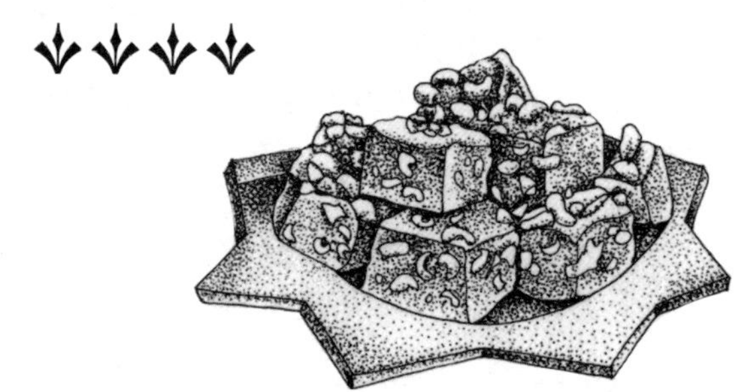

Peanut Butter Fudge

12 ounces chunky peanut butter
1 (12 ounce) package milk chocolate chips
1 (14 ounce) can sweetened condensed milk
1 cup chopped pecans

- In saucepan, combine peanut butter, chocolate chips and condensed milk. Heat on low, stirring constantly, until chocolate melts.
- Add pecans and mix well. Pour into 9 x 9-inch buttered dish.

Raisin Fudge

1 (12 ounce) package semi-sweet chocolate chips
1 cup chunky peanut butter
3 cups miniature marshmallows
¾ cup raisins

- In saucepan melt chocolate chips and peanut butter over medium to low heat.
- Fold in marshmallows and raisins and stir until marshmallows melt. Pour into 7 x 11-inch pan.
- Chill until firm. Cut into squares. Store where it is cool.

If you've ever over-beaten fudge so that it is too thick to pour into a pan, use your hands to shape it into logs. Then wrap the logs with plastic wrap, cool until firm, unwrap and slice.

Microwave Fudge

3 cups semi-sweet chocolate morsels
1 (14 ounce) can sweetened condensed milk
¼ cup (½ stick) butter, sliced
1 cup chopped walnuts

- Combine chocolate morsels, condensed milk and butter in 2-quart glass bowl.
- Microwave at MEDIUM for 4 to 5 minutes, stirring at 1½-minute intervals.
- Stir in walnuts and pour into buttered 8-inch square dish. Chill 2 hours. Cut into squares.

Dream Candy

2 (8 ounce) cartons whipping cream
3 cups sugar
1 cup light corn syrup
1 cup chopped pecans

- In saucepan combine whipping cream, sugar and corn syrup. Cook to soft-boil stage.
- Stir and beat until candy is cool.
- Add pecans and pour into 9-inch buttered pan.

Candy can be stored in an airtight container for 2 to 3 weeks. Keep in a cool, dry place.

Chocolate Toffee

1 cup sugar
1 cup (2 sticks) butter
1 (6 ounce) package chocolate chips
1 cup chopped pecans

- In heavy saucepan, combine sugar and butter. Cook until candy reaches hard-crack stage. Pour onto greased baking sheet.
- Melt chocolate in double boiler and spread over toffee.
- Sprinkle with pecans and press pecans into chocolate.
- Chill briefly to set chocolate. Break into pieces.

Quick Pralines

1 (3 ounce) box butterscotch cook-and-serve pudding
1¼ cups sugar
½ cup evaporated milk
2 cups pecan pieces

- In large saucepan, mix butterscotch pudding, sugar and milk.
- Bring to boil, stirring constantly, for 2 minutes. Add pecans and boil another 1½ minutes, stirring constantly.
- Remove from heat. Beat until candy begins to cool and drop by tablespoonfuls on wax paper.

Date-Loaf Candy

3 cups sugar
1 cup milk
1 (16 ounce) box chopped dates
1 cup chopped pecans

- Combine sugar and milk in large saucepan.
- Cook to soft-boil stage (234° on candy thermometer). Stir in dates. Cook to hard boil stage (260°), stirring constantly.
- Remove from heat, add pecans and mix well. Stir and cool until stiff. Pour mixture onto damp tea towel.
- Roll into log. Let stand until set. When candy is set, remove tea towel and slice.

Pecan-Topped Toffee

1 cup (2 sticks) butter
1¼ cups packed brown sugar
6 (1.5 ounce) milk chocolate bars
⅔ cup finely chopped pecans

- In saucepan combine butter and sugar. Cook on medium high heat, stirring constantly, until mixture reaches 300° on candy thermometer. Pour immediately into greased 9-inch baking pan.
- Lay chocolate bars evenly over hot candy. When candy is soft, spread into smooth layer.
- Sprinkle pecans over chocolate and press lightly with back of spoon. Chill in refrigerator for about 1 hour.
- Invert candy onto wax paper and break into small irregular pieces.

Yummy Pralines

½ cup (1 stick) butter
1 (16 ounce) box light brown sugar
1 (8 ounce) carton whipping cream
2½ cups whole pecans

- In heavy saucepan, combine butter, brown sugar and whipping cream.
- Cook until temperature comes to soft-ball stage (about 20 minutes), stirring constantly. Remove from heat and set aside for about 5 minutes.
- Fold in pecans and stir until ingredients are glassy. (This will take several minutes of stirring.)
- With large spoon, drop on wax paper. Remove after pralines cool.

Divinity Heaven

1 pint marshmallow cream
3 cups sugar
Pinch salt
⅔ cup chopped pecans

- Put marshmallow cream in large bowl.
- In saucepan, combine ½ cup water with sugar and salt. Bring to rolling boil for exactly 2 minutes.
- Pour sugar mixture into marshmallow cream and stir quickly.
- Add pecans and drop by teaspoonfuls onto wax paper.

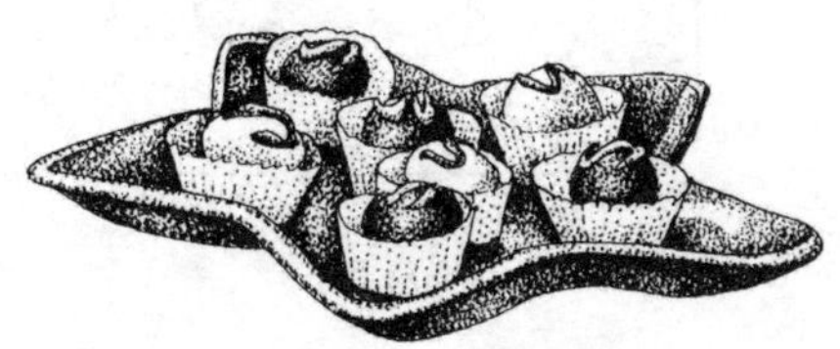

Butter Cookie Special

1 (18 ounce) box butter cake mix
1 (3.4 ounce) package butterscotch instant pudding mix
1 cup oil, 1 egg, beaten
1¼ cups chopped pecans

- Mix by hand cake mix, pudding mix, oil and egg. Beat thoroughly.
- Stir in pecans. With teaspoon place cookie dough on cookie sheet about 2 inches apart.
- Bake at 350° for about 8 minutes. Do not overcook.

Cheesecake Cookies

1 cup (2 sticks) butter, softened
2 (3 ounce) packages cream cheese, softened
2 cups sugar
2 cups flour

- Cream butter and cream cheese. Add sugar and beat until light and fluffy. Add flour and beat well.
- Drop by teaspoons onto cookie sheet and bake at 350° for 12 to 15 minutes or until edges are golden.

Tip: These are even better if you add 1 cup chopped pecans.

Cookies should always be completely cool before storing or they will get soggy.

Double-Chocolate Cookies

6 egg whites
3 cups powdered sugar
¼ cup cocoa
3½ cups finely chopped pecans

- Beat egg whites until light and frothy. Fold sugar and cocoa into egg whites and beat lightly. Fold in pecans.
- Drop by teaspoons on lightly greased, floured cookie sheet.
- Bake at 325° for about 20 minutes. Do not overbake and cool completely before removing from cookie sheet.

Nutty Fudgies

1 (18 ounce) package fudge cake mix
1 (8 ounce) carton sour cream
⅔ cup peanut butter chips
½ cup chopped peanuts

- Beat cake mix and sour cream until mixture blends well and is smooth. Stir in peanut butter chips and peanuts.
- Drop by teaspoonfuls onto greased cookie sheet.
- Bake at 350° for 10 to 12 minutes.
- Remove from oven and cool.

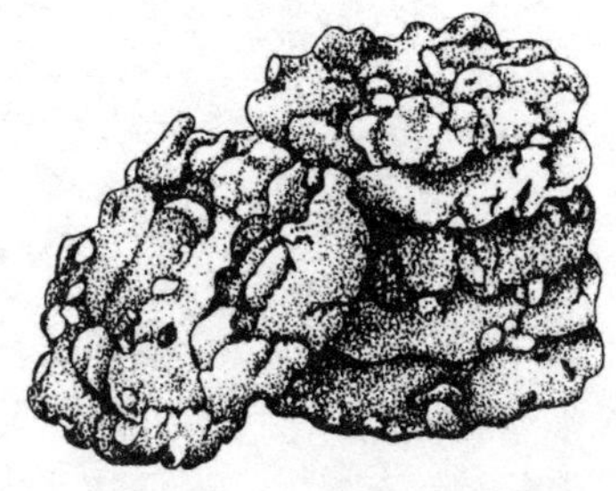

Peanut Butter Cookies

1 cup sugar
¾ cup light corn syrup
1 (16 ounce) jar crunchy peanut butter
4½ cups chow mein noodles

- In saucepan over medium heat bring sugar and corn syrup to boil and stir in peanut butter.
- Remove from heat and stir in noodles.
- Drop by spoonfuls onto wax paper and allow to cool.

Butterscotch Cookies

1 (12 ounce) and 1 (6 ounce) package butterscotch chips
2¼ cups chow mein noodles
½ cup chopped walnuts
¼ cup flaked coconut

- Melt butterscotch chips in double boiler. Add noodles, walnuts and coconut.
- Drop by tablespoonfuls onto wax paper.

Pecan Puffs

2 egg whites
¾ cup packed light brown sugar
1 teaspoon vanilla
1 cup chopped pecans

- Beat egg whites until foamy. Gradually add, ¼ cup at a time, brown sugar and vanilla. Continue beating until stiff peaks form (about 3 or 4 minutes). Fold in pecans.
- Line cookie sheet with freezer paper. Drop by teaspoonfuls onto freezer paper.
- Bake at 250° for 45 minutes.

No-Cook Lemon Balls

2 cups graham cracker crumbs, almond or pecan shortbread cookie crumbs, divided
1 (6 ounce) can frozen lemonade concentrate, thawed
½ cup (1 stick) butter, softened
1 (16 ounce) box powdered sugar, sifted

- Combine 1½ cups cookie crumbs, lemonade concentrate, butter and powdered sugar. Shape into small balls.
- Roll in reserved cookie crumbs and put on wax paper.
- Refrigerate 3 to 4 hours in sealed container or freeze to serve later.

Nutty Blonde Brownies

1 (1 pound) box light brown sugar
4 eggs
2 cups biscuit mix
2 cups chopped pecans

- In mixing bowl, beat brown sugar, eggs and biscuit mix. Stir in pecans and pour into greased 9 x 13-inch baking pan.
- Bake at 350° for 35 minutes. Cool and cut into squares.

Chocolate Chip Cheese Bars

1 (18 ounce) tube refrigerated chocolate chip cookie dough
1 (8 ounce) package cream cheese, softened
½ cup sugar
1 egg

- Cut cookie dough in half. For crust, press half dough onto bottom of greased 9-inch square baking pan or 7 x 11-inch baking pan.
- In mixing bowl, beat cream cheese, sugar and egg until smooth. Spread over crust. Crumble remaining dough over top.
- Bake at 350° for 35 to 40 minutes or until toothpick inserted near center comes out clean.
- Cool on wire rack. Cut into bars. Refrigerate leftovers.

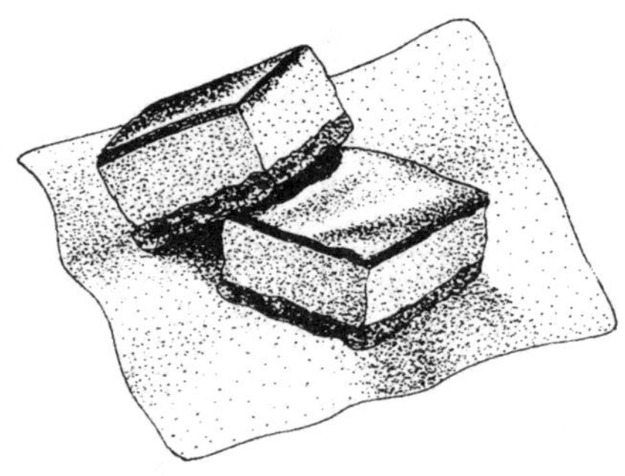

Walnut Bars

1 ⅔ cups graham cracker crumbs
1½ cups coarsely chopped walnuts
1 (14 ounce) can sweetened condensed milk
¼ cup flaked coconut, optional

- Place graham cracker crumbs and walnuts in bowl. Slowly add condensed milk, coconut and pinch of salt. Mixture will be very thick.
- Pack into 9-inch square greased pan. Pack mixture down with back of spoon.
- Bake at 350° for 35 minutes. When cool cut into squares.

Chocolate Drops

1 (12 ounce) package milk chocolate chips
⅔ cup chunky peanut butter
4 cups cocoa-flavored, crispy rice cereal
½ cup pecans, chopped

- In double boiler, melt chocolate chips. Stir in peanut butter, cereal and pecans.
- Press into 9 x 9-inch pan. Cut into bars.

Tip: Chocolate chips hold their shape when melted, so don't wait for them to "look" melted or you'll singe the chocolate.

Honey-Nut Bars

⅓ cup (⅔ stick) butter
¼ cup cocoa
1 (10 ounce) package miniature marshmallows
6 cups honey-nut clusters cereal

- Melt butter in large saucepan and stir in cocoa and marshmallows.
- Cook over low heat, stirring constantly, until marshmallows melt and mixture is smooth.
- Remove from heat and stir in honey-nut clusters.
- Pour into sprayed 7 x 11-inch pan. With spatula smooth mixture in pan.
- Cool completely and cut into bars.

Raisin Crunch

¾ cup light corn syrup
1 cup sugar
1 cup crunchy peanut butter
1 (20 ounce) box raisin bran

- In saucepan combine corn syrup and sugar. Heat until sugar thoroughly dissolves. Remove from heat and stir in peanut butter.
- Place raisin bran in large container and pour sauce over top. Mix thoroughly.
- Pat mixture into 9 x 13-inch pan and completely chill.
- Cut into squares and store in airtight container.

Peanut Clusters

1 (24 ounce) package almond bark
1 (12 ounce) package milk chocolate chips
4 cups salted peanuts
1 cup raisins

- In double boiler, melt almond bark and chocolate chips.
- Stir in peanuts and raisins. Drop by teaspoonfuls onto wax paper.
- Chill for 30 minutes to set. Store in airtight container.

Caramel-Apple Cupcakes

1 (18 ounce) package carrot cake mix
3 cups chopped, peeled tart apples
1 (12 ounce) package butterscotch chips
1 cup finely chopped pecans

- Make cake batter according to package directions. Fold in apples. Fill 12 greased or paper-lined jumbo muffin cups ¾ full.
- Bake at 350° for 20 minutes or until toothpick comes out clean.
- In saucepan on very low heat melt butterscotch chips. Spread over cupcakes and sprinkle with chopped pecans.

Always taste nuts before using them. Rancid nuts will ruin whatever food they flavor so buy in small amounts from super markets with rapid turn over.

Scotch Crunchies

½ cup crunchy peanut butter
1 (6 ounce) package butterscotch bits
2½ cups frosted flakes
½ cup peanuts

- Combine peanut butter and butterscotch bits in large saucepan and melt over low heat. Stir until butterscotch bits melt. Stir in cereal and peanuts. Drop by teaspoonfuls onto wax paper. Chill until firm. Store in airtight container.

Pumpkin Cupcakes

1 (18 ounce) package spice cake mix
1 (15 ounce) can pumpkin
3 eggs
⅓ cup oil

- Blend cake mix, pumpkin, eggs, oil and ⅓ cup water and beat for 2 minutes. Pour into 24 paper-lined muffin cups and fill ¾ full.
- Bake at 350° for 18 to 20 minutes or until toothpick inserted in center comes out clean. Spread with commercial icing if you like.

Tasty Treat

1 (12 ounce) package butterscotch morsels
2 cups salted peanuts
1 cup white raisins
2 cups cinnamon-swirl cereal

- Mix all ingredients and store in airtight container.

Macaroon Delight

12 soft coconut macaroons
1 (8 ounce) carton whipping cream, whipped
3 pints sherbet: 1 orange, 1 lime, 1 raspberry, softened

- Warm macaroons at 300° for 10 minutes, break into pieces and cool.
- Spoon macaroons into whipped cream.
- Completely line 9 x 5-inch loaf pan with foil. First spread 1 pint orange sherbet in loaf pan.
- Spread half whipped cream mixture, next lime sherbet and remaining whipped cream mixture. Raspberry sherbet goes on top.
- Freeze overnight.
- To serve remove from mold foil and slice.

Brown Sugar Cookies

¾ cup packed brown sugar
1 cup (2 sticks) butter, softened
1 egg yolk
2 cups flour

- Cream sugar and butter until light and fluffy. Mix in egg yolk. Blend in flour. Refrigerate dough for 1 hour.
- Form dough into 1-inch balls, flatten and criss-cross with fork on lightly greased baking sheet.
- Bake at 325° for 10 to 12 minutes or until golden brown.

Creamy Cherry-Lime Pie

2 (8 ounce) cartons lime yogurt
⅓ cup chopped maraschino cherries, divided
1 (8 ounce) carton frozen whipped topping, thawed
1 (9-inch) graham cracker piecrust

- Stir yogurt and ¼ cup cherries.
- Fold in whipped topping.
- Spoon mixture into graham cracker crust and garnish with chopped cherries.
- Refrigerate 6 to 8 hours or until firm.

Five-Citrus Cream Pie

1 (6 ounce) can frozen five-citrus concentrate, partially thawed
1 (4 ounce) can sweetened condensed milk
1 (8 ounce) carton frozen whipped topping, thawed
1 (9 inch) graham cracker piecrust

- Stir sweetened condensed milk and five-citrus concentrate until they blend well.
- Fold into whipped topping and spoon mixture into graham cracker crust.
- Refrigerate 6 to 8 hours.

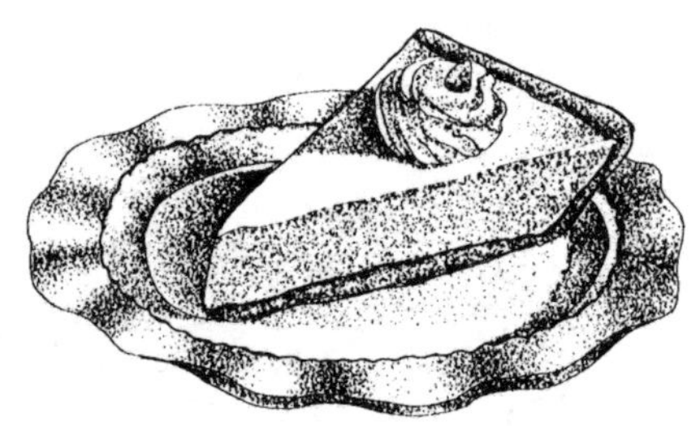

Million-Dollar Pie

24 round, buttery crackers, crumbled
1 cup chopped pecans
4 egg whites (absolutely no yolks at all)
1 cup sugar

- Mix cracker crumbs with pecans.
- In separate mixing bowl, beat egg whites until stiff and slowly add sugar while still mixing.
- Gently fold in crumbs and pecan mixture into egg whites. Pour into pie tin and bake at 350° for 20 minutes.
- Cool before serving.

Apricot Pie

2 (15 ounce) cans apricot halves, drained
1¼ cups sugar
¼ cup flour
1 (8 ounce) carton whipping cream

- Cut each apricot half into 2 pieces and arrange evenly in unbaked, 9-inch pie shell.
- Combine sugar and flour and sprinkle over apricots.
- Pour whipped cream over pie.
- Place 1-inch strips foil over edge of pie crust to keep from browning too much. Bake at 325° for 1 hour 20 minutes.

Tip: You might want to place pie on a cookie sheet to catch any possible spillovers.

Apricot-Chiffon Pie

2 (6 ounce) cartons apricot-mango yogurt
1 (3 ounce) box apricot gelatin
1 (8 ounce) carton whipped topping
1 (6 ounce) prepared shortbread piecrust

- In bowl, combine yogurt and gelatin and mix well.
- Fold in whipped topping, spread in piecrust and freeze.
- Take out of freezer 20 minutes before slicing.

Holiday Pie

1 (8 ounce) package cream cheese, softened
1 (14 ounce) can sweetened condensed milk
1 (3.4 ounce) box instant vanilla pudding mix
1½ cups whipped topping

- With mixer, beat cream cheese until smooth. Gradually add sweetened condensed milk and beat until smooth.
- Add ¾ cup water and pudding mix and beat until smooth.
- Fold in whipped topping and pour into graham cracker piecrust.
- Top with crumbled holiday candies and refrigerate.

Cheesecake Pie

1 (20 ounce) can strawberry pie filling, divided
2 cups milk
2 (3.4 ounce) packages instant cheesecake-flavored pudding mix
½ (8 ounce) carton whipped topping, thawed

- Spoon ¾ cup pie filling into graham cracker piecrust.
- In mixing bowl, combine milk and pudding mixes and beat for 2 minutes or until smooth. Mixture will be thick.
- Fold in whipped topping and spoon over pie filling in crust.
- Refrigerate at least 3 hours. When ready to serve, top with remaining pie filling.

Patrick's Pie

1 (8 ounce) package cream cheese, softened
Heaping ⅓ cup sugar
1 (8 ounce) carton frozen whipped topping, thawed
1 cup chopped grasshopper cookies

- With mixer, beat cream cheese and sugar and blend well.
- Fold in whipped topping and mix well.
- Add cookies and about 3 drops green food coloring, if you like.
- Pour into prepared, chocolate piecrust and garnish with extra crumbled cookies.
- Freeze.

Easy Pumpkin Pie

1 (9-inch) unbaked deep-dish pie shell
2 eggs
1 (30 ounce) can pumpkin pie mix
1 (5 ounce) can evaporated milk

- Beat eggs lightly in large bowl, stir in pumpkin pie mix and evaporated milk.
- Pour into pie shell.
- Cut 2-inch strips of foil and cover piecrust edges. This will keep piecrust from getting too brown.
- Bake at 400° for 15 minutes. Reduce temperature to 325° and bake for 40 more minutes or until knife inserted in center comes out clean. Cool.

Easy Chocolate Pie

1 frozen piecrust, cooked
1 (16 ounce) carton frozen whipped topping, thawed, divided
1 (8 ounce) milk chocolate candy bar
¾ cup chopped pecans

- In saucepan, break candy into small pieces and melt over low heat.
- Remove and cool several minutes.
- Fold in ⅔ whipped topping and mix well.
- Stir in chopped pecans and pour into piecrust.
- Spread remaining whipped topping over top of pie and refrigerate at least 8 hours.

Coffee Mallow

3 cups miniature marshmallows
½ cup hot, strong coffee
1 cup whipping cream, whipped
½ teaspoon vanilla

- In large saucepan, combine marshmallows and coffee. On low heat, stirring constantly, cook until marshmallows melt. Cool this mixture.
- Fold in whipped cream and vanilla.
- Pour into individual dessert glasses.
- Stir until ready to serve.

Brandied Apples

1 (10 ounce) loaf pound cake
1 (20 ounce) can apple pie filling
½ teaspoon allspice
2 tablespoons brandy

- Slice pound cake and place on dessert plates.
- In saucepan, combine pie filling, allspice and brandy. Heat and stir just until mixture heats thoroughly.
- Place several spoonfuls over cake.
- Top with scoop of vanilla ice cream.

Grape Fluff

1 cup grape juice
2 cups miniature marshmallows
2 tablespoons lemon juice
1 (8 ounce) carton whipping cream

- In saucepan heat grape juice to boiling. Add marshmallows and stir constantly until they melt.
- Add lemon juice and cool.
- Fold in whipped cream and spoon into individual serving dishes. Chill.

Blueberry Fluff

1 (20 ounce) can blueberry pie filling
1 (20 ounce) can crushed pineapple, drained
1 (14 ounce) can sweetened condensed milk
1 (8 ounce) carton whipped topping

- Mix pie filling, pineapple and condensed milk.
- Fold in whipped topping. (This dessert is even better if you add ¾ cup chopped pecans).
- Combine all ingredients and pour into parfait glasses. Chill.

Peachy Sundaes

1 pint vanilla ice cream
¾ cup peach preserves, warmed
¼ cup chopped almonds, toasted
¼ cup flaked coconut

- Divide ice cream into 4 sherbet dishes.
- Top with preserves.
- Sprinkle with almonds and coconut.

Peanut Butter Sundae

1 cup light corn syrup
1 cup chunky peanut butter
¼ cup milk
Ice cream or pound cake

- In mixing bowl, stir corn syrup, peanut butter and milk until they blend well.
- Serve over ice cream or pound cake. Store in refrigerator.

Nuts are one of the easiest dessert garnishes to create. You can chop them finely or grind and put them in a sieve for sprinkling over cakes, puddings or ice cream.

Amaretto Ice Cream

1 (8 ounce) carton whipping cream, whipped
1 pint vanilla ice cream, softened
⅓ cup amaretto
⅓ cup chopped almonds, toasted

- Combine whipped cream, ice cream and amaretto. Freeze in sherbet glasses.
- When ready to serve, drizzle a little additional amaretto over top of each individual serving and sprinkle with toasted almonds.

Mango Cream

2 soft mangoes
½ gallon vanilla ice cream, softened
1 (6 ounce) can frozen lemonade, thawed
1 (8 ounce) carton whipped topping

- Peel mangoes, cut slices around seed and cut into small chunks.
- In large bowl, mix ice cream, lemonade and whipped topping.
- Fold in mango chunks.
- Quickly spoon mixture into parfait glasses or sherbets and cover with plastic wrap. Place in freezer.

Tip: Select mangoes that are unblemished and have yellow skin blushed with red. The larger the mango, the higher the fruit-to-seed ratio.

Easy Cooking with 5 Ingredients

By Barbara C. Jones

cookbook resources® LLC

Easy Cooking with 5 Ingredients

Ist Printing – October 2001

2nd Printing – July 2002

3rd Printing – November 2002

4th Printing – January 2003

5th Printing – September 2004

6th Printing – February 2005

ISBN 1-931294-86-0 (hard bound)

Library of Congress Number 2004115661

ISBN 1-931294-87-9 (paper cover)

Library of Congress Number: 2004115660

Illustrations by Nancy Murphy Griffith

Edited, Designed, Published and Manufactured in the United States of America by

Cookbook Resources, LLC

541 Doubletree Drive

Highland Village, Texas 75077

Toll free 866-229-2665

www.cookbookresources.com

Introduction

We are all in a hurry today and **Easy Cooking With 5 Ingredients** is the "hurry up" way to great meals, easy cooking and the best way to get those compliments from family and friends. Raves are in order when you make the Unbelievable Crab Dip, the Great Guacamole Dip or the Fiesta Dip. Crabmeat is the wonderful seafood that is just as good canned or fresh. And the Fiesta Dip has a little different twist to the typical Mexican Dip. Stretch your world to the luscious mango and papaya - - eating healthy at the same time. The Tropical Mango Salad is hard to beat!

Whoever heard of spinach sandwiches? They are delicious, creamy and flavorful - - perfect for home or afternoon snack. You'll never go wrong on the Butter-Mint Salad - -it has a fabulous Hawaiian flavor and goes well with any entrée. It is so good you could even use it as a dessert.

Now when you're looking for a wonderful chicken dinner for family or friends, the Chicken Marseilles will set your meal apart while taking only a few minutes to "put together." And the Green Bean Revenge will call for a large glass of cold water, but the "hot and spicy" will put your taste buds in high gear. Mash potatoes are usually family fare, but Ranch Mashed Potatoes will give the potatoes a company taste. Any when you are looking for the extra special company flair, try the Chicken Ole or the Carnival Couscous. The couscous has your colorful vegetables and makes a really special dish. For the great ending, the Sunny Lime Pie or the Apricot Cobbler are so quick and easy to make (and good), you'll put it on the menu often.

How many times have you needed to rush foods to the home of a friend in need? The Favorite Cake will be the one you choose - - and all the ingredients can be kept on your pantry shelf (except the eggs, but you will have them in the refrigerator). Your **Easy Cooking With 5 Ingredients** Cookbook will give you lots of ideas for "easy fixin" foods to take for that best friend, your church or party where everybody pitches in.

"Dig In" to the cookbook with great dishes that have only 5 ingredients and give you 3 easy steps to "kitchen fame."

Barbara C. Jones

Contents

Easy Cooking with 5 Ingredients

Hurrah for Shrimp

The creole (or cajun) seasoning is the key to this great dip!

1 (8 ounce) package cream cheese, softened
½ cup mayonnaise
1 (6 ounce) can tiny, cooked shrimp, drained
1¼ teaspoons creole (or cajun) seasoning
1 tablespoon lemon juice

- Blend cream cheese and mayonnaise in mixer until creamy.
- Add shrimp, seasoning and lemon juice and whip only until they mix well.
- Serve with chips.

Favorite Stand-By Shrimp Dip

2 cups cooked, veined shrimp, finely chopped
2 tablespoons horseradish
½ cup chili sauce
¾ cup mayonnaise
1 tablespoon lemon juice

- Combine all ingredients with a few sprinkles of salt and refrigerate. (If shrimp is frozen, be sure to drain well.)
- Serve with cucumber or zucchini slices.

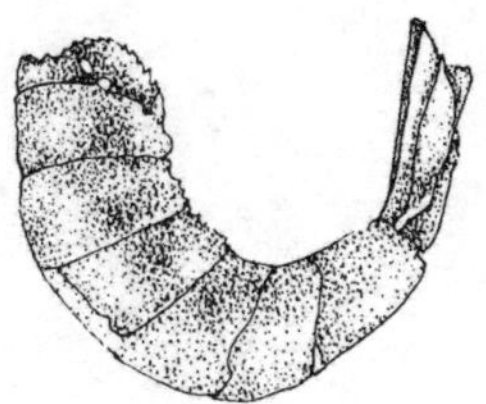

Fiesta Dip

1 (15 ounce) can tamales
1 (16 ounce) can chili without beans
1 cup picante sauce
2 (5 ounce) jars Old English cheese
1 cup finely chopped onion

- Mash tamales with fork.
- In saucepan, combine all ingredients and heat to mix.
- Serve hot with crackers or chips.

Unbelievable Crab Dip

Absolutely delicious!

1 (16 ounce) box processed cheese
2 (6½ ounce) cans crabmeat, drained
1 bunch fresh green onions with tops, chopped
2 cups mayonnaise
½ teaspoon seasoned salt

- Melt cheese in top of double boiler. Add remaining ingredients.
- Serve hot or at room temperature with wheat crackers.

Tip: Don't count on your guests leaving the dip table until this dip is gone!

❖❖❖❖❖

Jump-In Crab Dip

This is so good you will wish you had doubled the recipe!

1 (6 ounce) can white crabmeat
1 (8 ounce) package cream cheese
½ cup (1 stick) butter
Chips for dipping

- In saucepan, combine crabmeat, cream cheese and butter. Heat and mix thoroughly.
- Transfer to hot chafing dish.
- Serve with chips.

Seafood-Dip Kick

1 (8 ounce) package cream cheese, softened
3 tablespoons salsa
2 tablespoons prepared horseradish
1 (6 ounce) can crabmeat, drained, flaked
1 (6 ounce) can shrimp, drained, flaked

- In mixing bowl, beat cream cheese until creamy, add salsa and horseradish and mix well.
- Stir in the crabmeat and shrimp. Chill.
- Serve with assorted crackers.

Zippy Broccoli-Cheese Dip

1 (10 ounce) package frozen chopped broccoli, thawed, drained
2 tablespoons butter
2 ribs celery, chopped
1 small onion, finely chopped
1 (1 pound) box mild Mexican processed cheese, cubed

- Make sure broccoli is thoroughly thawed and drained. Place butter in large saucepan and saute broccoli, celery and onion at medium heat for about 5 minutes. Stir often.
- Add cheese and heat, stirring constantly, just until cheese melts.
- Serve hot with chips.

Tip: If you want the "zip" to be zippier, use hot Mexican processed cheese instead of mild.

Spicy Beef and Cheese Dip

1 (10 ounce) can tomatoes and green chilies
½ teaspoon garlic powder
1 teaspoon seasoned salt
1 (2 pound) package cubed processed cheese
1 pound lean ground beef, browned, cooked

- In large saucepan, place tomatoes and green chilies, garlic, seasoned salt and cheese. (Use a mild Mexican processed cheese if you prefer spicy.)
- Heat on low until cheese melts.
- Add ground beef and mix well.
- Serve with tortilla chips.

Veggie Dive Dip

1 cup mayonnaise
1 (8 ounce) carton sour cream
1½ teaspoons Beau Monde seasoning
1 teaspoon dill weed
2 tablespoons parsley
1 bunch green onions, chopped

- Stir all ingredients and chill. Better if made a day ahead.
- Serve with celery sticks, broccoli florets, jicama sticks or carrot sticks.

The Big Dipper

1 (15 ounce) can chili (no beans)
1 (10 ounce) can tomatoes and green chilies
1 (16 ounce) package cubed processed cheese
½ cup chopped green onions
½ teaspoon cayenne pepper

- In saucepan, combine all ingredients. Heat just until cheese melts, stirring constantly.
- Serve warm with assorted dippers or toasted French breadsticks.

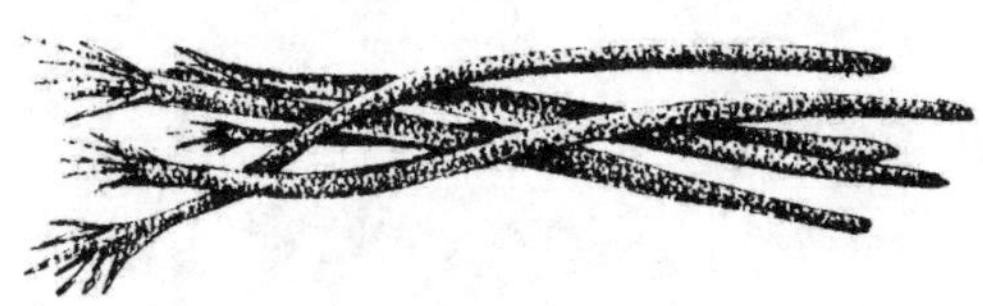

Sassy Onion Dip

Plain and simple, but great!

1 (8 ounce) package cream cheese, softened
1 (8 ounce) carton sour cream
½ cup chili sauce
1 (1 ounce) package dry onion soup mix
1 tablespoon lemon juice

- In mixing bowl, beat cream cheese until fluffy. Add remaining ingredients and mix well.
- Cover and chill. Serve with strips of raw zucchini, celery, carrots, or other veggies.

Hot Corn Dip

1 (15 ounce) can whole kernel corn, drained
1 (7 ounce) can chopped green chilies, drained
½ cup chopped sweet red pepper
1½ cups shredded Colby and Monterey Jack cheese
¼ cup mayonnaise

- In bowl, combine corn, chilies, red pepper and cheeses. Stir in mayonnaise. (Adding ½ cup chopped walnuts makes this dip even better.)
- Transfer to ungreased 2-quart baking dish.
- Cover and bake at 325° for 35 minutes. Serve hot with tortilla chips.

Tip: Sometimes the green chilies are not very hot, so I like to add a pinch or two of red pepper.

Ham-It-Up Dip

2 (8 ounce) packages cream cheese, softened
2 (6 ounce) cans deviled ham
2 heaping tablespoons horseradish
¼ cup minced onion
¼ cup finely chopped celery

- In mixing bowl, beat cream cheese until creamy.
- Add all other ingredients
- Chill and serve with crackers.

Tip: This will also make little party sandwiches with party rye bread.

Roquefort Dip

1 (8 ounce) package cream cheese, softened
2 cups mayonnaise
1 small onion, finely grated
1 (3 ounce) package roquefort cheese, crumbled
⅛ teaspoon garlic powder

- In mixing bowl, combine cream cheese and mayonnaise. Beat until creamy.
- Add onion, roquefort cheese and garlic powder and mix well. Refrigerate.
- Serve with zucchini sticks, turnip sticks or cauliflower flowerets.

Great Guacamole

4 avocados, peeled
1 tablespoon lemon juice
About ½ cup salsa
¼ cup sour cream
1 teaspoon salt

- Split avocados and remove seeds. Mash avocado with fork.
- Add lemon juice, salsa, sour cream and salt.
- Serve with tortilla chips.

Avocado-Onion Dip

1 (1 ounce) package dry golden onion soup mix
1 (8 ounce) carton sour cream
½ cup mayonnaise
2 ripe avocados, mashed
1 tablespoon lemon juice

- Mix all ingredients, but work quickly so avocados do not turn dark.
- Serve with wheat crackers.

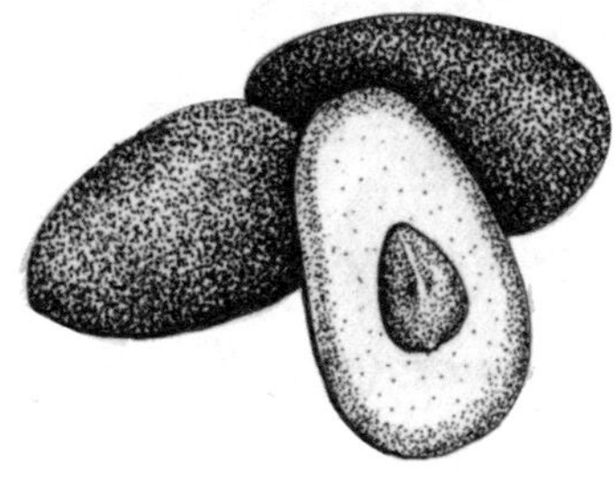

Tasty Tuna Spread

1 (6 ounce) can solid white tuna, drained, flaked
1 (1 ounce) package dry zesty Italian salad dressing mix
1 tablespoon lemon juice
1 (8 ounce) carton sour cream
3 green onions with tops, chopped

- Combine all ingredients and stir until they blend. Chill.
- Serve with melba rounds.

Cucumber Dip or Spread

2 medium cucumbers
2 (8 ounce) packages cream cheese, softened
Several drops hot sauce
1 (1 ounce) package dry ranch dressing mix
½ teaspoon garlic powder

- Peel cucumbers, cut in half lengthwise and scoop out seeds. Chop cucumbers in very fine pieces (or in food processor).
- In mixing bowl, combine cream cheese, hot sauce, dressing mix and garlic powder and beat until creamy.
- Combine cucumbers and cream cheese mixture and mix well. Serve with chips.

Tip: About ½ cup chopped pecans makes this dip even better.

Tip: This dip makes great "party" sandwiches made with thin, sliced white bread. If you do use it for sandwiches, make sure you squeeze all the water out of the cucumbers.

Blue Cheese Crisps

2 (4 ounce) packages crumbled blue cheese
½ cup (1 stick) butter, softened
1 ⅓ cups flour
⅓ cup poppy seeds
¼ teaspoon ground red pepper

- Beat blue cheese and butter at medium speed until fluffy. Add flour, poppy seeds and red pepper and beat until they blend.
- Divide dough in half, shape each portion into 9-inch log. Cover and refrigerate 2 hours.
- Cut each log into ¼-inch slices and place on ungreased baking sheet. Bake at 350° for 13 to 15 minutes or until golden grown. Cool.

Party Smokies

1 cup ketchup
1 cup plum jelly
1 tablespoon lemon juice
4 tablespoons prepared mustard
1 (5 ounce) packages tiny smoked sausages

- In saucepan, combine all ingredients except sausages, heat and mix well.
- Add sausages and simmer for 10 minutes.
- Serve hot with cocktail toothpicks.

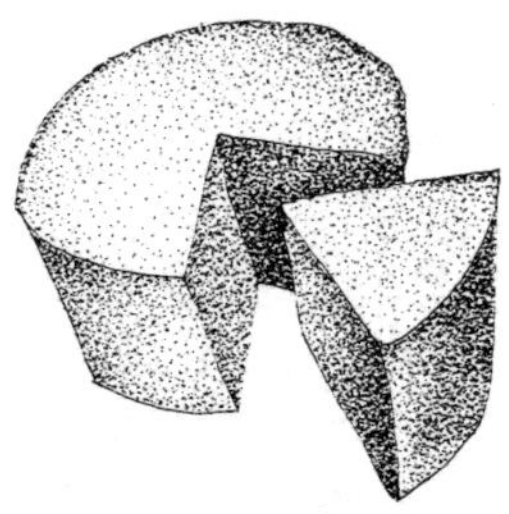

Sausage-Pineapple Bits

The "sweet and hot" makes a delicious combo.

1 pound link sausage, cooked, skinned
1 pound hot bulk sausage
1 (15 ounce) can crushed pineapple with juice
2 cups packed brown sugar
1 tablespoon white wine worcestershire sauce

- Slice link sausage into ⅓-inch pieces. Shape bulk sausage into 1-inch balls.
- In skillet, brown sausage balls.
- In large saucepan, combine pineapple, brown sugar and white worcestershire.
- Heat and add both sausages. Simmer for 30 minutes. Serve from chafing dish or small slow cooker with cocktail picks.

Sausage Balls

2 cups biscuit mix
1 pound hot sausage
1 cup shredded cheddar cheese

- Mix biscuit mix, sausage and cheese with wooden spoon. (You may want use your own hands to mix.)
- Shape into 1-inch balls, place on cookie sheet and bake at 350° for about 20 minutes.

Tip: These will freeze nicely.

Raspberry-Glazed Wings

¾ cup seedless raspberry jam
¼ cup cider vinegar
¼ cup soy sauce
1 teaspoon garlic powder
16 (about 3 pounds) whole chicken wings

- In saucepan, combine jam, vinegar, soy sauce, garlic and 1 teaspoon black pepper. Bring to a boil for 1 minute.
- Cut chicken wings into 3 sections and discard wing tips. Place wings in large bowl, add raspberry mixture and toss to coat. Cover and refrigerate for 4 hours.
- Line 10 x 15 inch-baking pan with foil and grease foil. Use slotted spoon to place wings in pan and reserve marinade.
- Bake at 350° for 30 minutes ad turn once. Cook reserved marinade for 10 minutes, brush over wings and bake 25 minutes longer.

Cocktail Ham Roll-Ups

1 (3 ounce) package cream cheese, softened
1 teaspoon finely grated onion
Mayonnaise
1 (3 ounce) package sliced ham
1 (15 ounce) can asparagus spears

- Combine cream cheese, grated onion and enough mayonnaise to make spreading consistency.
- Separate sliced ham, spread mixture on slices, place 1 or 2 asparagus spears on ham and roll. Cut each roll into 4 pieces.
- Spear each piece with toothpick for serving and chill.

Tip: This is great for a salad luncheon.

Green Eyes

Here's lookin' at ya!

4 medium dill pickles
4 slices boiled ham
Light cream cheese, softened
Black pepper
Seasoned salt

- Dry pickles with paper towels. Lightly coat 1 side of ham slices with cream cheese and sprinkle on a little pepper and seasoned salt. Roll pickle up in ham slice coated with cream cheese.
- Chill and slice into circles to serve.

Mini-Reubens

½ cup Thousand Island salad dressing
24 slices party rye bread
1⅓ cups well drained, chopped sauerkraut
½ pound thinly sliced, corned beef
¼ pound sliced Swiss cheese

- Spread dressing on slices of bread. Place 1 slice corned beef on bread and top with sauerkraut.
- Cut cheese same size of bread and place over sauerkraut.
- Place open-face sandwiches on cookie sheet. Bake at 375° for 10 minutes or until cheese melts.

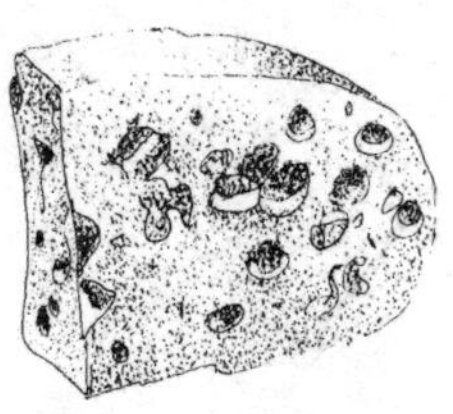

Oyster-Bites Bacon

1 (5 ounce) can smoked oysters, drained, chopped
⅔ cup herb-seasoned stuffing mix, crushed
½ teaspoon black pepper
¼ cup water
8 slices bacon, halved, partially cooked

- Combine oysters, stuffing mix, black pepper and water. Add another teaspoon water if mixture seems too dry. Form into balls with about 1 tablespoon mixture for each.
- Wrap ½ slice bacon around each and secure with toothpick. Place on rack in shallow baking pan.
- Cook at 350° for 25 to 30 minutes or until bacon is crisp.

No-Fuss Meatballs

1 (14 ounce) package frozen cooked meatballs, thawed
1 tablespoon soy sauce
½ cup chili sauce
⅔ cup grape or plum jelly
¼ cup Dijon-style mustard

- In skillet, cook meatballs in soy sauce until heated through.
- Combine chili sauce, jelly and mustard and pour over meatballs. Cook and stir until jelly dissolves and mixture comes to a boil.
- Reduce heat, cover and simmer for about 5 minutes.

Olive-Cheese Balls

2¼ cups shredded sharp cheddar cheese
1 cup flour
⅛ teaspoon cayenne pepper
½ cup (1 stick) butter, melted
1 (5 ounce) jar green olives

- In large bowl, combine cheese, flour and cayenne pepper. Add butter and mix well.
- Cover olives with mixture and form into balls.
- Bake at 350° for about 15 minutes or until light brown.

Caviar-Artichoke Delights

2 (8 ounce) packages cream cheese, softened
1 (14 ounce) can artichoke hearts, drained, chopped
½ cup finely grated onion
1 (3 ounce) jar caviar, drained
3 hard-boiled eggs, grated

- Beat cream cheese until smooth and add artichoke hearts and onion.
- Spread in 8 or 9-inch glass pie plate and chill.
- Before serving, spread caviar on top of cream cheese mixture and place grated, hard-boiled eggs on top. Serve with crackers.

Hot Artichoke Spread

1 (14 ounce) can artichoke hearts, drained, finely chopped
1 (4 ounce) can chopped green chilies
1 cup mayonnaise
1 (8 ounce) package shredded mozzarella cheese
½ teaspoon garlic powder

- Remove any spikes or tough leaves from artichoke hearts.
- Combine all ingredients and mix thoroughly. Pour into 9-inch square baking pan and sprinkle some paprika over top.
- Bake at 325° for 25 minutes. Serve hot with assorted crackers.

Walnut-Cheese Spread

1 (16 ounce) package shredded cheddar cheese
3 green onions, chopped
¾ cup walnuts, roasted, chopped
½ to ¾ cup mayonnaise
½ teaspoon liquid smoke

- Combine all ingredients and let stand in refrigerator overnight. (To roast walnuts, place in oven set on 250° for 10 minutes.)
- Spread on assorted crackers.

Smoked Oyster Spread

1 (8 ounce) package cream cheese, softened
3 tablespoons mayonnaise
1 (3½ ounce) can smoked oysters, chopped
½ teaspoon onion salt
2 tablespoons grated parmesan cheese

- Whip cream cheese and mayonnaise until creamy.
- Add oysters, onion salt and cheese.
- Mix well and dip or spread on crackers.

Ginger Fruit Dip

1 (3 ounce) package cream cheese, softened
1 (7 ounce) jar marshmallow cream
½ cup mayonnaise
1 teaspoon ground ginger
1 teaspoon grated orange rind

- Beat cream cheese at medium speed until smooth, add marshmallow cream and next 3 ingredients. Stir until smooth.
- Serve with fresh fruit sticks.

Kahlua-Fruit Dip

1 (8 ounce) package cream cheese, softened
1 (8 ounce) carton whipped topping
⅔ cup packed brown sugar
⅓ cup kahlua
1 (8 ounce) carton sour cream

- With mixer, whip cream cheese until creamy and fold in whipped topping.
- Add sugar, kahlua and sour cream and mix well.
- Chill for 24 hours before serving with fresh fruit.

Peanut Butter Spread

1 (8 ounce) package cream cheese, softened
1 ⅔ cups creamy peanut butter
½ cup powdered sugar
¼ teaspoon ground cinnamon
1 tablespoon milk

- In mixer, cream all ingredients.
- Serve spread with apple wedges or graham crackers.

Ambrosia Spread

1 (11 ounce) can mandarin orange sections, drained
1 (8 ounce) container soft cream cheese with pineapple, softened
¼ cup flaked coconut, toasted
¼ cup almonds, slivered, chopped, toasted

- Chop orange sections and set aside.
- Whip cream cheese and fold in coconut and almonds.
- Spread on date-nut bread, banana bread, etc.

Green-Olive Spread

1 (8 ounce) package cream cheese, softened
½ cup mayonnaise
½ cup sour cream
¾ cup chopped pecans
1 cup green olives, drained, chopped
¼ teaspoon black pepper

- In mixer, blend cream cheese, sour cream and mayonnaise until smooth.
- Add remaining ingredients, mix well and chill.
- Serve on crackers or make sandwiches with party rye bread.

Beef or Ham Spread

1 pound leftover roast beef or ham
¾ cup sweet pickle relish
½ onion, finely diced
2 celery ribs, chopped
2 hard-boiled eggs, chopped
Mayonnaise

- Chop meat in food processor and add relish, onion, celery and eggs.
- Add a little salt and pepper. Fold in enough mayonnaise to make mixture spread easily.
- Refrigerate. Spread on crackers or bread for sandwiches.

Mexican-Cheese Dip

1 (16 ounce) package cheddar cheese
1 (5 ounce) can evaporated milk
1 teaspoon cumin
1 tablespoon chili powder
1 (10 ounce) can tomatoes and green chilies

- Melt cheese with evaporated milk in double boiler.
- In blender, mix cumin, chili powder and tomatoes and green chilies. (Add dash of garlic powder if you like.)
- Add tomato mixture to melted cheese and mix well. Serve hot with chips.

Best Coffee Punch

This is so good you will want a big glass of it instead of a punch cup full.

1 gallon very strong, brewed coffee
½ cup sugar
3 tablespoons vanilla
2 pints half-and-half cream
1 gallon vanilla ice cream, softened

- Add sugar to coffee and chill. (Add more sugar if you like it sweeter.)
- Add vanilla and half-and-half.
- When ready to serve, combine coffee mixture and ice cream in punch bowl.

Pineapple-Citrus Punch

1 (46 ounce) can pineapple juice, chilled
1 quart apple juice, chilled
1 (2 liter) bottle lemon-lime carbonated beverage, chilled
1 (6 ounce) can frozen lemonade concentrate, thawed
1 orange, sliced

- Combine pineapple juice, apple juice, lemon-lime beverage and lemonade in punch bowl.
- Add orange slices for decoration.

Sparkling Punch

6 oranges, unpeeled, thinly sliced
1 cup sugar
2 (750 milliliter) bottles dry white wine
3 (750 milliliter) bottles sparkling wine, chilled

- Place orange slices in large nonmetallic container and sprinkle with sugar. Add white wine. Cover and chill at least 8 hours.
- Stir in sparkling wine.

Cranberry-Pineapple Punch

1 (48 ounce) bottle cranberry juice drink
1 (48 ounce) can pineapple juice
½ cup sugar
2 teaspoons almond extract
1 (2 liter) bottle ginger ale, chilled

- Combine cranberry juice, pineapple juice, sugar and almond extract and stir until sugar dissolves.
- Cover and chill 8 hours.
- When ready to serve, add ginger ale and stir.

Easiest Grape Punch

½ gallon ginger ale
Red seedless grapes
Green seedless grapes
Sparkling white grape juice, chilled

- Make ice ring of ginger ale and seedless grapes.
- When ready to serve, pour sparkling white grape juice in punch bowl with ice ring.

Tip: Sparkling white grape juice is great just by itself!

Ginger Ale Nectar Punch

1 (12 ounce) cans apricot nectar
1 (6 ounce) can frozen orange juice concentrate, thawed
1 cup water
2 tablespoons lemon juice
1 (2 liter) bottle ginger ale, chilled

- Combine apricot nectar, orange juice concentrate, water and lemon juice and chill.
- When ready to serve, stir in ginger ale.

Mocha Punch

4 cups brewed coffee
½ cup sugar
2 cups milk
1 pint half-and-half
2 pints chocolate ice cream, softened

- In container, combine coffee and sugar and stir until sugar dissolves. Chill for 2 hours.
- Just before serving, pour into punch bowl.
- Add milk and half-and-half and mix well. Top with scoops of ice cream and stir well.

Strawberry Smoothie

2 medium bananas, peeled, sliced
1 pint fresh strawberries, washed, quartered
1 (8 ounce) container strawberry yogurt
¼ cup orange juice
Crushed ice

- Place all ingredients in blender. Process until smooth.
- Serve as is or over crushed ice.

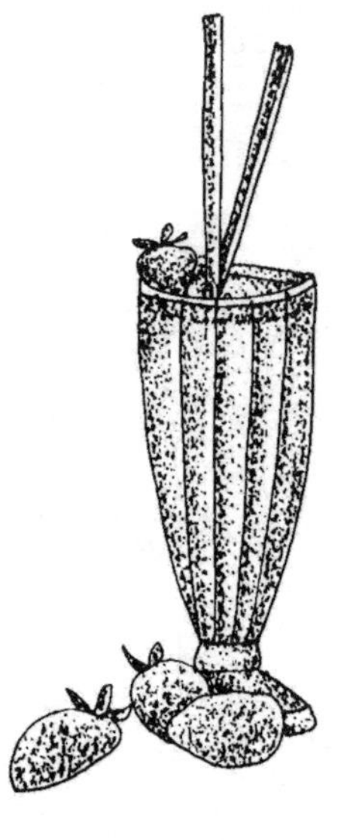

Kahlua Frosty

1 cup kahlua
1 pint vanilla ice cream
1 cup half-and-half cream
⅛ teaspoon almond extract
1 ⅔ cups crushed ice

- Combine all ingredients in blender and process until smooth.
- Serve immediately.

Pink Fizz

3 (6 ounce) cans frozen pink lemonade concentrate
1 (750 milliliter) bottles pink sparkling wine
3 (2 liter) bottles lemon-lime carbonated beverage, divided, chilled
Crushed ice

- Combine concentrate, wine and 2 bottles carbonated beverage in airtight container, cover and freeze 8 hours or until firm.
- Rest punch at room temperature for 10 minutes and place in punch bowl. Add remaining bottle carbonated beverage and stir until slushy.
- Mixture can be poured over crushed ice in glasses instead of serving in punch bowl.

Apple-Party Punch

3 cups sparkling apple cider
2 cups apple juice
1 cup pineapple juice
½ cup brandy, optional

- Combine all ingredients and freeze 8 hours.
- Remove punch from freezer 30 minutes before serving. Place in small punch bowl and break into chunks. Stir until slushy.

Champagne Punch

1 fifth dry white wine, chilled
1 cup apricot brandy
1 cup Triple Sec
2 bottles dry champagne, chilled
2 quarts club soda

- In large pitcher, combine white wine, apricot brandy and Triple Sec. Cover and chill until ready to use.
- At serving time, add champagne and club soda, stir to blend and pour in punch bowl.
- Add ice ring to punch bowl and serve.

Kahula

3 cups hot water
1 cup instant coffee granules
4 cups sugar
1 quart vodka
1 vanilla bean, split

- In large saucepan, combine hot water, coffee granules and sugar and mix well.
- Boil for 2 minutes and cool.
- Add vodka and vanilla bean. Pour into bottle or jar and let rest for 30 days before serving. Shake occasionally.

Tip: If you happen to have some Mexican vanilla, make "instant" kahula by using 3 tablespoons Mexican vanilla instead of 1 vanilla bean. You don't have to wait 30 days.

Amaretto

3 cups sugar
2¼ cups water
1 pint vodka
3 tablespoons almond extract
1 tablespoon vanilla (not the imitation)

- Combine sugar and water in large pan. Bring mixture to a boil.
- Reduce heat and simmer 5 minutes, stirring occasionally. Remove from stove.
- Add vodka, almond extract and vanilla and stir to mix. Store in airtight jar.

Cheddar-Butter Toast

½ cup (1 stick) butter, softened
1¼ cups shredded cheddar cheese
1 teaspoon worcestershire sauce
¼ teaspoon garlic powder
Thick-sliced bread

- Combine all ingredients and spread on thick-sliced bread.
- Turn on broiler to preheat.
- Turn off broiler, put in toast and heat for about 15 minutes.

Crispy Herb Bread

1½ teaspoons basil
1 teaspoon rosemary
½ teaspoon thyme
¾ cup (1½ sticks) butter, melted
1 package hot dog buns

- Combine first 4 ingredients and set aside several hours at room temperature.
- Spread on buns and cut into strips.
- Bake at 300° for 15 to 20 minutes or until crisp.

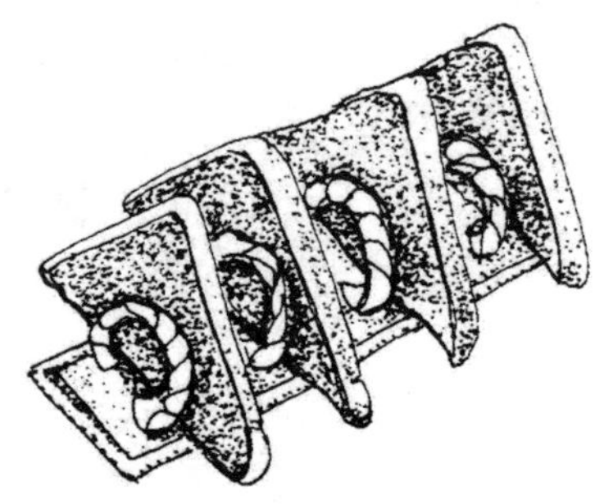

Crunchy Breadsticks

This is an all-time favorite of our family. I keep these made up in the freezer. We have served these several times at our Cancer Society luncheons and everybody loves them. No one can believe they are hot dog buns.

1 package hot dog buns
1 cup (2 sticks) butter, melted
Garlic powder
Paprika

- Take each half piece and slice in half lengthwise. Use pastry brush to spread butter over all breadsticks.
- Sprinkle a little garlic powder and a couple sprinkles of paprika.
- Place on cookie sheet and bake at 225° for about 45 minutes.

Garlic Toast

1 loaf French bread
1 tablespoon garlic powder
2 tablespoons dried parsley flakes
½ cup (1 stick) butter, melted
1 cup grated parmesan cheese

- Slice bread into 1-inch slices diagonally. In small bowl combine rest of ingredients except cheese and mix well.
- Use brush or knife to spread mixture on bread slices and sprinkle with parmesan cheese.
- Place on cookie sheet and bake at 225° for about 1 hour.

Mozzarella Loaf

1 (12 inch) loaf French bread
12 slices mozzarella cheese
¼ cup grated parmesan cheese
6 tablespoons (¾ stick) butter, softened
½ teaspoon garlic salt

- Cut loaf into 1-inch thick slices. Place mozzarella slices between bread slices.
- Combine parmesan cheese, butter and garlic salt and spread mixture on each slice of bread.
- Reshape loaf, press firmly together and brush remaining mixture on outside of loaf.
- Bake at 375° for 8 to 10 minutes.

Parmesan Bread Deluxe

1 loaf Italian bread
½ cup refrigerated creamy Caesar dressing and dip
⅓ cup grated parmesan cheese
3 tablespoons finely chopped green onions

- Cut 24 (½-inch thick) slices from bread. Reserve remaining bread for other use.
- In small bowl, combine dressing, cheese and onion. Spread 1 teaspoon dressing mixture onto each bread slice.
- Place bread on baking sheet. Broil 4 inches from heat until golden brown.
- Serve warm.

Poppy Seed Bread

3¾ cups biscuit mix
1½ cups shredded cheddar cheese
1 tablespoon poppy seed
1 egg, beaten
1½ cups milk

- Combine all ingredients and beat vigorously for 1 minute. Pour into greased loaf pan.
- Bake at 350° for 50 to 60 minutes. Test for doneness with toothpick.
- Remove from pan and cool before slicing.

Quick Pumpkin Bread

1 (16 ounce) package pound cake mix
1 cup canned pumpkin
2 eggs
⅓ cup milk
1 teaspoon allspice

- With mixer, combine, beat and blend all ingredients well. Pour into greased, floured 9 x 5-inch loaf pan.
- Bake at 350° for 1 hour. Use toothpick to check to be sure bread is done.
- Cool and turn out onto cooling rack.

Butter Rolls

2 cups biscuit mix
1 (8 ounce) carton sour cream
½ cup (1 stick) butter, melted
½ teaspoon salt, optional

- Combine all ingredients and mix well. Spoon into sprayed muffin tins and fill only half full.
- Bake at 400° for 12 to 14 minutes or until light brown.

Cheddar Cheese Loaf

3¾ cups biscuit mix
¾ cup shredded sharp cheddar cheese
1½ cups milk
2 small eggs
⅛ teaspoon ground red pepper

- Combine biscuit mix and cheese. Add milk, eggs and pepper and stir 2 minutes or until they blend. Spoon into 9 x 5-inch sprayed loaf pan.
- Bake at 350° for 45 minutes. Cool before slicing.

Orange French Toast

1 egg, beaten
½ cup orange juice
5 slices raisin bread
1 cup crushed graham crackers
2 tablespoons butter

- Combine egg and orange juice. Dip bread in mixture and then in crumbs. Fry in butter until brown.

Popovers

2 cups flour
1 teaspoon salt
6 eggs, beaten
2 cups milk
Butter

- Combine flour and salt in bowl. Add eggs and milk and mix. Add dry ingredients and mix well. (The batter will be like heavy cream.)
- Coat popover pans with butter and heat in oven. Fill each cup half full.
- Bake at 425° for 20 minutes. Reduce heat to 375° and bake for 25 more minutes.
- Serve immediately.

Cream Biscuits

2 cups flour
3 teaspoons baking powder
½ teaspoon salt
1 (8 ounce) carton whipping cream

- Combine flour, baking powder and salt. In mixing bowl, beat whipping cream only until it holds shape. Combine flour mixture and cream and mix with fork.
- Put dough on lightly floured board and knead for about 1 minute. Pat dough to ¾-inch thickness. Cut out biscuits with small biscuit cutter.
- Place on baking sheet and bake at 375° for about 12 minutes or until light brown.

Sour Cream Biscuits

2 cups plus 1 tablespoon flour
3 teaspoons baking powder
½ teaspoon baking soda
½ cup shortening
1 (8 ounce) carton sour cream

- Combine dry ingredients, add a little salt and cut in shortening.
- Gradually add sour cream and mix lightly. Turn on lightly floured board and knead a few times. Roll to ½-inch thick.
- Cut with biscuit cutter and place on greased baking sheet.
- Bake at 400° for 15 minutes or until light brown.

Spicy Cornbread Twists

2½ tablespoons (⅓ stick) butter
⅓ cup cornmeal
¼ teaspoon salt
¼ teaspoon red pepper
1 (11 ounce) can refrigerated soft breadsticks

- Place butter in pie plate and melt in oven.
- Remove from oven. On wax paper, mix cornmeal, salt and red pepper. Roll breadsticks in butter and cornmeal mixture.
- Twist breadsticks according to package directions and place on cookie sheet.
- Bake at 350° for 15 to 18 minutes.

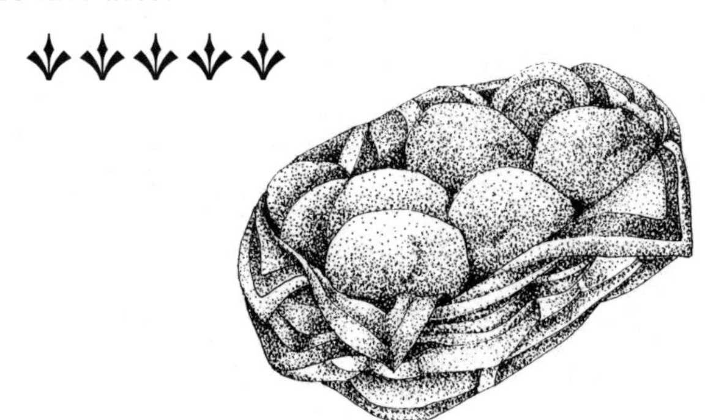

Souper-Sausage Cornbread

1 (10 ounce) can golden corn soup
2 eggs
¼ cup milk
1 (12 to 14 ounce) package corn muffin mix
¼ pound pork sausage, cooked, drained, crumbled

- In bowl, combine soup, eggs and milk. Stir in muffin mix and blend well.
- Fold in sausage. Spoon mixture into greased 9-inch baking pan.
- Bake at 400° for about 20 minutes or until light brown.

French Toast

4 eggs
1 cup whipping cream
2 thick slices bread, cut into 3 strips
Powdered sugar
Maple syrup

- Place a little oil in skillet. Beat eggs, cream and pinch of salt. Dip bread into batter and allow batter to soak in. Fry bread in skillet until brown, turn and fry on other side.
- Transfer to cookie sheet and bake at 325° for about 4 minutes or until puffed.
- Sprinkle with powdered sugar and serve with maple syrup.

Breakfast Bake

This is a favorite of ours for overnight guests or special enough for Christmas morning.

1 pound hot sausage, cooked, crumbled
1 cup grated cheddar cheese
1 cup biscuit mix
5 eggs, slightly beaten
2 cups milk

- Place cooked and crumbled sausage in sprayed 9 x 1-inch baking dish and sprinkle with cheese.
- In mixing bowl, combine biscuit mix, a little salt and eggs and beat well. Add milk and stir until fairly smooth. Pour over sausage mixture.
- Bake at 350° for 35 minutes. You can mix this the night before cooking and refrigerate. To cook the next morning, add 5 minutes to cooking time.

Christmas Breakfast

12 to 14 eggs, slightly beaten
1 pound sausage, cooked, drained, crumbled
2 cups whole milk
1½ cups grated cheddar cheese
1 (5 ounce) box seasoned croutons

- Mix all ingredients and pour into 9 x 13-inch baking dish.
- Bake at 350° for 40 minutes. Let cool for about 10 minutes before serving.

Bacon-Sour Cream Omelet

2 eggs
5 strips bacon, fried, drained, crumbled
⅓ cup sour cream
3 green onions, chopped
1 tablespoon butter

- Use fork to beat eggs with 1 tablespoon water.
- Combine cooked bacon and sour cream.
- Saute onions in remaining bacon drippings and add to bacon-sour cream mixture.
- Melt butter in omelet pan and pour in egg mixture and cook.
- When omelet is set, spoon bacon-sour cream mixture along center and fold omelet out onto warm plate.

Huevos Rancheros

8 eggs
3 tablespoons oil
4 corn tortillas
1 cup grated Monterrey Jack cheese
Enchilada sauce

- Fry tortillas in hot oil and drain.
- Lightly scramble 2 eggs at a time and place on tortillas.
- Pour enchilada sauce over eggs, top with cheese and serve.

Sunrise Eggs

6 eggs
2 cups milk
1 pound sausage, cooked, browned
¾ cup grated processed cheese
6 slices white bread, trimmed, cubed

- Beat eggs. Add milk, sausage and cheese. Pour over bread and mix well.
- Pour into greased 9 x 13-inch baking pan and cover with foil.
- Bake at 350° for 20 minutes.
- Remove foil and turn oven up to 375° and bake for another 10 minutes.

Mexican Breakfast Eggs

4 tablespoons butter
9 eggs
3 tablespoons milk
5 tablespoons salsa
1 cup crushed tortilla chips

- Melt butter in skillet. In mixing bowl, beat eggs and add milk and salsa.
- Pour into skillet and stir until eggs cook lightly.
- Stir in tortilla chips and serve hot.

Chiffon-Cheese Souffle

12 slices white bread with crusts trimmed
2 (5 ounce) jars Old English cheese spread, softened
6 eggs, beaten
3 cups milk
¾ cup (1½ sticks) butter, melted

- Spray 9 x 13-inch baking dish. Cut each slice of bread into 4 triangles. Place dab of cheese on each triangle and place triangles evenly in layers in baking dish. (You could certainly prepare this in a souffle dish if you have one.)
- Combine eggs, milk, butter and a little salt and pepper. Pour over layers, cover and chill 8 hours.
- Remove from refrigerator 10 to 15 minutes before baking.
- Bake at 350° uncovered for 1 hour.

Tip: This breakfast soufflé is light and fluffy, but still very rich. I believe it is the Old English cheese that gives it that special cheese flavor.

Green Chile Squares

2 cups chopped green chilies
1 (8 ounce) package shredded sharp cheddar cheese
8 eggs, beaten
Salt and pepper
½ cup half-and-half cream

- Place green chilies on bottom of 9 x 13-inch baking pan and cover with cheese.
- Combine eggs, salt, pepper and cream. Pour over chilies and cheese.
- Bake at 350° for 30 minutes. Let rest at room temperature for a few minutes before cutting into squares.

Pineapple-Cheese Casserole

This is really a different kind of recipe –and so good.

2 (20 ounce) cans unsweetened pineapple chunks, drained
1 cup sugar, 5 tablespoons flour
1½ cups grated cheddar cheese
1 stack Townhouse or Ritz crackers, crushed
½ cup (1 stick) butter, melted

- Grease 9 x 13-inch baking dish and layer in following order: pineapple, sugar-flour mixture, grated cheese and cracker crumbs.
- Drizzle butter over casserole and bake at 350° for 25 minutes or until bubbly.

Tip: This can be served at brunch and it's great with sandwiches at lunch.

Crabmeat Quiche

3 eggs, beaten
1 (8 ounce) carton sour cream
1 (6 ounce) can crabmeat, rinsed, drained, flaked
½ cup grated Swiss cheese
1 (9-inch) pie shell

- In bowl, combine eggs and sour cream. Mix crabmeat and cheese, add a little garlic salt and pepper and pour into egg mixture.
- Pour into 9-inch unbaked pie shell.
- Bake at 350° for 35 minutes.

Apricot Casserole

4 (15 ounce) cans apricot halves, drained
1 (16 ounce) box light brown sugar
¼ teaspoon ground cinnamon
1 stack Ritz crackers, crumbled
½ cup (1 stick) butter, sliced

- Grease 9 x 13-inch baking dish and line bottom of dish with 2 cans drained apricots.
- Sprinkle half brown sugar, cinnamon and half cracker crumbs over apricots. Dot with half butter and repeat layers.
- Bake at 300° for 1 hour.

Cinnamon Souffle

1 loaf cinnamon-raisin bread
1 (20 ounce) can crushed pineapple with juice
1 cup (2 sticks) butter, melted
½ cup sugar
5 eggs, slightly beaten

- Slice very thin amount of crusts off. Tear bread into small pieces and place in buttered 9 x 13-inch baking dish.
- Pour pineapple and juice over bread and set aside. Cream butter and sugar, add eggs and mix well.
- Pour creamed mixture over bread and pineapple. Bake at 350° uncovered for 40 minutes.

Tip: If you have some pecans handy, add ½ cup chopped pecans for extra texture and flavor.

Light, Crispy Waffles

2 cups biscuit mix
1 egg
½ cup oil
¼ teaspoon vanilla
1⅓ cups club soda

- Preheat waffle iron. Combine all ingredients in mixing bowl and stir by hand.
- Pour just enough batter to cover waffle iron and cook.
- Prepare waffle mixture, freeze separately on cookie sheet and place in large baggies. When ready to use, bake at 350° for about 10 minutes.

Tip: To have waffles for a "company weekend", prepare them before guests arrive.

Melon Boats

2 cantaloupes, chilled
4 cups red and green seedless grapes, chilled
1 cup mayonnaise
⅓ cup frozen orange juice concentrate

- Prepare each melon in 6 lengthwise sections, remove seeds and peel.
- Place lettuce leaves on individual serving plates and arrange melon on top.
- Heap grapes over and around cantaloupe slices.
- Combine mayonnaise and juice concentrate and mix well. Ladle over fruit.

Curried Fruit Medley

1 (29 ounce) can sliced peaches
2 (15 ounce) cans pineapple chunks
1 (10 ounce) jar maraschino cherries
1 cup packed brown sugar
1 teaspoon curry powder
¼ cup (½ stick) butter, cut into pieces

- Drain fruit and place in 9 x 13-inch baking dish.
- Combine brown sugar and curry and stir well. Sprinkle over fruit and dot with butter.
- Bake covered at 350° for approximately 30 minutes.

Treasure-Filled Apples

6 medium-sized, tart apples
½ cup sugar
¼ cup red hot candies
¼ teaspoon ground cinnamon

- Cut off apple tops and set aside. Core apples to within ½-inch of bottom. Place in greased 8-inch baking dish.
- In bowl, combine sugar, candies and cinnamon. Spoon 2 tablespoons into each apple and replace tops.
- Spoon any remaining sugar mixture over apples and bake uncovered at 350° for 30 to 35 minutes or until apples are tender. Baste occasionally.

Ranch Sausage and Grits

1 cup quick-cooking grits
1 pound pork sausage
1 onion, chopped
1 cup salsa
1 (8 ounce) package shredded cheddar cheese, divided

- Cook grits according to package directions and set aside.
- Cook and brown sausage and onion. Drain well.
- Combine grits, sausage mixture, salsa and half cheese and spoon into greased 2-quart baking dish.
- Bake at 350° for 15 minutes. Remove from oven and add remaining cheese.
- Bake another 10 minutes and serve hot.

Baked Grits

2 cups quick grits
4 cups water
2 cups milk
¾ cup (1½ sticks) butter
4 eggs, beaten

- Stir grits in water over medium heat for about 5 minutes.
- Add milk and butter, cover and cook an additional 10 minutes.
- Remove from heat, add beaten eggs and pour in buttered casserole.
- Bake at 350° for 30 minutes.

Gingered-Cream Spread

1 (8 ounce) package cream cheese, softened
½ (1 stick) unsalted butter, softened
2 tablespoons milk
3 tablespoons finely chopped crystallized ginger
Fruit or nut bread

- Combine all ingredients in mixer and beat until creamy.
- Spread on your favorite fruit or nut breads.

Homemade Egg Substitute

6 egg whites
¼ cup instant nonfat dry milk powder
2 teaspoons water
2 teaspoons oil
¼ teaspoon ground turmeric

- Combine all ingredients in electric blender and process 30 seconds.
- Chill.

Tip: With this recipe, ¼ cup is the equivalent of 1 egg.

Blueberry Coffee Cake

1 (16 ounce) package blueberry muffin mix
⅓ cup sour cream
1 egg
⅔ cup powdered sugar
1 tablespoon water

- Stir muffin mix, sour cream, egg and ½ cup water to mix.
- Rinse blueberries, gently fold into batter and pour into sprayed 7 x 11-inch baking dish. Bake at 400° for about 25 minutes.
- Mix powdered sugar and 1 tablespoon water and drizzle over coffee cake while still hot.

Pineapple Coffee Cake

1 (18 ounce) box butter cake mix
½ cup oil
½ teaspoon vanilla extract
4 eggs, slightly beaten
1 (20 ounce) can pineapple pie filling

- In mixing bowl combine mix, oil, vanilla and eggs. Beat until they mix well.
- Pour batter into greased, floured 9 x 13-inch baking pan.
- Bake at 350° for 45 to 50 minutes. Test with toothpick to make sure cake is done.
- Punch holes in cake about 2 inches apart with knife. Spread 1 can pineapple pie filling over cake while it is hot.

Spicy Tomato Soup

2 (10 ounce) cans tomato soup
1 (10 ounce) can beef broth
1 (15 ounce) can Mexican stewed tomatoes
Sour cream
½ pound bacon, fried, drained, crumbled

- In saucepan, combine soup, broth and stewed tomatoes and heat.
- To serve, place dollop of sour cream on each bowl of soup and sprinkle crumbled bacon over sour cream.

Beef-Noodle Soup

1 pound lean ground beef
1 (46 ounce) can V8 juice
1 (1 ounce) package onion soup mix
1 (3 ounce) package beef-flavored ramen noodles
1 (16 ounce) package frozen mixed vegetables

- In large saucepan, cook beef over medium heat until no longer pink and drain. Stir in V8 juice, soup mix, contents of noodle seasoning packet and mixed vegetables.
- Bring to boil. Reduce heat and simmer, uncovered, for 6 minutes or until vegetables are tender.
- Return to boil and stir in noodles. Cook for 3 minutes or until noodles are tender. Serve hot.

Broccoli-Wild Rice Soup

This is a hardy and delicious soup – full of flavor.

1 (6 ounce) package chicken-flavored wild rice mix
1 (10 ounce) package frozen chopped broccoli, thawed
2 teaspoons dried minced onion
1 (10 ounce) can cream of chicken soup
1 (8 ounce) package cream cheese, cubed

- In large saucepan, combine rice, contents of seasoning packet and 6 cups water.
- Bring to boil, reduce heat, cover and simmer for 10 minutes, stirring once.
- Stir in broccoli and onion and simmer 5 minutes.
- Stir in soup and cream cheese. Cook and stir until cheese melts.

Warm-Your-Soul Soup

Great flavor – great soup!

3 (15 ounce) cans chicken broth
1 (10 ounce) can Italian stewed tomatoes with liquid
½ cup chopped onion
¾ cup chopped celery
½ (12 ounce) box fettuccine

- In large soup kettle, combine chicken broth, tomatoes, onion and celery. Bring to boil and simmer until onion and celery are almost done.
- Add pasta and cook according to package directions. Season with a little salt and pepper.

Crab Bisque

1 (10 ounce) can cream of celery soup
1 (10 ounce) can pepper pot soup
1 pint half-and-half cream
1 (6 ounce) can crabmeat, drained, flaked
A scant ⅓ cup sherry

- Mix soups and half-and-half. Stir in crabmeat and heat through.
- Just before serving, add sherry and stir.

Clam Chowder

1 (10 ounce) can New England clam chowder
1 (10 ounce) can cream of celery soup
1 (10 ounce) can cream of potato soup
1 (6.5 ounce) can chopped clams
1 (10 ounce) soup can milk

- Combine all ingredients in saucepan. Heat and stir.

Cream of Cauliflower Soup

1 onion, chopped
½ teaspoon garlic powder
2 (14 ounce) cans chicken broth
1 large cauliflower, cut into small florets
1½ cups whipping cream

- Saute onion and garlic powder in 1 tablespoon butter. Stir in broth and bring to boil. Add cauliflower and cook, stirring occasionally, for 15 minutes or until tender.
- In blender, process soup in batches until smooth and return to pan.
- Stir in cream and add a little salt and white pepper. Cook over low heat, stirring often, until it heats thoroughly.

Cream of Zucchini Soup

1 pound fresh zucchini, grated
1 onion, chopped
1 (15 ounce) can chicken broth
½ teaspoon sweet basil
2 cups half-and-half cream

- In saucepan, combine zucchini, onion, broth, basil and a little salt and pepper. Bring to boil and simmer until soft. Empty into food processor and puree.
- Gradually add ½ cup half-and-half and blend. (You could add ¼ teaspoon curry powder if you like its flavor.)
- Return zucchini mixture to saucepan and add remaining half-and-half. Heat, but do not boil.

Creamy Butternut Soup

4 cups cooked, mashed butternut squash
2 (14 ounce) cans chicken broth
½ teaspoon sugar
1 (8 ounce) carton whipping cream, divided
¼ teaspoon ground nutmeg

- In saucepan, combine mashed squash, broth, sugar and a little salt. Bring to boil and gradually stir in half of whipping cream. Cook until it heats thoroughly.
- Beat remaining whipping cream. When ready to serve, place dollop of whipped cream on soup and sprinkle of nutmeg.

Easy Potato Soup

1 (16 ounce) package frozen hash brown potatoes
1 cup chopped onion
1 (14 ounce) can chicken broth
2 (10 ounce) cans soup: 1 cream of celery and 1 cream of chicken soup
2 cups milk

- In large saucepan, combine potatoes, onion and 2 cups water. Bring to boil.
- Cover, reduce heat and simmer 30 minutes.
- Stir in broth, soups and milk and heat thoroughly.
- If you like, garnish with shredded cheddar cheese or diced, cooked ham.

Navy Bean Soup

3 (14 ounce) cans navy beans with liquid
1 (14 ounce) can chicken broth
1 cup chopped ham
1 large onion, chopped
½ teaspoon garlic powder

- In large saucepan, combine beans, broth, ham, onion and garlic powder. Add 1 cup water and bring to boil.
- Simmer until onion is tender crisp and serve hot with cornbread.

Peanut Soup

2 (10 ounce) cans cream of chicken soup
1 (10 ounce) can cream of celery soup
2 soup cans of milk
1¼ cups crunchy-style peanut butter
½ teaspoon black pepper

- In saucepan on medium heat, blend soups and milk.
- Stir in peanut butter, black pepper and heat until it blends well.

✦✦✦✦✦

Cold Cucumber Soup

3 medium cucumbers, peeled, seeded , cut into chunks
1 (14 ounce) can chicken broth, divided
1 (8 ounce) carton sour cream
3 tablespoons fresh chives, minced
2 teaspoon fresh dill, minced

- In blender, combine cucumbers, 1 cup chicken broth and dash of salt.
- Cover and process until smooth. Transfer to medium bowl and stir in remaining chicken broth. Whisk in sour cream, chives and dill.
- Cover and chill well before serving. Garnish with dill sprig.

Chilled Squash Soup

2 pounds yellow squash, thinly sliced
1 onion, chopped
1 (14 ounce) can chicken broth
1 (8 ounce) package cream cheese, softened
¼ teaspoon freshly ground pepper

- Combine squash, onion and chicken broth in saucepan and bring to boil. Cover, reduce heat and simmer 10 minutes or until tender. Set aside to cool.
- Spoon half each of squash mixture and cream cheese into blender. Process until smooth and stop once to scrape down sides. Repeat procedure.
- Stir in pepper and chill.

Avocado-Cream Soup

4 ripe avocados, peeled, diced
1½ cups whipping cream
2 (14 ounce) cans chicken broth
1 teaspoon salt
¼ cup dry sherry

- With blender, cream half avocados and half whipping cream. Repeat with remaining avocados and cream.
- Bring chicken broth to boil, reduce heat and stir in avocado puree. Add salt and sherry and chill thoroughly.
- To serve, place in individual bowls and sprinkle a little paprika on top.

Asparagus Chiller

1 (10 ounce) can cream of asparagus soup
⅔ cup plain yogurt
½ cup chopped cucumber
2 tablespoon chopped red onion

- Blend soup, yogurt and 1 soup can water. Add cucumber and onion.
- Chill at least 4 hours and serve in chilled bowls.

Cold Strawberry Soup

$2\frac{1}{4}$ cups strawberries
$\frac{1}{3}$ cup sugar
$\frac{1}{2}$ cup sour cream
$\frac{1}{2}$ cup whipping cream
$\frac{1}{2}$ cup light red wine

- Place strawberries and sugar in blender and puree. Pour into pitcher, stir in creams and blend well.
- Add $1\frac{1}{4}$ cups water and red wine. Stir and chill.

Strawberry Soup

$1\frac{1}{2}$ cups fresh strawberries
1 cup orange juice
$\frac{1}{4}$ cup honey
$\frac{1}{2}$ cup sour cream
$\frac{1}{2}$ cup white wine

- Combine all ingredients in blender. Process until strawberries are pureed.
- Chill thoroughly.
- Stir before serving.

Hot Bunwiches

8 hamburger buns
8 slices Swiss cheese
8 slices ham
8 slices turkey
8 slices American cheese

- Lay out all 8 buns. On bottom, place slices of Swiss cheese, ham, turkey and American cheese. Place top bun over American cheese. Wrap each bunwich individually in foil and place in freezer.
- Remove from freezer 2 to 3 hours before serving.
- Heat at 325° for about 30 minutes and serve hot.

Grilled Bacon-Banana Sandwiches

Peanut butter
8 slices English muffins
2 bananas
8 slices bacon, cooked crispy
Butter, softened

- Spread layer of peanut butter over 8 slices of muffins. Slice bananas and arrange on top of 4 slices.
- Place 2 strips bacon on each of 4 slices. Top with remaining muffin slices. Spread top slice with butter.
- Brown sandwiches butter side down. Turn, spread butter and cook other side until golden brown. Serve hot.

Reuben Sandwiches

For each sandwich:
2 slices rye bread
1 slice Swiss cheese
Generous slices corned beef
2 tablespoons sauerkraut
Dijon mustard

- Butter 1 slice bread on 1 side. Place butter side down in skillet over low heat.
- Layer cheese, corned beef, sauerkraut on bread and spread mustard on 1 side of other slice. Butter opposite side of bread. Place butter side up on sauerkraut.
- Cook until bottom browns, turn carefully and brown other side.

Turkey-Cranberry Croissant

1 (8 ounce) package cream cheese, softened
¼ cup orange marmalade
6 large croissants, split
Lettuce leaves
1 pound thinly sliced, cooked turkey
¾ cup whole berry cranberry sauce

- Beat cream cheese and orange marmalade. Spread evenly on cut sides of croissants.
- Place lettuce leaves and turkey on croissant bottoms and spread with cranberry sauce.
- Cover with croissant tops.

Turkey-Asparagus Sandwiches

4 (1 ounce) slices cheddar cheese
2 English muffins, split, toasted
½ pound thinly sliced turkey
1 (15 ounce) can asparagus spears, drained
1 package hollandaise sauce mix

- Place 1 cheese slice on each muffin half and top evenly with turkey.
- Cut asparagus spears to fit muffin halves and top each sandwich with 3 or 4 asparagus spears.
- Prepare sauce mix according to package directions. Pour evenly over sandwiches and sprinkle with paprika, if desired.

Provolone-Pepper Burgers

⅓ cup finely cubed provolone cheese
¼ cup diced roasted red peppers
¼ cup finely chopped onion
1 pound lean ground beef
4 hamburger buns, split

- In bowl, combine cheese, red peppers, onion and a little salt and pepper.
- Add beef and mix well. Shape into 4 patties.
- Grill covered, over medium-hot heat for 5 minutes on each side or until all pink is gone from meat.

When buying ground beef, remember that fat content contributes to its flavor. The lower the fat, the drier it will be once cooked.

Party Sandwiches

1 (8 ounce) package cream cheese, softened
⅓ cup chopped stuffed olives
2 tablespoons olive juice
⅓ cup chopped pecans
6 slices bacon, cooked, crumbled

- Beat cream cheese with mixer until smooth.
- Add remaining ingredients and spread on party rye bread.

Spinach Sandwiches

1 (10 ounce) package chopped spinach, thawed, well drained
1 cup mayonnaise
1 (8 ounce) carton sour cream
½ cup finely minced onion
1 (1 ounce) package dry vegetable soup mix

- Make sure spinach is WELL drained. Combine all ingredients and mix well.
- Chill for 3 to 4 hours before making sandwiches.
- Use thin white bread to make sandwiches

Sandwiches Extraordinaire

Here are some new or different combinations for sandwiches you may not have tried before. You'll get some "ooh's" and "aah's" and maybe even a raised eyebrow or two.

Sandwich Inspiration I
Pumpernickel bread
Mayonnaise
Deli sliced corned beef
Slices of Swiss cheese
Lettuce

Sandwich Inspiration II
Dark rye bread
2 slices corned beef
2 slices Swiss cheese
4 tablespoons sauerkraut
Russian dressing

Sandwich Inspiration III
Hoagie Rolls
Grey Poupon mustard
Slices of pastrami
Slices of mozzarella cheese
Deli cold slaw

Sandwich Inspiration IV
Pita bread
Ham slices
Mozzarella cheese slices
Slices of sweet pickles
Bean sprouts and mayonnaise

Sandwich Inspiration V
Rye bread
Slices mozzarella cheese
Deli ham salad
Avocado slices
Lettuce

Sandwich Inspiration VI
French bread slices
Turkey and deli beef slices
Slices of American cheese
Slices of Monterey jack cheese
Lettuce with mayonnaise

Sandwich Inspiration VII
Whole wheat bread
Slices of American cheese
Deli shrimp or crab salad
Slices of avocados
Lettuce

Sandwich Inspiration VIII
Kaiser Rolls
Spread with softened cream cheese
Deli egg salad
Slices of dill pickles
Bean sprouts

Sandwich Inspiration IX
Multi-grain bread
Deli turkey breasts
Slices havarti cheese
Fresh spinach
Garlic mayonnaise

Sandwich Inspiration X
Pumpernickel bread
Deli roast beef
Fresh spinach
Tomato slices
Quick guacamole

Sandwich Inspiration XI
French rolls
Thin slices brie cheese
Deli turkey breast slices
Chutney spread
Mayonnaise

Sandwich Inspiration XII
Kaiser rolls
Grilled chicken breasts
Canned pineapple slices
Leaf lettuce
Sesame-ginger mayonnaise

Sandwich Inspiration XIII
Slices marble rye bread
Slices deli peppered roast beef
Slices sweet onion, separated into rings
Leaf lettuce
Horseradish mayonnaise

Sandwich Inspiration XIV
Honey nut bread
Crisp cooked bacon slices
Tomato slices
Bibb lettuce
Remoulade mayonnaise

Sandwich Spreads:

Horseradish Mayonnaise
½ cup mayonnaise
1 tablespoon chopped fresh chives
1 tablespoon prepared horseradish
⅛ teaspoon seasoned salt
Combine ingredients. Chill.

Garlic Mayonnaise
⅔ cup mayonnaise
1 tablespoon chopped roasted garlic
1 teaspoon finely chopped onion
⅛ teaspoon salt
Combine ingredients. Chill.

Remoulade Mayonnaise
½ cup mayonnaise
2 tablespoons chunky salsa
1 teaspoon chopped fresh parsley
1 teaspoon sweet pickle relish
1 teaspoon dijon mustard
Combine ingredients. Chill.

Chutney Spread
⅓ cup peach preserves
½ cup chopped fresh peaches
2 teaspoons finely chopped green onion
½ teaspoon balsamic vinegar
¼ teaspoon crushed red pepper flake
Combine ingredients. Chill.

Sesame-Ginger Mayonnaise
⅔ cup mayonnaise
1 tablespoon honey
1 tablespoon sesame toasted sesame seeds
2 teaspoon grated fresh gingerroot
Combine ingredients. Chill.

Quick Guacamole
1 package onion soup mix (dry)
2 (8 ounce) cartons avocado dip
2 green onions, chopped, tops too
½ teaspoon crushed dill weed
Combine ingredients. Chill.

Burgers With Flair

Basic Burger:

1¼ pounds ground chuck
1 egg
2 teaspoons worcestershire sauce
½ teaspoon salt
¼ teaspoon black pepper

- Mix ground chuck with egg, worcestershire, salt and pepper. Form into 4 or 5 patties about ¼-inch thick and about 4 inches in diameter. Cook on grill for 5 to 6 minutes on each side or in skillet for 4 to 5 minutes on each side. (Ground beef should never be rare. Always cook until well done.)
- Toast 4 buns and spread with mayonnaise or mustard.
- Serve with lettuce, tomatoes and slice of onion.

Here are suggested additions to your basic hamburger for a little change of taste:

Super Hamburger I
Add 2 slices of crisp, cooked bacon and American cheese slices for each bun.

Super Hamburger II
Spread some deli prepared guacamole and sliced hot peppers.

Super Hamburger III
Instead of lettuce, spread about 3 tablespoons of deli prepared slaw and few sunflower seeds.

Super Hamburger IV
Add thin slices of apples and some chopped peanuts.

Super Hamburger V
Add thin slices of cucumber and sliced olives.

Super Hamburger VI
Instead of American cheese, use Monterey jack cheese and instead of mayonnaise or mustard, use prepared guacamole as spread.

Super Hamburger VII
Add slices of pastrami and slices of mozzarella cheese.

Super Hamburger VIII
Add slices of salami and slices of Swiss cheese.

Super Hamburger IX
Add slices of avocados (mayonnaise, not mustard) and slices of crisp, cooked bacon.

Broccoli-Waldorf Salad

6 cups fresh broccoli florets
1 large red apple with peel, chopped
½ cup golden raisins
½ cup chopped pecans
½ cup prepared coleslaw dressing

- In large bowl, combine broccoli, apple, raisins and pecans.
- Drizzle with dressing and toss to coat. Chill.

Broccoli-Noodle Salad

2 (3 ounce) packages chicken-flavored ramen noodles
1 package broccoli slaw
1 cup almonds, slivered, toasted
1 cup sunflower seeds, toasted
1 (8 ounce) bottle Italian salad dressing

- Break up noodles and mix with slaw, almonds and sunflower seeds.
- Toss with dressing and chill.

Tip: To toast almonds and sunflower seeds heat in oven at 275° for about 10 minutes. Toasting really brings out their flavors.

To increase the flavor of nuts and add an extra crunch in recipes, toast nuts before using. Toasted nuts also aren't as likely to sink in cake, bread and other batter baking.

Broccoli-Cauliflower Salad

1 small head cauliflower
3 stalks broccoli, 1 cup mayonnaise
1 tablespoon vinegar, 1 tablespoon sugar
1 bunch fresh green onions with tops, chopped
8 ounces mozzarella cheese, cubed

- Cut up cauliflower and broccoli into bite-size florets.
- Combine mayonnaise, vinegar and sugar and add to cauliflower-broccoli mixture.
- Add onions and cheese to mixture with a little salt if you like. Toss and chill.

Winter Salad

1 (15 ounce) can cut green beans, drained
1 (15 ounce) can English peas, drained
1 (15 ounce) can whole kernel corn, drained
1 (15 ounce) can jalapeno black-eyed peas, drained
1 (8 ounce) bottle Italian dressing

- Combine all vegetables in large bowl. Pour dressing over vegetables.
- Cover and chill

Tip: This is a great make-ahead salad and will stay fresh at least a week.

Keep you salads crispier longer by chilling the salad plates or serving bowls.

Sunflower Salad

2 apples, cored, chopped
1 cup seedless green grapes, halved
½ cup chopped celery
¾ cup chopped pecans
⅓ cup mayonnaise

- Combine all ingredients and chill.

Avocado-Green Bean Salad

2 (15 ounce) cans French-cut green beans, drained
8 green onions with tops, chopped
¾ cup Italian salad dressing
2 avocados, chopped
1 (8 ounce) can artichoke hearts, drained, chopped

- Place green beans and onions in serving dish. Pour dressing over mixture and chill several hours or overnight.
- When ready to serve, stir in avocado and artichoke hearts.

Marinated Black-Eyed Peas

3 can jalapeno black-eyed peas, drained
1 cup chopped celery
1 bunch fresh green onions with tops, chopped
1 (4 ounce) jar pimentos, drained
1 (8 ounce) bottle Italian dressing

- Mix all ingredients and chill. Let rest several hours before serving.

Cold Butter Bean Salad

2 (10 ounce) packages frozen baby lima beans
1 (15 ounce) can shoe-peg corn, drained
1 bunch fresh green onions with tops, chopped
1 cup mayonnaise
2 teaspoons Hidden Valley ranch seasoning

- Cook beans according to package directions and drain.
- Add corn, onions, mayonnaise and seasoning. Mix well and chill.

Nutty Green Salad

6 cups torn, mixed salad greens
1 medium zucchini, sliced
1 can sliced water chestnuts
½ cup peanuts
⅓ cup Italian salad dressing

- Toss greens, zucchini, water chestnuts and peanuts.
- When ready to serve, add dressing and toss.

Green Pea Salad

1 (16 ounce) bag frozen green peas
1 bunch fresh green onions with tops, chopped
½ cup chopped celery
½ cup sweet pickle relish
Mayonnaise

- Mix peas, onions, celery and relish.
- Add enough mayonnaise to hold salad together and chill.

Spinach-Apple Salad

1 (10 ounce) package fresh spinach
⅓ cup frozen orange juice concentrate, thawed
¾ cup mayonnaise
1 red apple with peel, diced
5 slices bacon, fried, crumbled

- Tear spinach into small pieces. Mix orange juice concentrate and mayonnaise.
- When ready to serve, mix spinach and apple, pour dressing over salad and top with bacon.

City-Slicker Salad

2 (10 ounce) packages fresh spinach
1 quart fresh strawberries, halved
1 green apple, with peel, chopped
½ cup slivered almonds, toasted
1 (8 ounce) bottle poppy seed dressing

- Tear spinach into smaller pieces and add strawberries, apple and almonds.
- Refrigerate until ready to serve. Toss with dressing.

Merry-Berry Salad

1 (10 ounce) package mixed salad greens
2 apples: red and green, diced
1 cup shredded parmesan cheese
½ cup dried cranberries
½ cup slivered almonds, toasted

- In large salad bowl, toss greens, apples, cheese, cranberries and almonds.
- Drizzle poppy seed dressing over salad and toss.

Marinated Corn Salad

3 (15 ounce) cans whole kernel corn, drained
1 red bell pepper, chopped
1 cup chopped walnuts
¾ cup chopped celery
1 (8 ounce) bottle Italian salad dressing

- In bowl with lid, combine corn, bell pepper, walnuts and celery. Pour dressing over vegetables. Refrigerate several hours before serving.

Tip: For a special little zip, add several dashes of hot sauce.

Calypso Coleslaw

1 (16 ounce) package shredded cabbage
1 bunch green onions with tops, sliced
2 cups cubed cheddar or mozzarella cheese
¼ cup sliced ripe olives
1 (15 ounce) can whole kernel corn with peppers, drained

- Combine all slaw ingredients and add a few sprinkles of salt.

Dressing for Calypso Coleslaw:

1 cup mayonnaise
2 tablespoons sugar
1 tablespoon prepared mustard
2 tablespoons vinegar

- Combine dressing ingredients and mix well.
- Add dressing to slaw. Toss, cover and refrigerate.

Easy Guacamole Salad

4 avocados, softened
1 (8 ounce) package cream cheese, softened
1 (10 ounce) can diced tomatoes and green chilies
1½ teaspoons garlic salt
About 1 tablespoon lemon juice

- Peel avocados and mash with fork. In mixing bowl, beat cream cheese until smooth.
- Add avocados and remaining ingredients and mix well.
- Serve on lettuce leaf with a few chips beside salad.

Terrific Tortellini Salad

2 (14 ounce) packages frozen cheese tortellini
1 green and 1 red bell pepper, diced
1 cucumber, chopped
1 (14 ounce) can artichoke hearts, rinsed, drained
1 (8 ounce) bottle creamy Caesar salad dressing

- Prepare tortellini according to package directions and drain. Rinse with cold water, drain and chill.
- Combine tortellini and remaining ingredients in large bowl, cover and chill at least 2 hours.

Fancy Eggs

12 large hard-boiled eggs
1 (4 ounce) package crumbled blue cheese
¼ cup half-and-half cream
2 tablespoons lime juice
2 tablespoons black caviar

- Cut eggs in half lengthwise and carefully remove yolks. Mash yolks with fork.
- Add cheese, half-and-half and lime juice and stir until smooth.
- Spoon mixture back into egg whites and top with caviar. Chill.

Chicken Salad

3 cups finely chopped, cooked chicken breasts
1½ cups chopped celery
½ cup sweet pickle relish
2 hard-boiled eggs, chopped
¾ cup mayonnaise

- Combine all ingredients and several sprinkles of salt and pepper.

Tip: If you have some pecans, ½ cup chopped pecans gives the chicken salad a special crunchy texture.

Fantastic Fruit Salad

2 (11 ounce) cans mandarin oranges
2 (15 ounce) cans pineapple chunks
1 (16 ounce) carton frozen strawberries, thawed
1 (20 ounce) can peach pie filling
1 (20 ounce) can apricot pie filling

- Drain oranges, pineapple and strawberries.
- Combine all ingredients and fold together gently.

Peachy Fruit Salad

2 (20 ounce) cans peach pie filling
1 (20 ounce) can pineapple chunks, drained
1 (11 ounce) can mandarin oranges, drained
1 (8 ounce) jar maraschino cherries, drained
1 cup miniature marshmallows

- Combine all ingredients in large bowl. Fold together gently and chill.

Angel Salad

1 (8 ounce) package cream cheese, softened
½ cup sugar
1 (16 ounce) can chunky fruit cocktail, drained
1 (15 ounce) can pineapple chunks, drained
1 (8 ounce) carton whipped topping

- With mixer, beat cream cheese and sugar until creamy. Add fruit and mix gently.
- Fold in whipped topping. Pour into crystal bowl and chill.

Tropical-Mango Salad

2 (15 ounce) cans mangoes with juice
1 (6 ounce) package orange gelatin
1 (8 ounce) can crushed pineapple with juice
1 (8 ounce) package cream cheese, softened
½ (8 ounce) carton whipped topping

- Place all mango slices on dinner plate and cut into bite-size pieces. Pour 1½ cups mango juice and water, if necessary, in saucepan and bring to boil. Pour over gelatin in mixing bowl and mix well. Add crushed pineapple.
- Add cream cheese and start mixer very slowly. Gradually increase speed until cream cheese mixes into gelatin. Pour in mango pieces and place in refrigerator until it congeals lightly.
- Fold in whipped topping. Pour into 7 x 11-inch dish and chill.

Butter-Mint Salad

1 (6 ounce) box lime gelatin
1 (20 ounce) can crushed pineapple with juice
½ (10 ounce) bag miniature marshmallows
1 (8 ounce) carton whipped topping
1 (8 ounce) bag butter mints, crushed

- Pour dry gelatin over pineapple. Add marshmallows and let set overnight.
- Fold in whipped topping and butter mints. Pour into 9 x 13-inch dish and freeze.

Tip: This salad is so good served with the Hawaiian Chicken recipe on page 399.

Pistachio Salad or Dessert

1 (20 ounce) can crushed pineapple with juice
1 (3 ounce) package instant pistachio pudding mix
2 cups miniature marshmallows
1 cup chopped pecans
1 (8 ounce) carton whipped topping

- Place pineapple in large bowl. Sprinkle with dry pudding mix.
- Add marshmallows and pecans and fold in whipped topping. Pour into crystal serving dish and chill.

Add flavor to a recipe by substituting other liquids for all or part of the water called for in gelatin mixes.

Divinity Salad

1 (6 ounce) package lemon gelatin
1 (8 ounce) package cream cheese, softened
¾ cup chopped pecans
1 (15 ounce) can crushed pineapple with juice
1 (8 ounce) carton whipped topping

- With mixer, mix gelatin with 1 cup boiling water until it dissolves.
- Add cream cheese, beat slowly at first and beat until smooth. Add pecans and pineapple. Cool in refrigerator until nearly set.
- Fold in whipped topping. Pour into 9 x 13-inch dish and chill.

Frozen Dessert Salad

1 (8 ounce) package cream cheese, softened
1 cup powdered sugar
1 (10 ounce) box frozen strawberries, thawed
1 (15 ounce) can crushed pineapple, drained
1 (8 ounce) carton whipped topping

- In mixing bowl, beat cream cheese and sugar.
- Fold in remaining ingredients. Pour into 9 x 9-inch pan and freeze.
- Cut into squares to serve.

Asparagus Bake

4 (10.5 ounce) cans asparagus
3 eggs, hard-boiled, sliced
⅓ cup milk
1½ cups grated cheddar cheese
1¼ cups cheese cracker crumbs

- Place asparagus in 7 x 11-inch baking dish. Place hard-boiled eggs on top and pour milk over casserole. Sprinkle cheese on top and add cracker crumbs.
- Bake uncovered at 350° for 30 minutes.

Fantastic Fried Corn

Yes, I know this has too many calories, but it's a favorite vegetable of my grandkids' and who can turn them down! Actually, I only fix it a couple of times a year.

2 (16 ounce) packages frozen whole kernel corn
½ cup (1 stick) butter
1 cup whipping cream
1 tablespoon sugar
1 teaspoon salt

- Place corn in large skillet and turn on medium heat.
- Add butter, whipping cream, sugar and salt.
- Stirring constantly, heat until most of whipping cream and butter is absorbed into corn.

Super Corn Casserole

1 (15 ounce) can whole kernel corn
1 (15 ounce) can cream-style corn
½ cup (1 stick) butter, melted
1 (8 ounce) carton sour cream
1 (6 ounce) package jalapeno cornbread mix

- Mix all ingredients and pour into greased 9 x 13-inch baking dish.
- Bake uncovered at 350° for 35 minutes.

Tip: It is really tasty if you add ½ cup grated cheese on top immediately after the dish comes out of oven.

Corn-Vegetable Medley

1 (10 ounce) can golden corn soup
½ cup milk
2 cups fresh broccoli florets
2 cups cauliflower florets
1 cup shredded cheddar cheese

- In saucepan over medium heat, heat soup and milk to boil. Stir often.
- Stir in broccoli and cauliflowerets and return to boil.
- Reduce heat to low, cover and cook 20 minutes or until vegetables are tender. Stir occasionally.
- Add cheese and heat until cheese melts.

Almond Green Beans

⅓ cup almonds, slivered
¼ cup (½ stick) butter
¾ teaspoon garlic salt
3 tablespoons lemon juice
2 (16 ounce) cans French-style green beans

- In saucepan, cook almonds in butter, garlic salt and lemon juice until slightly golden brown.
- Add drained green beans to almonds and heat.

Green Bean Revenge

3 (16 ounce) cans green beans, drained
1 (8 ounce) can sliced water chestnuts, drained, chopped
2 (8 ounce) jars jalapeno processed cheese spread
1½ cups cracker crumbs
¼ cup (½ stick) butter, melted

- Place green beans in greased 9 x 13-inch baking dish and cover with water chestnuts.
- Heat both jars cheese in microwave just until they can be poured (take lids off).
- Pour cheese over green beans and water chestnuts.
- Combine cracker crumbs and butter and sprinkle over casserole.
- Bake at 350° for 30 minutes.

Cheesy Green Beans

¾ cup milk
1 (8 ounce) package cream cheese
½ teaspoon garlic powder
½ cup fresh parmesan cheese
2 (16 ounce) cans green beans

- In saucepan, combine milk, cream cheese, garlic and parmesan cheese. Heat until cheeses melt.
- Heat green beans in pan, drain and cover with cream cheese mixture.
- Toss to coat evenly and serve hot.

Broccoli Supreme

2 (10 ounce) packages broccoli spears
1 (6 ounce) stick garlic-cheese roll
1 (10 ounce) can cream of mushroom soup
1 (3 ounce) can mushrooms, drained
¾ cup herb dressing, crushed

- Boil broccoli for 3 minutes and drain.
- In saucepan, melt cheese on medium heat in mushroom soup, add mushrooms and combine with broccoli.
- Pour into 2-quart greased baking dish and top with dressing. Bake uncovered at 350° for 30 minutes.

Tip: For change of pace, use cream of chicken soup instead of mushroom soup and leave out mushrooms.

Heavenly Broccoli

2 (16 ounce) packages frozen broccoli spears
1 (8 ounce) container cream cheese and chives
2 (10 ounce) cans cream of shrimp soup
2 teaspoons lemon juice
¼ cup (½ stick) butter, melted

- Trim stems off broccoli and discard. Cook broccoli in microwave according to package directions and place in 2-quart baking dish.
- In saucepan, combine cream cheese, soup, lemon juice and butter.
- Heat just enough to mix thoroughly and pour over broccoli.
- Bake at 350° just until hot and bubbly.

Best Cauliflower

1 (16 ounce) package frozen cauliflower
Salt and pepper
1 (8 ounce) carton sour cream
1½ cups grated American or cheddar cheese
4 teaspoons sesame seeds, toasted

- Cook cauliflower according to package directions. Drain and place half of cauliflower in 2-quart baking dish.
- Sprinkle a little salt and pepper on cauliflower and spread half sour cream and half cheese. Top with 2 teaspoons sesame seed and repeat layers.
- Bake at 350° for about 15 to 20 minutes.

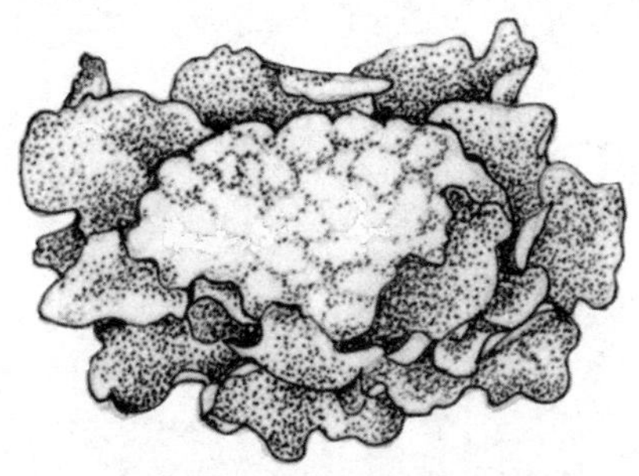

Cauliflower Medley

1 head cauliflower, cut into florets
1 (15 ounce) can Italian stewed tomatoes
1 bell pepper and 1 onion, chopped
¼ cup (½ stick) butter
1 cup shredded cheddar cheese

- In large saucepan, place cauliflower, stewed tomatoes, bell pepper, onion and butter.
- Add about 2 tablespoons water, salt and pepper.
- Cook in saucepan with lid until cauliflower is done, about 10 to 15 minutes. Do not let cauliflower get mushy.
- Place in 2-quart casserole, sprinkle cheese on top and bake at 350° just until cheese melts.

Chile-Cheese Squash

1 pound yellow squash
⅔ cup mayonnaise
1 (4 ounce) can diced green chilies, drained
⅔ cup grated longhorn cheese
⅔ cup breadcrumbs

- Cook squash in salted water just until tender-crisp and drain.
- Return to saucepan, stir in mayonnaise, chilies, cheese and breadcrumbs.
- Serve hot.

Zucchini Patties

$1\frac{1}{2}$ cups grated zucchini
1 egg, beaten
2 tablespoons flour
$\frac{1}{3}$ cup finely minced onion
$\frac{1}{2}$ teaspoon seasoned salt

- Mix all ingredients and heat skillet with about 3 tablespoons oil.
- Drop zucchini mixture by tablespoons into skillet at medium-high heat.
- Turn and brown both sides, remove and drain on paper towels.

Creamed Green Peas

1 (16 ounce) package frozen English peas
2 tablespoons ($\frac{1}{4}$ stick) butter
1 (10 ounce) can cream of celery soup
1 (3 ounce) package cream cheese
1 (8 ounce) can water chestnuts, drained

- Place peas in microwave dish and cook in microwave for 4 minutes. Turn dish and cook another 4 minutes.
- In large saucepan, combine butter, soup and cream cheese. Cook on medium heat while stirring, until butter and cream cheese melt.
- Add peas and water chestnuts, mix and serve hot.

Tasty Black-Eyed Peas

2 (10 ounce) packages frozen black-eyed peas
1¼ cups chopped green pepper
¾ cup chopped onion
3 tablespoons butter
1 (15 ounce) can stewed tomatoes with liquid

- Cook black-eyed peas according to package directions. Drain.
- Saute green pepper and onion in butter.
- Add peas, tomatoes and a little salt and pepper.
- Cook over low heat until it heats thoroughly. Stir often.

Sour Cream Cabbage

1 medium head cabbage, cooked tender crisp, drained
2 tablespoons (¼ stick) butter
1 tablespoon sugar
¼ teaspoon nutmeg
1 (4 ounce) jar pimentos, drained
1 (8 ounce) package cream cheese

- Combine cabbage, butter, sugar, nutmeg and pimentos in saucepan.
- Cook until cabbage is tender-crisp but don't overcook.
- Add cream cheese while on low heat and stir until it melts.

Creamed Spinach Bake

2 (10 ounce) packages frozen chopped spinach
2 (3 ounce) packages cream cheese, softened
3 tablespoons butter
Salt
1 cup seasoned breadcrumbs

- Cook spinach according to package directions and drain.
- Combine cream cheese and butter with spinach and heat until they melt.
- Mix well with spinach and pour into greased baking dish. Sprinkle a little salt over spinach and cover with breadcrumbs
- Bake at 350° for 15 to 20 minutes.

Cheese-Please Spinach

1 (16 ounce) package frozen chopped spinach
3 eggs
½ cup flour
1 (16 ounce) carton small curd cottage cheese
2 cups shredded cheddar cheese

- Cook spinach, drain and set aside. Beat eggs. Add flour, cottage cheese and a little salt and pepper.
- Stir in spinach and cheddar cheese and pour into 1½-quart baking dish.
- Bake uncovered at 350° for 35 minutes.

Baked Tomatoes

2 (16 ounce) cans diced tomatoes, drained
1½ cups toasted breadcrumbs, divided
A scant ¼ cup sugar
½ onion, chopped
¼ cup (½ stick) butter, melted

- Combine tomatoes, 1 cup breadcrumbs, sugar, onion and butter.
- Pour into buttered baking dish and cover with remaining breadcrumbs.
- Bake at 325° for 25 to 30 minutes or until crumbs are light brown.

Mixed Vegetable-Cheese Casserole

These vegetables are worthy of Sunday dinner and a way to get kids to eat vegetables.

1 (16 ounce) packages frozen mixed vegetables
1½ cups shredded American cheese
¾ cup mayonnaise
1 tube round buttery crackers, crushed
6 tablespoons (¾ stick) butter, melted

- Cook vegetables according to package directions and drain. Place in 2-quart buttered casserole dish.
- Mix cheese and mayonnaise and spread over vegetables.
- Mix cracker crumbs and butter and sprinkle on top.
- Bake at 350° for 35 minutes.

Creamy Vegetable Casserole

1 (16 ounce) package frozen broccoli, carrots and cauliflower
1 (10 ounce) can cream of mushroom soup with liquid
1 (8 ounce) carton garden vegetable cream cheese
1 cup seasoned croutons

- Cook vegetables according to package directions, drain and place in large bowl.
- In saucepan, place soup and cream cheese and heat just enough to mix easily. Pour into vegetable mixture, mix well and pour into 2-quart baking dish.
- Sprinkle with croutons and bake uncovered at 375° for 25 minutes or until bubbly.

Zucchini Bake

4 cups grated zucchini
1½ cups grated Monterey Jack cheese
1 teaspoon seasoned salt
4 eggs, beaten
2 cups cheese cracker crumbs

- In mixing bowl, combine zucchini, cheese, seasoned salt and eggs and mix well.
- Spoon into buttered 3-quart baking dish and sprinkle cracker crumbs over top.
- Bake uncovered at 350° for 35 minutes.

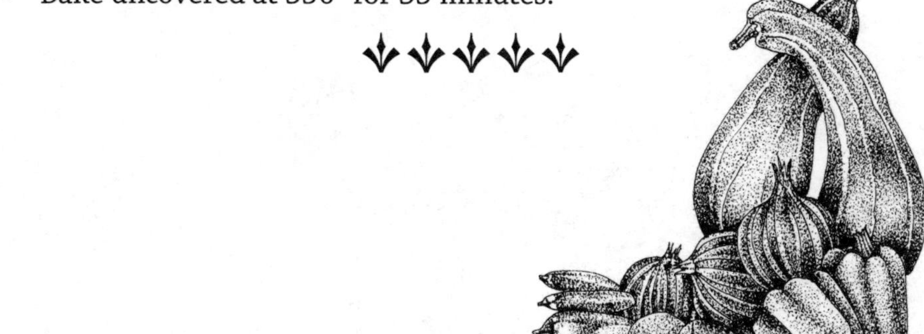

Baked Broccoli

2 (10 ounce) packages frozen broccoli spears
1 can cream of chicken soup
⅔ cup mayonnaise
¾ cup breadcrumbs
Paprika

- Place broccoli spears in 9 x 13-inch baking dish.
- In saucepan, combine and heat soup and mayonnaise. Pour mixture over broccoli and sprinkle with breadcrumbs and paprika.
- Bake at 325° for 45 minutes.

Parmesan Broccoli

1 (16 ounce) package frozen broccoli spears
½ teaspoon garlic powder
½ cup breadcrumbs
¼ cup (½ stick) butter, melted
½ cup grated parmesan cheese

- Cook broccoli according to package directions. Drain.
- Add remaining ingredients to cooked broccoli and salt if desired. Toss.
- Heat and serve.

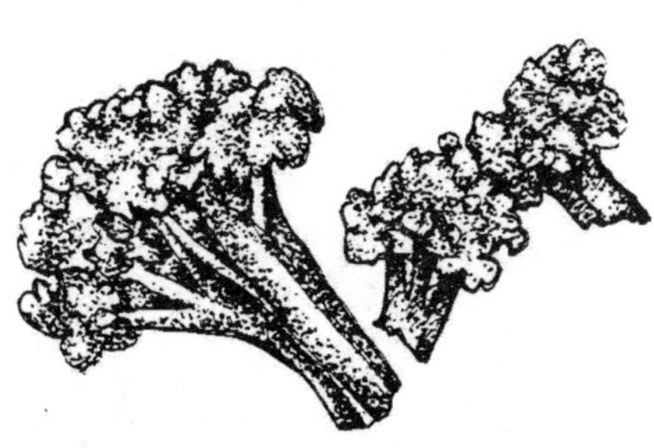

Country Baked Beans

4 (16 ounce) cans baked beans, drained
1 (12 ounce) bottle chili sauce
1 large onion, chopped
½ pound bacon, cooked and crumbled
2 cups packed brown sugar

- Combine all ingredients in an ungreased 3-quart baking dish. Mix well.
- Bake uncovered at 325° for 55 minutes or until it heats thoroughly.

Spinach Casserole

1 (16 ounce) package frozen chopped spinach
1 (8 ounce) package cream cheese and chives
1 can cream of mushroom soup
1 egg, beaten
Cracker crumbs

- Cook spinach according to package directions and drain. In mixing bowl, blend cream cheese and soup with egg.
- Combine mixture with spinach and pour into buttered casserole dish.
- Top with cracker crumbs and bake at 350° for 35 minutes.

Scalloped Potatoes

6 medium potatoes
½ cup (1 stick) butter, divided
1 tablespoon flour
2 cups grated cheddar cheese
¾ cup milk

- Peel and slice half potatoes and place in 3-quart greased baking dish.
- Slice half butter over potatoes, sprinkle flour over potatoes and cover with half cheese. Repeat layers with cheese on top.
- Pour milk over casserole and sprinkle a little pepper. Prepare potatoes as fast as you can to prevent them from turning dark. Cover and bake at 350° for 1 hour.

Cheddar Potato Strips

3 large potatoes, cut into ½ inch strips
½ cup milk
2 tablespoons (¼ stick) butter
½ cup shredded cheddar cheese
1 tablespoon minced fresh parsley

- In greased 9 x 13-inch baking dish, arrange potatoes in single layer. Pour milk over potatoes and dot with butter. Sprinkle a little salt and pepper.
- Cover and bake at 400° for 30 minutes or until potatoes are tender.
- Sprinkle with cheese and parsley and bake uncovered for another 5 minutes.

Oven Fries

5 medium baking potatoes
⅓ cup oil
¼ teaspoon black pepper
¾ seasoned salt
Paprika

- Scrub potatoes and cut each in 6 lengthwise wedges. Place potatoes in shallow baking dish.
- In bowl, combine oil, pepper and seasoned salt and brush potatoes. Sprinkle lightly with paprika and bake at 375° for about 50 minutes or until potatoes are tender and light brown.
- Baste twice with remaining oil mixture while baking.

Terrific 'Taters

5 to 6 medium potatoes
1 (8 ounce) carton sour cream
1 (1 ounce) package dry ranch-style salad dressing mix
1½ cups shredded cheddar cheese
3 pieces bacon, fried, drained and crumbled

- Peel, slice and boil potatoes. Drain and place potatoes in 2-quart baking dish.
- Combine sour cream and dressing mix. Toss until potatoes coat well in mixture. Sprinkle cheese on top.
- Bake at 350° for about 20 minutes. Sprinkle bacon on top and serve hot.

Mashed Potatoes Supreme

1 (8 ounce) package cream cheese, softened
½ cup sour cream
2 tablespoons (¼ stick) butter, softened
1 (1 ounce) package ranch salad dressing mix
6 to 8 cups warm mashed potatoes

- With mixer, combine cream cheese, sour cream, butter and dressing and mix well.
- Add potatoes and stir well.
- Transfer to 2-quart casserole dish and bake at 350° for 25 minutes or until it heats well.

Tip: Use instant mashed potatoes to make 6 to 8 cups mashed potatoes.

Ranch-Mashed Potatoes

4 cups prepared, unsalted mashed potatoes
1 (1 ounce) package ranch-style dressing mix
¼ cup (½ stick) butter
½ cup half-and-half cream
1 (2.8 ounce) can French fried onions, optional

- Combine all ingredients in saucepan.
- Heat on low until potatoes heat thoroughly.
- Top with fried onions if you like and heat an additional 5 minutes.

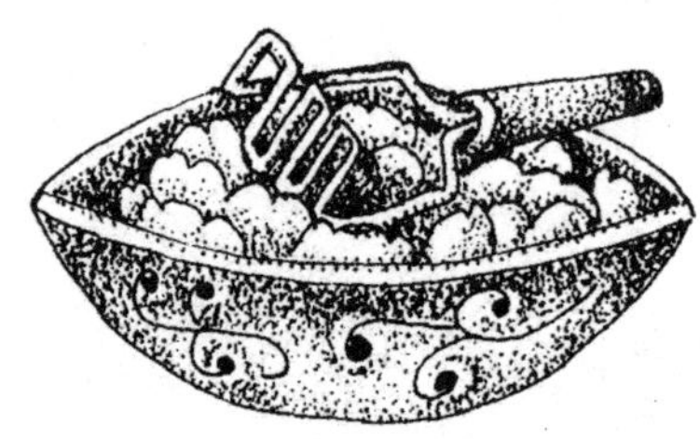

Loaded Baked Potatoes

6 medium potatoes
1 (1 pound) hot sausage
1 (16 ounce) package cubed processed cheese
1 (10 ounce) can tomatoes and green chilies
½ teaspoon minced garlic

- Wrap potatoes in foil and bake at 375° for 1 hour or until done.
- Brown sausage and drain. Cut cheese into chunks and add to sausage.
- Heat until cheese melts and add tomatoes and green chilies and garlic.

Broccoli-Cheese Potato Topper

1 (10 ounce) can fiesta nacho cheese soup
2 tablespoons sour cream
½ teaspoon dijon-style mustard
1 (10 ounce) box frozen broccoli florets, cooked
4 medium potatoes, baked, fluffed

- In 1-quart microwave baking dish, stir soup, sour cream, mustard and broccoli.
- Heat in microwave for 2 to 2½ minutes and spoon over potato halves.

Potatoes Au Gratin

1 (8 ounce) package cubed processed cheese
1 (16 ounce) carton half-and-half cream
1 cup shredded cheddar cheese
½ cup (1 stick) butter
1 (2 pound) package frozen hash brown potatoes

- In double boiler, melt processed cheese, cream, cheddar cheese and butter.
- Place hash browns in greased 9 x 13-inch baking dish and pour cheese mixture over potatoes.
- Bake uncovered at 350° for 1 hour.

Chive-Potato Souffle

3 eggs, separated
2 cups hot mashed potatoes
½ cup sour cream
2 heaping tablespoons chopped chives
1 teaspoon seasoned salt

- Beat egg whites until stiff and set aside. Beat yolks until smooth and add to potatoes.
- Fold in beaten egg whites, sour cream, chives and salt and pour into buttered 2-quart baking dish.
- Bake at 350° for 45 minutes.

Tip: Use instant potatoes to make 6 to 8 cups mashed potatoes.

Herbed New Potatoes

1½ pounds new potatoes
6 tablespoons (¾ stick) butter, sliced
¼ teaspoon thyme
½ cup chopped fresh parsley
½ teaspoon rosemary

- Scrub potatoes, cut in halves, but do not peel.
- In medium saucepan, boil in lightly salted water for about 20 minutes or until potatoes are tender and drain.
- Add butter, thyme, parsley and rosemary and toss gently until butter melts. Serve hot.

Carnival Couscous

This is a delicious, colorful dish that easily replaces rice or a vegetable.

1 (5.7 ounce) box herbed chicken couscous
¼ cup (½ stick) butter
1 red bell pepper, minced
1 yellow squash, seeded, minced
¾ cup fresh broccoli flowerets, finely chopped

- Cook couscous according to package directions but leave out butter.
- With butter in saucepan, saute bell pepper, squash and broccoli and cook about 10 minutes or until vegetables are almost tender.
- Combine couscous and vegetables.

Tip: If you want to do this a little ahead of time, place couscous and vegetable in sprayed non-stick baking dish and heat at 325° for about 20 minutes.

Macaroni, Cheese and Tomatoes

2 cups elbow macaroni, uncooked
1 (14 ounce) can stewed tomatoes with liquid
1 (8 ounce) package shredded cheddar cheese
2 tablespoons sugar
1 (6 ounce) package cheese slices

- Cook macaroni according to package directions and drain.
- In large mixing bowl, combine macaroni, tomatoes, shredded cheese, sugar, ¼ cup water and a little salt and mix well.
- Pour into 9 x 13-inch baking dish and place cheese slices on top.
- Bake at 350° for 30 minutes or until bubbly.

Red Rice

1 (16 ounce) package smoked sausage, sliced
2 (10 ounce) cans diced tomato and green chilies
3 cups chicken broth
2 teaspoons Creole seasoning
1½ cups uncooked, long-grain rice

- Saute sausage in Dutch oven until brown.
- Stir in tomato and green chilies, broth and seasoning and bring to boil.
- Stir in rice, cover and reduce heat.
- Simmer 25 minutes, uncover and cook until liquid absorbs.

Grits Souffle

1½ cups grits
1½ teaspoons salt
½ cup (1 stick) butter
1½ cups shredded cheddar cheese
5 eggs, beaten

- Boil grits in 6 cups salted water. Stir in butter and cheese until cheese melts.
- Cool until lukewarm and add eggs.
- Pour into greased 2-quart baking dish and bake at 350° for 45 minutes.

Favorite Pasta

4 ounces spinach linguine, uncooked
1 cup whipping cream
1 cup chicken broth
½ cup freshly grated parmesan cheese
½ cup frozen English peas

- Cook linguine according to package directions, drain and keep warm.
- Combine whipping cream and chicken broth in saucepan and bring to boil.
- Reduce heat and simmer mixture 25 minutes or until it thickens and reduces to 1 cup.
- Remove from heat and add cheese and peas, stirring until cheese melts.
- Toss with linguine and serve immediately.

Pasta with Basil

2½ cups uncooked small tube pasta
1 small onion, chopped
2 tablespoons oil
2½ tablespoons dried basil
1 cup shredded mozzarella cheese

- Cook pasta according to package directions. In skillet, saute onion in oil.
- Stir in basil, 1 teaspoon salt and ¼ teaspoon pepper and cook and stir 1 minute.
- Drain pasta leaving about ½ cup so pasta won't be too dry and add to basil mixture.
- Remove from heat and stir in cheese just until it melts. Serve immediately.

Speedy Sweet Potatoes

2 (16 ounce) cans sweet potatoes, drained
1 (8 ounce) can crushed pineapple with juice
½ cup chopped pecans
⅓ cup packed brown sugar
1 cup miniature marshmallows

- In 2-quart microwave dish, layer sweet potatoes, a little salt, pineapple, pecans, brown sugar and ½ cup marshmallows. Cover and microwave on HIGH for 6 minutes or until bubbly around edges.
- Top with remaining marshmallows and heat uncovered on HIGH for 30 seconds or until marshmallows puff. If you like, sprinkle sweet potatoes with little nutmeg.

Festive Cranberry Stuffing

1 (14 ounce) can chicken broth
1 rib celery, chopped
½ cup fresh or frozen cranberries
1 small onion, chopped
4 cups herb-seasoned stuffing

- Mix broth, dash of black pepper, celery, cranberries and onion in saucepan and heat to boil. Cover and cook over low heat 5 minutes.
- Add stuffing, mix lightly and spoon into baking dish.
- Bake at 325° just until it heats thoroughly.

Whipped Sweet Potatoes

1 (28 ounce) can sweet potatoes
1 cup (2 sticks) butter, melted, divided
1 cup packed light brown sugar
½ teaspoon ground cinnamon
1½ cups crushed corn flakes

- Drain most of liquid from sweet potatoes. Place sweet potatoes in mixing bowl and cut large pieces of potatoes into small pieces.
- Beat sweet potatoes until creamy and fold in ¾ cup (1½ sticks) melted butter, brown sugar and cinnamon.
- Beat until butter and sugar thoroughly combine with sweet potatoes and pour into buttered 2-quart baking dish.
- Combine crushed corn flakes and remaining melted butter and sprinkle over sweet potato casserole.
- Bake uncovered at 350° for 40 minutes.

Spiced Beef

1 pound lean ground beef
1 (1 ounce) package taco seasoning mix
1 (16 ounce) can Mexican stewed tomatoes with liquid
1 (15 ounce) can kidney beans with liquid
1 (1 pound) package egg noodles

- Cook beef in skillet and drain. Add taco seasoning and ½ cup water and simmer 15 minutes.
- Add stewed tomatoes and kidney beans. (You may need to add ¼ teaspoon salt.)
- Cook egg noodles according to package directions.

Tip: This is excellent serve over noodles.

Asian Beef and Noodles

1¼ pounds ground beef
2 (3 ounce) packages Oriental-flavored ramen noodles
1 (16 ounce) package frozen Oriental stir-fry mixture
½ teaspoon ground ginger
3 tablespoons thinly sliced green onions

- In large skillet, brown ground beef and drain. Add ½ cup water, salt and pepper and simmer 10 minutes. Transfer to separate bowl.
- In same skillet, combine 2 cups water, vegetables, noodles (broken up), ginger and both seasoning packets. Bring to boil and reduce heat.
- Cover and simmer 3 minutes or until noodles are tender. Stir occasionally.
- Return beef to skillet and stir in green onions. Serve right from skillet.

Pinto Bean Pie

1 pound lean ground beef
1 onion, chopped
2 (16 ounce) cans pinto beans with liquid, divided
1 (10 ounce) can tomatoes and green chilies with liquid
1 can french-fried onion rings

- In skillet, brown beef and onion and drain.
- In 2-quart casserole dish, layer 1 can beans, beef-onion mixture and ½ can tomatoes and green chilies. Repeat layer.
- Top with onion rings and bake uncovered at 350° for 30 minutes.

Chili Casserole

1 (40 ounce) can chili with beans
1 (4 ounce) can chopped green chilies
1 (2¼ ounce) can sliced ripe olives, drained
1 (8 ounce) package shredded cheddar cheese
2 cups ranch-flavored tortilla chips, crushed

- Combine all ingredients and transfer to greased 3-quart casserole dish.
- Bake uncovered at 350° for 35 minutes or until bubbly.

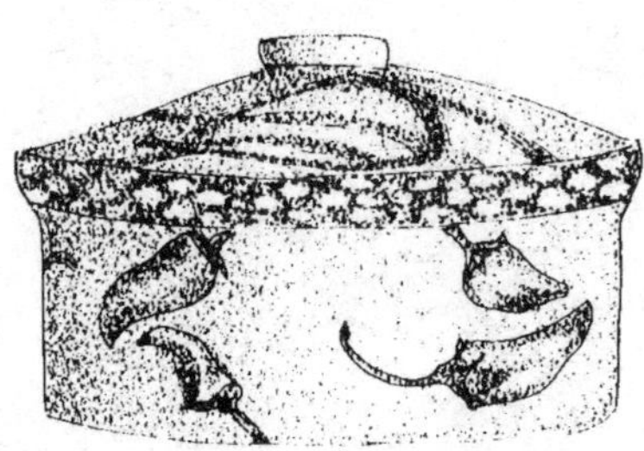

Easy Chili

2 pounds lean ground chuck
1 onion, chopped
4 (16 ounce) cans chili-hot beans with liquid
1 (1¾ ounce) package chili seasoning mix
1 (46 ounce) can tomato juice

- Cook beef and onion in Dutch oven, stir until meat crumbles and drain.
- Stir in remaining ingredients and bring mixture to a boil. Reduce heat and simmer, stirring occasionally, for 2 hours.

Oven Brisket

1 (5 to 6 pound) trimmed brisket
1 (1 ounce) package onion soup mix
1 (12 ounce) can cola
1 (10 ounce) bottle Heinz 57 sauce
1 teaspoon garlic, minced

- Place brisket, fat side up, in roasting pan.
- Combine remaining ingredients and pour over brisket. Cover and bake at 325° for 4 to 5 hours or until tender.
- Remove brisket from pan and pour off drippings. Chill both, separately, overnight.
- The next day, trim all fat from meat, slice and reheat. Skim fat off drippings and reheat. Serve sauce over brisket.

Great Brisket

2 onions, sliced
Paprika
Seasoned salt
5 to 6 pound trimmed brisket
1 (12 ounce) Pepsi-Cola

- Place onions in bottom of roaster. Sprinkle with paprika and seasoned salt.
- Lay brisket on top of onions and sprinkle more seasoned salt.
- Bake uncovered at 450° for 30 minutes. Pour Pepsi over roast and reduce oven to 325°. Cover with foil and bake for approximately 4 hours or until tender,
- Baste occasionally with Pepsi and juices from brisket.

Sweet and Savory Brisket

1 (3 to 4 pound) trimmed beef brisket, halved
⅓ cup grape or plum jelly
1 cup ketchup
1 (1 ounce) packet dry onion soup mix
¾ teaspoon black pepper

- Place half of brisket in slow cooker. In bowl, combine jelly, ketchup, soup mix and pepper and spread half over meat.
- Top with remaining brisket and ketchup mixture. Cover and cook on low for 8 to 10 hours or until meat is tender. Slice brisket and serve with cooking juices.

Lemon-Herb Pot Roast

1 (3 to 3½ pound) boneless beef chuck roast
1 teaspoon garlic powder
2 teaspoons lemon-pepper seasoning
1 teaspoon dried basil
1 tablespoon oil

- Combine garlic, lemon pepper and basil and press evenly into surface of beef.
- In Dutch oven, heat oil over medium-high heat until hot. Brown roast.
- Add 1 cup water, bring to boil and reduce heat to low.
- Cover tightly and simmer for 3 hours.

Tip: Vegetables may be added to roast the last hour of cooking.

Prime Rib of Beef

⅓ cup each: chopped onion and chopped celery
1 teaspoon salt
½ teaspoon garlic powder
1 (6 to 8 pounds) beef rib roast
1 (14 ounce) can beef broth

- Combine onion and celery and place in greased roasting pan. Combine salt, garlic powder and a little black pepper and rub over roast. Place roast over vegetables with fat side up.
- Bake uncovered at 350° for 2½ to 3½ hours or until meat reaches desired doneness. (medium-rare 145°, medium 160°, well-done 170°)
- Let stand for about 15 minutes before carving. Skim fat from pan drippings, add beef broth and stir to remove browned bits. Heat and strain, discarding vegetables. Serve au jus with roast.

Delicious Meat Loaf

1½ pounds lean ground beef
⅔ cup Italian-seasoned dry breadcrumbs
1 eggs, beaten
1 (10 ounce) can golden mushroom soup
2 tablespoons butter

- Combine beef, breadcrumbs, ½ mushroom soup and egg and blend well. In baking pan, shape firmly into 8 x 4-inch loaf. Bake at 350° for 45 minutes.
- In small saucepan, mix 2 tablespoons butter, remaining soup and ¼ cup water.
- Heat thoroughly and serve with meat loaf.

Spanish Meatloaf

1½ pounds lean ground beef
1 (16 ounce) can Spanish rice
1 egg, beaten
¾ cup round, buttery cracker crumbs
Chunky salsa

- Combine beef, rice, egg and crumbs and shape into loaf in greased pan.
- Bake at 350° for 1 hour and serve with salsa on top of meat loaf.

Chicken Ole

6 boneless, skinless chicken breast halves
1 (8 ounce) package cream cheese, softened
1 (16 ounce) jar hot sauce
2 teaspoons cumin
1 cup fresh green onion with tops, chopped

- Pound chicken breasts flat. In mixing bowl, beat cream cheese until smooth and add hot sauce, cumin and onions.
- Place 1 heaping spoonful of mixture on each chicken breast and roll. Place seam side down in shallow baking pan.
- Pour remaining sauce over top of chicken rolls.
- Bake uncovered at 350° for 50 minutes.

Chicken Crunch

4 chicken boneless, skinless breast halves
½ cup Italian salad dressing
½ cup sour cream
2½ cups corn flakes, crushed

- Place chicken in plastic bag and add dressing and sour cream. Seal and refrigerate 1 hour.
- Remove chicken from marinade and discard marinade.
- Dredge chicken in corn flakes and place in 9 x 13-inch sprayed baking dish.
- Bake at 375° for 45 minutes.

Favorite Chicken Breasts

6 to 8 boneless, skinless chicken breast halves
1 (10 ounce) can cream of mushroom soup
¾ cup white wine or white cooking wine
1 (8 ounce) carton sour cream

- Place chicken breasts in large, shallow baking pan. Sprinkle on a little salt and pepper.
- Bake uncovered at 350° for 30 minutes.
- In saucepan, combine soup, wine and sour cream and heat just enough to mix.
- Remove chicken from oven and pour sour cream mixture over chicken.
- Return to oven to cook another 30 minutes. Baste twice and serve over rice.

Broccoli-Cheese Chicken

1 tablespoon butter
4 boneless, skinless chicken breasts
1 (10 ounce) can broccoli-cheese soup
1 (10 ounce) package frozen broccoli spears
⅓ cup milk

- In skillet, heat butter and cook chicken 15 minutes or until brown on both sides.
- Remove and set aside. In same skillet, combine soup, broccoli, milk and a little black pepper. Heat to boiling.
- Return chicken to skillet and reduce heat to low. Cover and cook another 25 minutes until chicken is no longer pink and broccoli is tender. Serve over rice.

Hawaiian Chicken

2 small, whole chickens, quartered
Flour to coat chicken
Oil
1 (20 ounce) can sliced pineapple with juice
2 bell peppers, cut in strips

- Wash and pat chicken dry with paper towels. Coat chicken with salt, pepper and flour. Brown chicken in oil and place in shallow pan.
- Drain pineapple into 2-cup measure. Add water (or orange juice if you prefer) to make 1½ cups liquid. Reserve juice for sauce.

Sauce for Hawaiian Chicken:

1 cup sugar
3 tablespoons corn starch
¾ cup vinegar, 1 tablespoon lemon juice
1 tablespoon soy sauce
2 teaspoons chicken bouillon

- In medium saucepan, combine 1½ cups juice, sugar, corn starch, vinegar, lemon juice, soy sauce and chicken bouillon.
- Bring to boil and stir constantly until thick and clear. Pour over chicken and bake at 350° covered for 40 minutes.
- Place pineapple slices and bell pepper on top of chicken and bake another 10 minutes.
- Serve on fluffy white rice.

Apricot Chicken

1 cup apricot preserves
1 (8 ounce) bottle Catalina salad dressing
1 (1 ounce) package onion soup mix
6 to 8 boneless, skinless chicken breast halves

- Combine apricot preserves, dressing and soup mix.
- Place chicken breasts in large, buttered baking dish and pour apricot mixture over chicken. (For change of pace, use Russian dressing instead of Catalina).
- Bake uncovered at 325° for 1 hour 20 minutes. Serve over hot rice.

Hurry-Up Chicken Enchiladas

2½ to 3 cups cooked, cubed chicken breasts
1 (10 ounce) can cream of chicken soup
1½ cups chunky salsa
8 (6 inch) flour tortillas
1 (10 ounce) can fiesta-nacho cheese soup

- In saucepan, combine chicken, soup and ½ cup salsa and heat through.
- Spoon about ⅓ cup chicken mixture down center of each tortilla and roll up tortilla around filling. Place, seam-side down in sprayed 9 x 13-inch baking dish.
- Mix nacho cheese, remaining salsa and ¼ cup water. Pour over enchiladas.
- Cover with wax paper and microwave on HIGH, turning several times, for 5 minutes or until bubbly.

Chicken Marseilles

3 tablespoons butter
5 to 6 boneless, skinless chicken breast halves
1 (1 ounce) package vegetable soup-dip mix
½ teaspoon dill weed
½ cup sour cream

- Melt butter in skillet and brown chicken, turning occasionally, for about 10 to 15 minutes.
- Stir 2 cups water, soup mix and dill into skillet and bring to boil.
- Reduce heat, cover and simmer, stirring occasionally, for 25 to 30 minutes or until chicken is tender. Remove chicken to heated plate.
- After removing chicken, add sour cream to skillet and stir until creamy.
- Spoon sauce over chicken.

Tip: This chicken is terrific with instant brown rice. Place chicken on cooked rice and cover with sauce. It is a simple, but very delicious dinner.

Grilled Chicken Cordon Bleu

6 boneless, skinless chicken breast halves
6 slices Swiss cheese
6 thin slices deli ham
3 tablespoons oil
1 cup seasoned breadcrumbs

- Flatten chicken to ¼-inch thickness. Place 1 slice cheese and ham on each half to within ¼ inch of edge.
- Fold in half and secure with toothpicks. Brush with oil and roll in breadcrumbs.
- Grill, covered, over medium-hot heat for 15 to 18 minutes or until juices run clear.

✤✤✤✤✤

One-Dish Chicken Bake

1 (6 ounce) package chicken stuffing mix
1⅔ cups water
4 boneless, skinless chicken breast halves
1 (10 ounce) can cream of mushroom soup
⅓ cup sour cream

- Toss together stuffing mix, vegetable-seasoning packet included in stuffing mix and water. Set aside.
- Place chicken in greased 9 x 13-inch baking dish.
- Mix soup and sour cream in saucepan over low heat and pour over chicken. Spoon stuffing evenly over top and bake uncovered at 375° for 40 minutes.

Honey-Baked Chicken

2 whole chickens, quartered
½ cup (1 stick) butter, melted
⅔ cup honey
¼ cup dijon-style mustard
1 teaspoon curry powder

- Place chicken pieces skin side up in large shallow baking dish. Sprinkle a little salt over chicken.
- Combine butter, honey, mustard and curry powder. Pour over chicken and bake uncovered at 350° for 1 hour 5 minutes. Baste every 20 minutes.

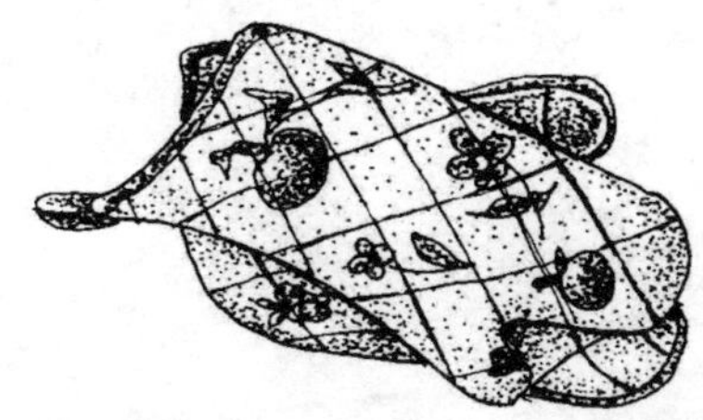

Sweet and Sour Chicken

6 to 8 boneless, skinless chicken breast halves
Oil
1 (1 ounce) package dry onion soup mix
1 (6 ounce) can frozen orange juice concentrate, thawed
⅔ cup water

- Brown chicken in a little oil or butter. Place chicken in greased 9 x 13-inch baking dish.
- In small bowl, combine onion soup mix, orange juice and water and mix well. Pour over chicken and bake uncovered at 350° for 45 to 50 minutes.

Bacon-Wrapped Chicken

6 boneless, skinless chicken breast halves
1 (8 ounce) carton whipped cream cheese with onion and chives
Butter
Salt
6 bacon strips

- Flatten chicken to ½-inch thickness. Spread 3 tablespoons cream cheese over each. Dot with butter and a little salt and roll up.
- Wrap each with 1 bacon strip.
- Place seam side down in greased 9 x 13-inch baking dish.
- Bake uncovered at 375° for 40 to 45 minutes or until juices run clear.
- To brown, broil 6 inches from heat for about 3 minutes or until bacon is crisp.

Oven-Fried Chicken

⅔ cup fine dry breadcrumbs
⅓ cup grated parmesan cheese
½ teaspoon garlic salt
6 boneless, skinless chicken breast halves
¼ cup Italian salad dressing

- In small bowl, combine breadcrumbs, cheese and garlic salt. Dip chicken in dressing and dredge in crumb mixture.
- Place chicken in 9 x 13-inch sprayed pan.
- Bake uncovered at 350° for 50 minutes.

Party Chicken Breasts

6 to 8 boneless, skinless chicken breast halves
8 strips bacon
1 (1.5 ounce) jar chipped beef
1 (10 ounce) can cream of chicken soup
1 (8 ounce) carton sour cream

- Wrap each chicken breast with 1 strip bacon and secure with toothpicks.
- Place chipped beef in bottom of large, shallow baking pan. Top with chicken.
- Heat soup and sour cream, just enough to pour over chicken.
- Bake uncovered at 325° for 1 hour.

Ranch Chicken

2 pounds chicken drumsticks
½ cup (1 stick) butter, melted
½ cup grated parmesan cheese
1½ cups corn flakes
1 (1 ounce) package dry ranch dressing mix

- Dip washed, dried chicken in melted butter. Combine cheese, corn flakes and dressing mix and dredge chicken in mixture.
- Bake uncovered at 350° for 50 minutes or until golden brown.

Pineapple-Pork Chops

6 to 8 thick, boneless pork chops
1 (6 ounce) can frozen pineapple juice concentrate, thawed
3 tablespoons brown sugar
⅓ cup wine or tarragon vinegar
⅓ cup honey

- Place pork chops in a little oil in skillet and brown. Remove to shallow baking dish.
- Combine pineapple juice, sugar, vinegar and honey. Pour over pork chops.
- Cook covered at 325° for about 50 minutes. Serve over hot rice.

Tip: I like to thicken the sauce made when pork chops are done. I mix corn starch with a little water and stir into sauce. I also like to put pork chops over Uncle Ben's instant brown rice.

Orange-Pork Chops

6 to 8 medium thick pork chops
Flour
¼ cup (½ stick) butter
2 cups orange juice
Hot, cooked rice

- Dip pork chops in flour and brown in skillet with butter. Place chops in 9 x 13-inch baking pan and pour remaining butter over top of pork chops.
- Pour orange juice over chops.
- Cover and bake at 325° for 55 minutes. Uncover for last 15 minutes.
- Serve over hot, cooked rice.

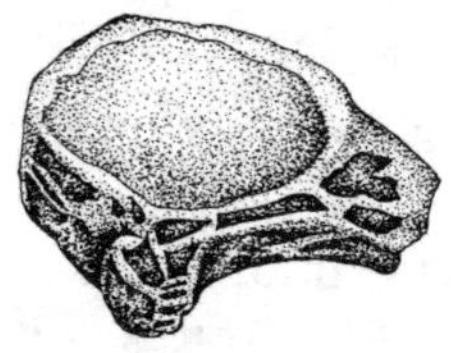

Oven Pork Chops

6 to 8 medium thick pork chops
1 (10 ounce) can cream of chicken soup
3 tablespoons ketchup
1 tablespoon worcestershire
1 medium onion, chopped

- Brown pork chops in a little oil and season with salt and pepper. Place drained pork chops in shallow baking dish.
- In saucepan, combine soup, ketchup, worcestershire and onion. Heat just enough to mix and pour over pork chops.
- Bake covered at 350° for 50 minutes. Uncover the last 15 minutes.

Onion-Smothered Pork Chops

1 tablespoon oil
6 (½ inch) thick pork chops
1 onion, chopped
2 tablespoons butter
1 (10 ounce) can cream of onion soup

- In skillet, brown pork chops in oil and simmer about 10 minutes.
- In same skillet, add butter and saute chopped onion. (Pan juices are brown from pork chops so onions will be brown from juices already in skillet.)
- Add onion soup and ½ cup water. Stir well to create pretty, light brown color.
- Pour onion-soup mixture over pork chops. Cover and bake at 325° for 40 minutes. Serve with Uncle Ben's brown rice.

Pork Chops in Cream Gravy

4 (¼ inch) thick pork chops
Salt and pepper
Flour
Oil
2¼ cups milk

- Trim all fat off pork chops. Dip chops in flour with a little salt and pepper.
- Brown pork chops on both sides in a little oil. Remove chops from skillet.
- Add about 2 tablespoons flour to skillet, brown lightly and stir in a little salt and pepper. Slowly stir in milk to make gravy.
- Return chops to skillet with gravy. Cover and simmer on low burner for about 40 minutes. Serve over rice or noodles.

✦✦✦✦✦

Grilled Pork Loin

1 (4 pound) boneless pork loin roast
1 (8 ounce) bottle Italian salad dressing
1 cup dry white wine
3 cloves garlic, minced
10 black peppercorns

- Pierce roast at 1-inch intervals with fork and set aside. (Piercing allows marinade to penetrate meat better.)
- Combine dressing and remaining ingredients in large plastic bag. Reserve ½ cup mixture for basting during grilling.
- Add roast to remaining mixture in bag, chill 8 hours and turn occasionally.
- Remove roast from marinade and discard marinade. Place roast on grill rack. Cook, covered with grill lid, for 35 minutes or until meat thermometer inserted into thickest portion reaches 160°.
- Turn and baste with reserve ½ cup dressing mixture.

Apricot-Baked Ham

This is the ham you will want for Easter dinner!

1 (12 to 20 pound) whole ham, fully cooked
Whole cloves
2 tablespoons dry mustard
1¼ cups apricot jam
1¼ cups packed light brown sugar

- Heat oven to 450°. Place ham on rack in large roasting pan. Insert cloves in ham every inch or so.
- Combine dry mustard and jam and spread over entire surface of ham. Pat brown sugar over jam mixture.
- Reduce heat to 325°. Bake uncovered at 15 minutes per pound.

Baked Ham and Pineapple

1 (6 to 8 pound) fully cooked, bone-in ham
Whole cloves
½ cup packed brown sugar
1 (8 ounce) can sliced pineapple
5 maraschino cherries

- Place ham in roasting pan. Score surface with shallow diagonal cuts making diamond shapes and insert cloves into diamonds.
- Cover and bake at 325° for 1 hour 30 minutes.
- Combine brown sugar and juice from pineapple and pour over ham.
- Arrange pineapple slices and cherries on ham. Bake uncovered 40 minutes longer.

Praline Ham

2 (½ inch) thick ham slices, cooked
½ cup maple syrup
3 tablespoons brown sugar
1 tablespoon butter
⅓ cup chopped pecans

- Bake ham slices in shallow pan at 325° for 10 minutes.
- Bring syrup, sugar and butter to boil in small saucepan and stir often. Stir in pecans and spoon over ham.
- Bake another 20 minutes.

Tip: These 2 ham slices are about 2½ pounds.

Pineapple Sauce for Ham

Pre-sliced, cooked honey-baked ham slices
1 (15 ounce) can pineapple chunks with juice
1 cup apricot preserves
1¼ cups packed brown sugar
¼ teaspoon cinnamon

- Place ham slices in shallow baking pan. In saucepan, combine pineapple preserves, brown sugar and cinnamon and heat.
- Pour sauce over ham slices and heat.

Tangy Apricot Ribs

3 to 4 pounds baby back pork loin ribs
1 (16 ounce) jar apricot preserves
⅓ cup soy sauce
¼ cup packed light brown sugar
2 teaspoons garlic powder

- Place ribs in large roasting pan. Whisk preserves, soy sauce, brown sugar and garlic powder until they blend and pour over ribs. Cover and chill overnight.
- Remove ribs from marinade and reserve marinade in small saucepan.
- Line baking pan with foil, add ribs and sprinkle with a little salt and pepper.
- Bring marinade to boil, cover, reduce heat and simmer 5 minutes.
- Bake ribs at 325° for 1 hour 30 minutes or until tender and baste frequently with marinade.

Sweet and Sour Spareribs

3 to 4 pounds spareribs
3 tablespoons soy sauce
⅓ cup prepared mustard
1 cup packed brown sugar
½ teaspoon garlic salt

- Place spareribs in roaster. Bake at 325° for 45 minutes. Drain.
- Make sauce with remaining ingredients and brush on ribs.
- Return to oven, reduce heat to 300° and bake for 1 hour or until tender. Baste several times while cooking.

Orange Roughy with Peppers

1 pound orange roughy filets
1 onion, sliced
2 red bell peppers, cut into julienne strips
1 teaspoon dried thyme leaves
¼ teaspoon black pepper

- Cut fish into 4 serving pieces. Heat a little oil in skillet. Layer onion and bell peppers in skillet and sprinkle with half thyme and pepper.
- Place fish over peppers and sprinkle with remaining thyme and pepper.
- Turn burner on high until fish is hot enough to begin cooking. Lower heat, cover and cook fish for 15 to 20 minutes or until fish flakes easily.

Lemon-Dill Filets

½ cup mayonnaise
2 tablespoons lemon juice
½ teaspoon lemon peel
1 teaspoon dill weed
1 pound cod or flounder filets

- Combine all ingredients except filets and blend well.
- Place fish on greased grill or broiler rack. Brush with half of sauce. Grill or broil 5 to 8 minutes, turn and brush with remaining sauce.
- Continue grilling or broiling 5 to 8 minutes or until fish flakes easily with fork.

Flounder Au Gratin

½ cup fine dry breadcrumbs
¼ cup grated parmesan cheese
¼ teaspoon seasoned salt
1 pound flounder
⅓ cup mayonnaise

- In shallow dish combine crumbs, cheese and seasoned salt. Brush both sides of fish with mayonnaise. Coat with crumb mixture.
- Arrange in single layer in shallow pan and bake at 375° for 20 to 25 minutes or until fish flakes easily.

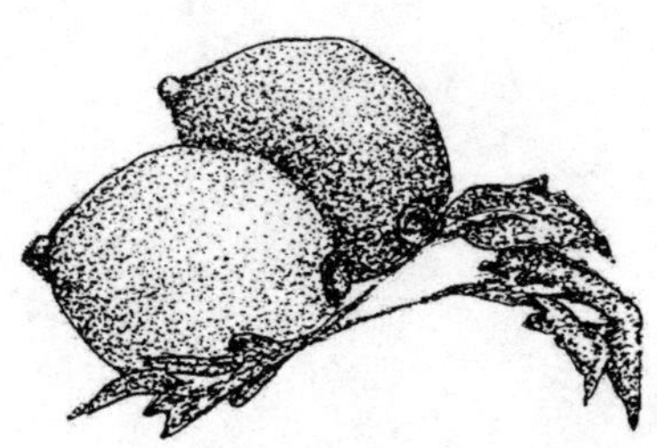

Baked Fish

1 pound fish filets
3 tablespoons butter
1 teaspoon tarragon
2 teaspoons capers
2 tablespoons lemon juice

- Place fish filets in greased shallow pan. Sprinkle with salt, pepper and a little butter. Bake at 375° for about 8 to 10 minutes, turn and bake another 6 minutes or until fish flakes.
- For sauce, melt butter with tarragon, caper and lemon juice. Serve over warm fish.

Spicy Catfish Amandine

¼ cup (½ stick) butter, melted
3 tablespoons lemon juice
6 to 8 catfish fillets
1½ teaspoons Creole seasoning
½ cup sliced almonds

- Combine butter and lemon juice and dip each fillet in butter mixture. Arrange in 9 x 13-inch baking dish.
- Sprinkle fish with Creole seasoning.
- Bake at 375° for 25 to 30 minutes or until fish flakes easily when tested with fork.
- Sprinkle almonds over fish for last 5 minutes of baking.

Golden Catfish Filets

3 eggs
¾ cup flour
¾ cup cornmeal
1 teaspoon garlic powder
6 to 8 (4 to 8 ounce) catfish filets

- In shallow bowl, beat eggs until foamy. In another shallow bowl, combine flour cornmeal, seasonings and a little salt.
- Dip fillets in eggs, then coat with cornmeal mixture.
- Heat ¼ inch oil in large skillet and fry fish over medium-high heat for about 4 minutes on each side or until fish flakes easily with fork.

Curried Red Snapper

1½ pounds fresh red snapper
2 medium onions, chopped
2 celery ribs, chopped
1 teaspoon curry powder
¼ cup milk

- Place snapper in greased 9 x 13-inch baking pan.
- In skillet, saute onions and celery in a little butter. Add curry powder and a little salt and mix well.
- Remove from heat and stir in milk. Spoon over snapper.
- Bake uncovered at 350° for 25 minutes or until fish flakes easily with fork.

Chipper Fish

2 pounds sole or orange roughy
½ cup Caesar salad dressing
1 cup crushed potato chips
½ cup shredded cheddar cheese
½ teaspoon black pepper

- Dip fish in dressing and place in greased baking dish.
- Combine remaining ingredients and sprinkle over fish.
- Bake at 375° for about 20 to 25 minutes.

Shrimp Newburg

1 (10 ounce) can cream of shrimp soup
¼ cup water
1 teaspoon seafood seasoning
1 (1 pound) package frozen cooked salad shrimp, thawed

- In saucepan, combine soup, water and seafood seasoning. Bring to a boil, reduce heat and stir in shrimp. Heat thoroughly.
- Serve over hot white rice.

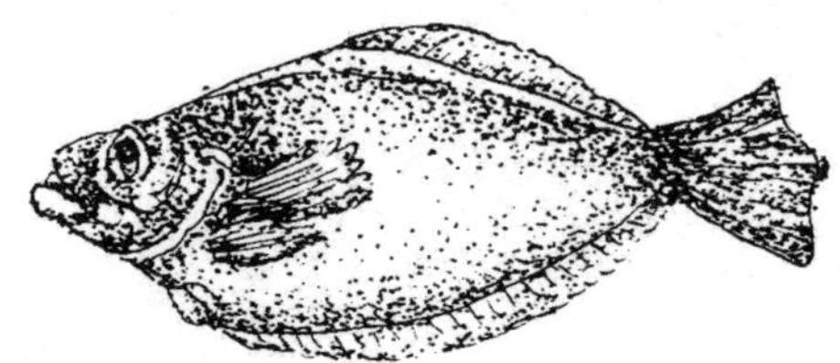

Shrimp Scampi

2 pounds raw shrimp, peeled
½ cup (1 stick) butter
3 cloves garlic, pressed
¼ cup lemon juice
Hot sauce

- Melt butter, saute garlic and add lemon juice and a few dashes of hot sauce.
- Arrange shrimp in single layer in shallow pan. Pour garlic butter over shrimp and salt lightly.
- Broil 2 minutes, turn shrimp and broil 2 more minutes. Reserve garlic butter and serve separately.

Tip: This recipe requires real butter, no substitutions.

Skillet Shrimp Scampi

2 teaspoons olive oil
2 pounds uncooked shrimp, peeled, veined
⅔ cup herb-garlic marinade with lemon juice
¼ cup finely chopped green onion with tops

- In large nonstick skillet, heat oil. Add shrimp and marinade.
- Cook, stirring often, until shrimp turn pink. Stir in green onions.
- Serve over hot, cooked rice or your favorite pasta.

Divine Strawberries

This is such a bright, pretty bowl of fruit and it's so delicious.

1 quart fresh strawberries
1 (20 ounce) can pineapple chunks, well drained
2 bananas, sliced
1 (18 ounce) carton strawberry glaze
Pound cake, optional

- Cut strawberries in half or in quarters if strawberries are large.
- Add pineapple chunks and bananas.
- Fold in strawberry glaze and chill.

Tip: This is wonderful served over pound cake or just served in sherbet glasses.

Coffee Surprise

1 cup strong coffee
1 (10 ounce) package large marshmallows
1 (8 ounce) package chopped dates
1¼ cups chopped pecans
1 (8 ounce) carton whipping cream, whipped

- Melt marshmallows in hot coffee. Add dates and pecans and chill.
- When mixture begins to thicken, fold in whipped cream.
- Pour into sherbet glasses. Place plastic wrap over top and refrigerate.

Tip: This is a super dessert – no slicing – no dishing up – just bring it from the refrigerator to the table.

Kahlua Mousse

1 (12 ounce) carton whipped topping
2 teaspoons dry instant coffee
5 teaspoons cocoa
5 tablespoons sugar
½ cup kahlua liqueur

- In large bowl, combine whipped topping, coffee, cocoa and sugar and blend well.
- Fold in kahlua. Spoon into sherbet dessert glasses.
- Place plastic wrap over dessert glasses until ready to serve.

Caramel-Amaretto Dessert

1 (9 ounce) bag small Heath bars, crumbled
30 caramels
⅓ cup amaretto liqueur
½ cup sour cream
1 cup whipping cream

- Reserve about ⅓ cup crumbled Heath bars (not in big chunks). In buttered 7 x 11-inch dish, spread candy crumbs.
- In saucepan, melt caramels with amaretto. Cool to room temperature.
- Stir in creams and whip until thick. Pour into individual dessert dishes and top with reserved candy crumbs. Cover and freeze. Cut into squares to serve

Tip: If you like, you can place the crumbs in individual dessert glasses. Pour caramel cream over crumbs and sprinkle remaining crumbs on top. Wrap plastic over top and freeze.

Strawberry-Angel Dessert

1 (6 ounce) package strawberry gelatin
1 cup boiling water
2 (10 ounce) cartons frozen strawberries with juice
2 (8 ounce) carton whipping cream, whipped
1 large angel food cake

- Dissolve gelatin in 1 cup boiling water and mix well. Stir in strawberries.
- Cool in refrigerator until mixture begins to thicken. Fold in whipped cream.
- Break cake into pieces and place in 9 x 13-inch dish.
- Pour strawberry mixture over cake. Refrigerate overnight. Cut into square to serve.

Pavlova

3 large egg whites
1 cup sugar
1 teaspoon vanilla
2 teaspoons white vinegar
3 tablespoons cornstarch

- Beat egg whites until stiff and add 3 tablespoons COLD water. Beat again.
- Add sugar very gradually white beating.
- While still beating slowly, add vanilla, vinegar and cornstarch.
- On parchment-covered cookie sheet, draw 9-inch circle and mound mixture within circle.
- Bake at 300° for 45 minutes. LEAVE in oven to cool.
- To serve, peel paper from bottom while sliding pavlova onto serving plate. Cover with whipped cream and top with assortment of fresh fruit such as kiwi, strawberries, blueberries, etc.

Oreo Sunday

A kid's favorite!

½ cup (1 stick) butter
1 (19 ounce) package Oreos, crushed
½ gallon vanilla ice cream, softened
2 jars fudge sauce
1 (12 ounce) carton whipped topping

- Melt butter in 9 x 13-inch pan. Reserve about ½ cup crushed Oreos for top and mix remaining with butter to form crust. Press crumbs in pan.
- Spread softened ice cream over crust (work fast). Add fudge sauce on top.
- Top with whipped topping, sprinkle with remaining crumbs and freeze.

Grasshopper Dessert

26 Oreo cookies, crushed
¼ cup (½ stick) butter, melted
¼ cup creme de menthe liqueur
2 (7 ounce) jars marshmallow creme
2 (8 ounce) cartons whipping cream

- Combine cookie crumbs and butter and press into bottom of greased 9-inch spring-form pan. Reserve about ⅓ cup crumbs for topping.
- Gradually add creme de menthe to marshmallow creme. Whip cream until very thick and fold into marshmallow mixture. Pour over crumbs.
- Sprinkle remaining crumbs on top and freeze.

Ice Cream Dessert

19 ice cream sandwiches
1 (12 ounce) carton whipped topping
1 (11¾ ounce) jar hot fudge ice cream topping
1 cup salted peanuts, divided

- Cut 1 ice cream sandwich in half. Place 1 whole and 1 half sandwich along short side of ungreased 9 x 13-inch pan. Arrange 8 sandwiches in opposite direction in pan.
- Spread with half whipped topping. Spoon fudge topping by teaspoonfuls onto whipped topping. Sprinkle with ½ cup peanuts.
- Repeat layers with remaining ice cream sandwiches, whipped topping and peanuts. (Pan will be full.)
- Cover and freeze. Take out of freezer 20 minutes before serving.

Twinkie Dessert

1 (10 count) box Hostess Twinkies
4 bananas, sliced
1 (15 ounce) package vanilla instant pudding
1 (20 ounce) can crushed pineapple, drained
1 (8 ounce) carton whipped topping

- Slice twinkies in half lengthwise and place in buttered 9 x 13-inch pan, cream side up.
- Make layer of sliced bananas over twinkies.
- Prepare pudding according to package directions and pour over bananas. Add pineapple.
- Top with whipped topping and refrigerate. Cut into squares to serve.

Creamy Banana Pudding

A quick and easy way to make the old favorite banana pudding

1 (14 ounce) can sweetened condensed milk
1 (3¾ ounce) package instant vanilla pudding mix
1 (8 ounce) carton whipped topping
36 vanilla wafers
3 bananas

- In large bowl, combine condensed milk and 1½ cups cold water. Add pudding mix and beat well. Chill 5 minutes. Fold in whipped topping.
- Spoon 1 cup pudding mixture into 3-quart glass serving bowl. Top with wafers, bananas and pudding. Repeat layering twice and end with pudding. Cover and chill.

Fruit Fajitas

1 (20 ounce) can cherry pie filling
8 large flour tortillas
1½ cups sugar
¾ cup (1½ sticks) butter
1 teaspoon almond flavoring

- Divide fruit equally on tortillas, roll up and place in 9 x 13-inch baking dish.
- Mix 2 cups water, sugar and butter in saucepan and bring to boil.
- Add almond flavoring and pour over flour tortillas.
- Place in refrigerator and soak 1 to 24 hours.
- Bake 350° for 20 minutes or until brown and bubbly. Serve hot or room temperature.

Tip: Use any flavor of pie filling you like.

Mango Cream

2 soft mangoes
½ gallon vanilla ice cream, softened
1 (6 ounce) can frozen lemonade, thawed
1 (8 ounce) carton whipped topping
Almonds, toasted, optional

- Peel mangoes, cut slices around seeds and cut into small chunks.
- In large bowl, mix ice cream, lemonade and whipped topping. Fold in mango chunks.
- Quickly spoon mixture into parfait glasses or sherbets and cover with plastic wrap.
- Place in freezer. When serving, sprinkle almonds over top.

Cinnamon Cream

This dessert must be made day before serving.

1 box cinnamon graham crackers
2 (5 ounce) packages instant French vanilla pudding mix
3 cups milk
1 (8 ounce) carton whipped topping
1 (18 ounce) prepared caramel frosting

- Line bottom of 9 x 13-inch casserole dish with graham crackers. (You will use one-third graham crackers.)
- With mixer, combine vanilla pudding and milk and whip until thick and creamy.
- Fold in whipped topping and pour half pudding mixture over graham crackers.
- Top with another layer of graham crackers. Add remaining pudding mixture.
- Top with final layer of graham crackers. (You will have a few crackers left.)
- Spread frosting over last layer of graham crackers and chill overnight.

Favorite Cake

1 (18 ounce) box yellow cake mix
3 eggs
1¼ cups water
1⅓ cup oil
1 (9.9 ounce) box dry coconut-pecan icing mix

- In mixing bowl, combine cake mix, eggs, 1¼ cups water and oil. Beat well.
- Stir in box of icing mix. Pour into greased, floured bundt pan.
- Bake at 350° for 45 minutes. Test with toothpick.

Tip: Some grocery stores do not carry coconut-pecan icing, but this recipe is worth looking for the icing. You can keep all these ingredients right in your pantry – to have on hand when you need to take food to a friend.

Cherry-Pineapple Cake

1 (20 ounce) can crushed pineapple, drained
1 (20 ounce) can cherry pie filling
1 (18 ounce) yellow cake mix
1 cup (2 sticks) butter, softened
1¼ cups chopped pecans

- Place all ingredients in mixing bowl and mix by hand.
- Pour into greased, floured 9 x 13-inch baking dish. Bake at 350° for 1 hour 10 minutes.

Pound Cake Deluxe

1 bakery pound cake
1 (15 ounce) can crushed pineapple with juice
1 (3.4 ounce) package coconut instant pudding mix
1 (8 ounce) carton whipped topping
½ cup flaked coconut

- Slice cake horizontally to make 3 layers.
- Mix pineapple, pudding and whipped topping and blend well.
- Spread on each layer, sprinkle cake with coconut and chill.

Easy Pineapple Cake

2 cups sugar
2 cups flour
1 (20 ounce) can crushed pineapple with juice
1 teaspoon baking soda
1 teaspoon vanilla

- Mix by hand and combine all cake ingredients. Pour into greased, floured 9 x 13-inch baking pan. Bake at 350° for 30 to 35 minutes.

Easy Pineapple Cake Icing:

1 (8 ounce) package cream cheese, softened
½ cup (1 stick) butter, melted
1 cup powdered sugar
1 cup chopped pecans

- Beat cream cheese, butter and powdered sugar with mixer. Add chopped pecans and pour over HOT cake.

Strawberry Pound Cake

1 (18 ounce) box strawberry cake mix
1 (3½ ounce) package instant pineapple pudding mix
⅓ cup oil
4 eggs
1 (3 ounce) package strawberry gelatin

- Mix all ingredients plus 1 cup water and beat for 2 minutes at medium speed. Pour into greased, floured bundt pan.
- Bake at 325° for 55 to 60 minutes. Cake is done when toothpick comes out clean.
- Cool for 20 minutes before removing cake from pan. If you would like an icing, use commercial vanilla icing.

Tip: If you like coconut better than pineapple, use coconut cream pudding mix.

Chocolate-Orange Cake

1 (16 ounce) loaf frozen pound cake, thawed
1 (12 ounce) jar orange marmalade
1 (16 ounce) can ready-to-spread chocolate-fudge frosting
½ cup pecans, chopped

- Cut cake horizontally into 3 layers. Place 1 layer on cake platter.
- Spread with half of marmalade. Place second layer over first and spread on remaining marmalade.
- Top with third cake layer and spread frosting liberally on top and sides of cake. Sprinkle pecans over top and chill.

Hawaiian Dream Cake

1 (18 ounce) yellow cake mix
4 eggs
¾ cup oil
1 teaspoon vanilla extract
½ (20 ounce) can crushed pineapple with ½ juice

- With mixer beat all ingredients for 5 minutes.
- Pour into greased, floured 9 x 13-inch baking pan.
- Bake at 350° for 30 to 35 minutes or until cake tests done with toothpick and cool.

Coconut-Pineapple Icing:

½ (20 ounce) can crushed pineapple with juice
½ cup (1 stick) butter
1 (16 ounce) box powdered sugar
1 (7 ounce) can coconut
½ cup almonds, slivered, toasted

- Heat pineapple and butter and boil for 2 minutes. Add remaining ingredients.
- Punch holes in cake with knife. Pour hot icing over cake.

Tip: This looks like a lot of trouble to make, but it really isn't. It's wonderful!

Angel Strawberry Delight Cake

1 cup sweetened condensed milk
¼ cup lemon juice
1 pint fresh strawberries, halved
1 angel food cake
1 pint heavy cream, whipped

- Combine condensed milk and lemon juice. Fold in strawberries.
- Slice cake in half. Spread strawberry filling on bottom layer. Place top layer over filling.
- Cover with whipped cream and top with extra strawberries.

Coconut Cake Deluxe

This is a fabulous cake!

1 (18 ounce) package yellow cake mix
1 (14 ounce) can sweetened condensed milk
1 can coconut cream
1 can flaked coconut
1 (8 ounce) carton whipped topping

- Mix yellow cake according to directions. Pour into greased, floured 9 x 13-inch baking pan. Bake at 350° for 30 to 35 minutes or until toothpick inserted in center comes out clean.
- While cake is warm, punch holes in cake about 2 inches apart. Pour sweetened condensed milk over cake and spread around until all milk soaks into cake.
- Pour coconut cream over cake and sprinkle coconut on top.
- Cool, frost with whipped topping and refrigerate.

Cherry Cake

1 (18 ounce) box French vanilla cake mix
½ cup (1 stick) butter, melted
2 eggs
1 (20 ounce) can cherry pie filling
1 cup chopped pecans

- In large bowl, mix all ingredients by hand. Pour into greased, floured bundt or tube pan and bake at 350° for 1 hour.

Golden Rum Cake

1 (18 ounce) box yellow cake mix with pudding
3 eggs
⅓ cup oil
½ cup rum
1 cup chopped pecans

- Mix cake mix, eggs, water, oil and rum and blend well.
- Stir in pecans. Pour into greased, floured 10-inch tube or bundt pan.
- Bake at 325° for 1 hour.

Tip: You might want to sprinkle powdered sugar over cooled cake.

Chocolate-Peanut Butter Drops

1 cup sugar
½ cup light corn syrup
¼ cup honey
1 (12 ounce) jar chunky peanut butter
4 cups chocolate-flavored frosted corn puff cereal

- Combine first 3 ingredients in Dutch oven and bring to boil, stirring constantly.
- Remove from heat, add peanut butter and stir until ingredients blend well.
- Stir in cereal and drop by tablespoonfuls onto wax paper. Cool.

White Chocolate Fudge

1 (8 ounce) package cream cheese, softened
4 cups powdered sugar
1½ teaspoons vanilla extract
12 ounces almond bark, melted
¾ cup chopped pecans

- Beat cream cheese at medium speed with mixer until smooth. Gradually add sugar and vanilla and beat well.
- Stir in almond bark and pecans. Spread into buttered 8-inch square pan.
- Refrigerate until firm. Cut into small squares.

Tip: This has a little different slant to fudge – really creamy and really good!

Creamy Peanut Butter Fudge

3 cups sugar
¾ cup (1½ sticks) butter
⅔ cup evaporated milk
1 (10 ounce) package peanut butter-flavored morsels
1 (7 ounce) jar marshmallow creme

- Combine sugar, butter and evaporated milk in large saucepan. Bring to boil over medium heat, stirring constantly.
- Cover and cook 3 minutes without stirring. Uncover and boil 5 minutes (do not stir).
- Remove from heat, add morsels and stir until morsels melt. Stir in marshmallow creme and 1 teaspoon vanilla.
- Pour into buttered 9 x 13-inch pan. Place in freezer for 10 minutes.

Peanut Brittle

2 cups sugar
½ cup light corn syrup
2 cups dry-roasted peanuts
1 tablespoon butter
1 teaspoon baking soda

- Combine sugar and corn syrup in saucepan, cook over low heat and stir constantly as sugar dissolves. Cover and cook over medium heat another 2 minutes.
- Uncover, add peanuts and cook, stirring occasionally to reach hard crack stage (300°). Stir in and baking soda. Pour into buttered jelly-roll pan and spread thinly.
- Cool and break into pieces.

✦✦✦✦✦

Easy Holiday Mints

1 (16 ounce) package powdered sugar
3 tablespoons butter, softened
3½ tablespoons evaporated milk
¼ to ½ teaspoon peppermint or almond extract
Few drops desired food coloring

- Combine all ingredients in large mixing bowl and knead mixture in bowl until smooth.
- Shape mints in rubber candy molds and place on baking sheets.
- Cover with paper towel and let dry. Store in airtight container.

Macadamia Candy

2 (3 ounce) jars macadamia nuts
1 (20 ounce) package of white almond bark
¾ cup flaked coconut

- Heat dry skillet and toast nuts until slightly golden. (Some brands of macadamia nuts are already toasted.) Set aside.
- In double boiler, melt 12 squares of almond bark. As soon as almond bark melts, pour nuts and coconut in with almond bark and stir well.
- Place wax paper on cookie sheet, pour candy on wax paper and spread out.
- Refrigerate 30 minutes to set. Break unto pieces.

Tip: When I want to make a candy that is special and one that most people have not eaten – this is the candy I choose. And is it ever great!

Apricot Cobbler

So easy and so good!

1 (20 ounce) can apricot pie filling
1 (20 ounce) can crushed pineapple with juice
1 cup chopped pecans
1 (18 ounce) yellow cake mix
1 cup (2 sticks) butter, melted

- Spray 9 x 13-inch baking dish with non-stick spray. Pour pie filling in pan and spread out.
- Spoon pineapple and juice over pie filling. Sprinkle pecans over pineapple.
- Sprinkle cake mix over pecans. Drizzle melted butter over cake mix.
- Bake at 375 ° for 40 minutes or until light brown and crunchy.
- Serve hot or room temperature.

Tip: It's great served with whipped topping.

Cherry-Strawberry Cobbler

1 can strawberry pie filling
1 (20 ounce) can cherry pie filling
1 (18 ounce) package white cake mix
1 cup (2 sticks) butter, melted
¾ cup package almonds, slivered

- Spread pie filling in greased 9 x 13-inch sprayed baking pan. Sprinkle cake mix over cherries.
- Drizzle melted butter over top and sprinkle almonds. Bake at 350° for 55 minutes.
- Serve with whipped topping.

Vanishing Butter Cookies

1 (18 ounce) box butter cake mix
1 (3 ounce) package butterscotch, instant pudding mix
1 cup oil
1 egg, beaten
1¼ cups chopped pecans

- Hand mix cake and pudding mixes. Stir in oil and egg and blend well. Stir in pecans.
- With teaspoon or small cookie scoop, place cookie dough on cookie sheet about 2 inches apart.
- Bake at 350° for 8 or 9 minutes. Do not overcook.

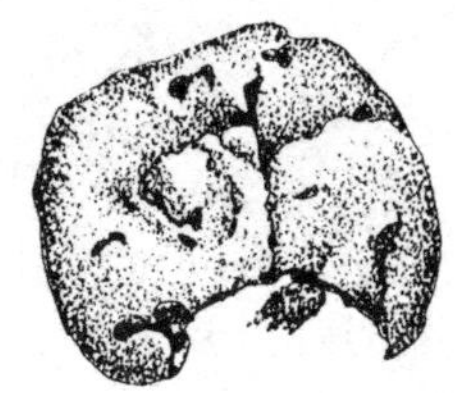

Chocolate Macaroons

1 (4 ounce) package sweet baking chocolate
2 egg whites, room temperature
½ cup sugar
¼ teaspoon vanilla
1 (7 ounce) can flaked coconut

- Place chocolate in top of double boiler. Cook until chocolate melts and stir occasionally. Remove from heat and cool.
- Beat egg whites at high speed for 1 minute. Gradually add sugar 1 tablespoon at a time and beat until stiff peaks form (about 3 minutes). Add chocolate and vanilla and beat well. Stir in coconut.
- Drop by teaspoonfuls onto cookie sheet lined with brown paper. Bake at 350° for 12 to 15 minutes. Transfer cookies on brown paper to cooling rack and cool. Carefully remove cookies from brown paper.

Chocolate Crunchies

1 (20 ounce) package chocolate
¾ cup light corn syrup
2 tablespoons (¼ stick) butter
2 teaspoons vanilla
8 cups crispy rice cereal

- Combine chocolate, corn syrup and butter in top of double boiler. Heat on low and cook until coating melts. Remove from heat and stir in vanilla.
- Place cereal in large bowl, pour chocolate mixture on top and stir until it coats well.
- Quickly spoon mixture into buttered 9 x 13-inch dish and press firmly, using back of spoon. Cool completely and cut into bars.

Chocolate Kisses

2 egg whites, room temperature
⅔ cup sugar
1 teaspoon vanilla
1¼ cups chopped pecans
1 (6 ounce) package chocolate chips

- Preheat oven to 375°. Beat egg whites until very stiff. Blend in sugar, vanilla and dash of salt. Fold in pecans and chocolate chips.
- Drop on shiny side of foil on cookie sheet. Put cookies in oven, TURN OVEN OFF and leave overnight.
- If cookies are a little sticky, leave out in air to dry.

Chocolate-Crunch Cookies

1 (18 ounce) package German chocolate cake mix with pudding
1 egg, slightly beaten
1 teaspoon vanilla extract
½ cup (1 stick) butter, melted
1 cup crisp rice cereal

- Combine cake mix, egg, vanilla and butter. Add cereal and stir until they blend well.
- Shape dough into 1-inch balls and place on lightly greased cookie sheet.
- Dip fork in flour and flatten cookies in crisscross pattern.
- Bake at 350° for 10 to 12 minutes and cool.

Tip: These cookies are so incredibly easy, they're wonderful for kids to bake.

Easy Peanut Butter Cookies

1 (18 ounce) package prepared sugar cookie dough
½ cup creamy peanut butter
½ cup miniature chocolate chips
½ cup peanut butter chips
½ cup chopped peanuts

- Beat cookie dough and peanut butter in large bowl until they blend and are smooth.
- Stir in remaining ingredients. Drop 1 heaping tablespoon dough onto ungreased baking sheet and bake at 350° for 15 minutes. Cool on wire rack.

Chinese Cookies

1 (6 ounce) package butterscotch chips
1 (6 ounce) package chocolate chips
1 (6 ounce) can cinnamon chips
1 (16 ounce) can chow mein noodles
1¼ cups salted peanuts

- On low heat, melt butterscotch, chocolate chips and cinnamon chips. Pour over noodles and peanuts and mix well. Drop by teaspoon onto wax paper.
- Refrigerate to harden and store in airtight container.

Potato Chip Crispies

These are really good and crunchy!

1 cup (2 sticks) butter, softened
⅔ cup sugar
1 teaspoon vanilla
1½ cups flour
½ cup crushed potato chips

- Cream butter, sugar and vanilla. Add flour and chips and mix well.
- Drop by teaspoonfuls onto ungreased cookie sheet.
- Bake at 350° for about 12 minutes or until light brown.

Angel Macaroons

1 (16 ounce) package 1-step angel food cake mix
½ cup water
1½ teaspoons almond extract
2 cups flaked coconut

- With mixer, beat cake mix, water and extract on low speed for 30 seconds. Scrape bowl and beat on medium for 1 minutes. Fold in coconut.
- Drop by rounded teaspoonfuls onto parchment paper-lined baking sheet.
- Bake at 350° for 10 to 12 minutes or until set. Remove paper with cookies to wire rack to cool.

Coconut Yummies

1 (12 ounce) package white chocolate baking chips
¼ cup (½ stick) butter
16 large marshmallows
2 cups quick-cooking oats
1 cup flaked coconut

- In saucepan over low heat, melt chocolate chips, butter and marshmallows and stir until smooth.
- Stir in oats and coconut and mix well.
- Drop by rounded teaspoonfuls onto wax paper-lined baking sheets. Chill until set. Store in airtight container.

Scotch Shortbread

1 cup butter
2 cups flour
¾ cup cornstarch
⅔ cup sugar
Granulated sugar

- Melt butter and stir in remaining ingredients.
- Press into 9-inch square pan and bake at 325° for 45 minutes.
- Cut into squares immediately after removing from oven.
- Sprinkle with colored sugar sprinkles or granulated sugar.

Orange Balls

1 (12 ounce) box vanilla wafers, crushed
½ cup (1 stick) butter, melted
1 (16 ounce) box powdered sugar
1 (6 ounce) can frozen orange juice concentrate
1 cup finely chopped pecans

- Combine wafers, butter, sugar and orange juice and mix well.
- Form into balls and roll in chopped pecans.
- Store in airtight container.

Tip: Make these in finger shapes for something different. They make neat cookies for a party or tea.

Nutty Blonde Brownies

So easy and so very good!

1 (1 pound) box light brown sugar
4 eggs
2 cups biscuit mix
2 cups chopped pecans

- In mixing bowl, beat brown sugar, eggs and biscuit mix.
- Stir in pecans and pour into greased 9 x 13-inch baking pan.
- Bake at 350° for 35 minutes.
- Cool and cut into squares.

Pecan-Cream Cheese Squares

1 (18 ounce) package yellow cake mix
3 eggs, divided
½ cup (1 stick) butter, softened
2 cups chopped pecans
1 (8 ounce) package cream cheese, softened
3⅔ cups powdered sugar

- In mixing bowl, combine cake mix, 1 egg and butter. Stir in pecans and mix well.
- Press into greased 9 x 13-inch baking pan.
- In mixing bowl, beat cream cheese, sugar and remaining eggs until smooth.
- Pour over pecan mixture and bake at 350° for 55 minutes or until golden brown.
- Cool and cut into squares.

Gooey Turtle Bars

½ cup (1 stick) butter, melted
2 cups vanilla wafer crumbs
1 (12 ounce) semi-sweet chocolate chips
1 cup pecan pieces
1 (12 ounce) jar caramel topping

- Combine butter and wafer crumbs in 9 x 13-inch baking pan and press into bottom of pan. Sprinkle with chocolate chips and pecans.
- Remove lid from caramel topping. Microwave on HIGH for 1 to 1½ minutes or until hot, stirring after 30 seconds. Drizzle over pecans.
- Bake at 350° for about 15 minutes or until morsels melt and cool in pan. Chill at least 30 minutes before cutting into squares.

Tip: Watch bars closely – you want the chips to melt, but you don't want the crumbs to burn.

Caramel-Chocolate Chip Bars

1 (18 ounce) package caramel cake mix
2 eggs
⅓ cup firmly packed light brown sugar
¼ cup (½ stick) butter, softened
1 cup semi-sweet chocolate chips

- Combine cake mix, eggs, ¼ cup water, brown sugar and butter in large bowl.
- Stir until thoroughly blended. Mixture will be thick.
- Stir in chocolate chips and spread in greased, floured 9 x 13-inch baking pan.
- Bake at 350° for about 25 to 30 minutes or until toothpick inserted in center comes out clean. Cool.

Tip: These bars are especially good when frosted with a prepared caramel icing.

Creamy Lemon Pie

1 (8 ounce) package cream cheese, softened
1 (14 ounce) can sweetened condensed milk
¼ cup lemon juice
1(20 ounce) can lemon pie filling
1 (9 inch) graham cracker piecrust

- In mixing bowl, cream cheese until creamy. Add sweetened condensed milk and lemon juice. Beat until mixture is very creamy.
- Fold in lemon pie filling and stir well.
- Pour into piecrust. Refrigerate several hours before slicing and serving.

Strawberry-Cream Cheese Pie

2 (10 ounce) packages frozen sweetened strawberries, thawed
2 (8 ounce) packages cream cheese, softened
⅔ cup powdered sugar
1 (8 ounce) carton whipped topping
1 prepared chocolate crumb crust

- Drain strawberries and save ¼ cup liquid. In mixing bowl, combine cream cheese, reserved liquid, strawberries and sugar. Beat well.
- Fold in whipped topping and spoon into crust. Refrigerate overnight.
- Garnish with fresh strawberries.

Cherry Pecan Pie

1 can sweetened condensed milk
¼ cup lemon juice
1 (8 ounce) carton whipped topping
1 cup chopped pecans
1 can cherry pie filling

- Combine condensed milk and lemon juice.
- Fold in whipped topping, pecans and pie filling into mixture and blend well.
- Spoon into 2 graham cracker crusts and chill overnight.

Chocolate-Cream Cheese Pie

1 (8 ounce) package cream cheese, softened
¾ cup powdered sugar
¼ cup cocoa
1 (8 ounce) container whipped topping, thawed
½ cup chopped pecans

- Combine first 3 ingredients in mixing bowl and beat at medium speed until creamy.
- Add whipped topping and fold until smooth.
- Spread in prepared crumb piecrust, sprinkle pecans over top and refrigerate.

Coffee-Mallow Pie

1 tablespoon instant coffee granules
4 cups miniature marshmallows
1 tablespoon butter
1 (8 ounce) carton whipping cream, whipped
½ cup chopped walnuts, toasted

- In heavy saucepan, bring 1 cup water to boil and stir in coffee until it dissolves.
- Reduce heat and add marshmallows and butter. Cook and stir over low heat until marshmallows melt and mixture is smooth.
- Set saucepan in ice and whisk mixture constantly until cooled.
- Fold in whipped cream and spoon into 9-inch graham cracker piecrust.
- Sprinkle with walnuts and refrigerate for at least 4 hours before serving.

Peach-Mousse Pie

1 (16 ounce) package frozen peach slices, thawed
1 cup sugar
1 (1 ounce) envelope unflavored gelatin
⅛ teaspoon ground nutmeg
¾ (8 ounce) carton whipped topping

- Place peaches in blender and process until smooth. Place in saucepan and bring to boil, stirring constantly.
- Combine sugar, gelatin and nutmeg and stir into hot puree until sugar and gelatin dissolve.
- Pour gelatin-peach mixture into large bowl and place in freezer until mixture mounds (about 20 minutes). Stir occasionally.
- Beat mixture at high speed about 5 minutes it becomes light and frothy. Fold in whipped topping and spoon into 9-inch graham cracker piecrust.

Black Forest Pie

1½ cups whipping cream, whipped
4 (1 ounce) bars unsweetened baking chocolate
1 (14 ounce) can sweetened condensed milk
1 teaspoon almond extract
1 (20 ounce) can cherry pie filling, chilled

- In saucepan over medium-low heat, melt chocolate with sweetened condensed milk and mix well. Remove from heat and stir in extract. (This mixture needs to cool.)
- When mixture is about room temperature, pour chocolate into whipped cream and fold gently until both blend well.
- Pour into prepared, cooked 9-inch piecrust. To serve, spoon heaping spoonful over each pie of pie.

Tip: This is definitely a party dessert, but the family will insist it should be served on a regular basis.

Peanut Butter Pie

⅔ cup crunchy peanut butter
1 (8 ounce) package cream cheese, softened
½ cup milk
1 cup powdered sugar
1 (8 ounce) carton whipped topping

- With mixer, blend peanut butter, cream cheese, milk and powdered sugar. Gently fold in whipped topping.
- Pour into graham cracker crust. Refrigerate several hour before serving.

Pineapple-Cheese Pie

1 (14 ounce) can sweetened condensed milk
¼ cup lemon juice
1 (8 ounce) package cream cheese, softened
1 (15 ounce) can crushed pineapple, well drained
1 (9 inch) graham cracker piecrust

- In mixing bowl, combine condensed milk, lemon juice and cream cheese. Beat slowly at first until smooth.
- Fold in well-drained pineapple and mix well.
- Pour into prepared graham cracker crust and chill 8 hours before slicing.

Pineapple-Lemon Pie

1 (14 ounce) can sweetened condensed milk
1 (20 ounce) can lemon pie filling
1 (20 ounce) can crushed pineapple, well drained
1 (8 ounce) carton whipped topping
2 cookie-flavored piecrusts

- Beat condensed milk and lemon pie filling and beat until smooth.
- Add pineapple and whipped topping and gently fold into pie filling mixture.
- Pour into 2 piecrusts. Refrigerate.

Tip: Eat one and freeze the other!

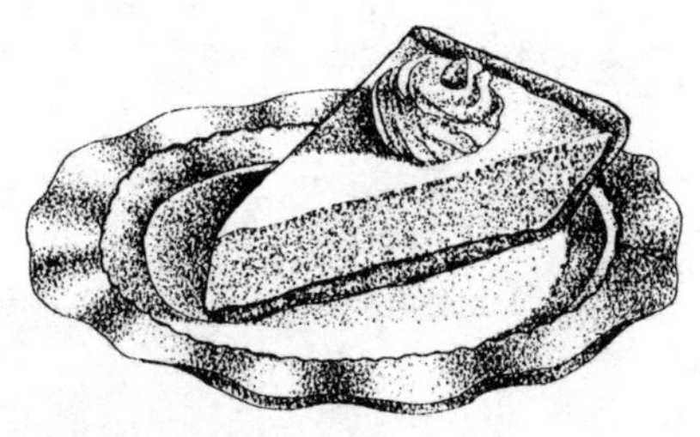

Sunny Lime Pie

2 (6 ounce) cartons key lime pie yogurt
1 (3 ounce) package lime gelatin
1 (8 ounce) carton whipped topping
1 (9 inch) graham cracker piecrust

- Combine yogurt and lime gelatin and mix well.
- Fold in whipped topping, spread in piecrust and freeze.
- Take out of freezer 20 minutes before slicing.

Grasshopper Pie

25 large marshmallows
⅓ cup creme de menthe
¼ cup milk
2 (8 ounce) cartons whipping cream, whipped
1 (9 inch) prepared chocolate piecrust

- In large saucepan, melt marshmallows with creme de menthe and milk over low heat.
- Cool and fold whipped cream into marshmallow mixture.
- Pour filling into piecrust and freeze until ready to serve.

Pink Lemonade Pie

1 (6 ounce) can frozen pink lemonade concentrate, thawed
1 (14 ounce) can sweetened condensed milk
1 (12 ounce) carton whipped topping
1 graham cracker piecrust

- In large bowl, combine lemonade concentrate and condensed milk and mix well.
- Fold in whipped topping and pour into piecrust. Chill 3 to 4 hours.

Sweet Potato Pie

1 (14 ounce) can sweet potatoes
¾ cup milk
1 cup firmly packed brown sugar
2 eggs
½ teaspoon ground cinnamon

- Combine all ingredients plus ½ teaspoon salt in mixing bowl and blend until smooth.
- Pour into 9-inch unbaked piecrust.
- Bake at 350° for 40 minutes or until knife inserted in center comes out clean.

Tip: Shield edges of pastry with aluminum foil to prevent excessive browning.

Easy Pumpkin Pie

1 unbaked 9-inch deep-dish pie shell
2 eggs
1 (30 ounce) can pumpkin pie mix
⅔ cup evaporated milk
¼ teaspoon ground cinnamon

- Beat eggs lightly in large bowl. Stir in pie mix, evaporated milk and cinnamon.
- Pour into pie shell and cut 2-inch wide strips of foil and cover piecrust edges. (This will keep piecrust from getting too brown.)
- Bake at 400° for 15 minutes. Reduce temperature to 350° and bake for 50 more minutes or until knife inserted in center comes out clean. Cool.

3-4-5 -INGREDIENT RECIPES